Efficient Vegetable Gardening

GETTING MORE OUT OF YOUR GARDEN IN LESS TIME

by

Paul Doscher,

Timothy Fisher,

and Kathleen Kolb

The Globe Pequot Press

Old Saybrook, Connecticut

Solar Pod® and Solar Frame® are registered trademarks of Solar Survival, Harrisville, New Hampshire
Drawings on pages 51, 85, 88, 90, 120, 139 by Coni Porter. All other drawings by Kathleen Kolb.

Photo credits: P. 14 bottom left: Jonathan Fisher. P. 28 top: SCS USDA photo by Morrison W. Liston. P. 71 left and 107 left: John P. Hamel/Rodale Stock Images. P. 160: Frank Oatman. Pp. 162 and 163 top: From *A History of Gardens and Gardening* by Edward Hyams; copyright © 1971 Praeger Publishers, an imprint of Greenwood Publishing Group, Inc., Westport, CT; reprinted with permission. P. 163 bottom: Illustration of "The Botanical Garden at Leiden" by J.C. Woudamus from *Folklore and Odyssey of Medicinal Plants* by Ernst and Johanna Lehner; copyright © 1962 by Tudor Publishing Company; reprinted by permission of Farrar, Straus and Giroux, Inc. P. 166: From *Early American Gardens* by Ann Leighton (Houghton Mifflin Company, copyright © 1970 by Isadore Leighton Luce Smith); Pp. 169 top, 170, and 171 bottom: From *The French Garden* by C. D. McKay (London: Associated Newspapers, 1908). Pp. 171 top, 176, and 179: From *Garden Farming* by Lee Cleveland Corbett (Boston: Ginn & Co., 1913). P. 172: From *The Book of Market Gardening* by R. Lewis Castle (London: John Lane, 1906). Pp. 177 and 178: From *Starting Early Vegetable and Flowering Plants Under Glass* by Charles Nissley (New York: Orange Judd, 1929). All other photos by the authors.

Book design by Nancy Freeborn

Library of Congress Cataloging-in-Publication Data

Doscher, Paul, 1950–
      Efficient vegetable gardening: getting more out of your garden in less time / by Paul Doscher, Timothy Fisher, and Kathleen Kolb. — 1st ed.
          p. cm.
      Includes index
      ISBN 1-56440-134-0
      1. Vegetable gardening. 2. Organic gardening. I. Fisher, Timothy. II. Kolb, Kathleen, 1954- III. Title.
   SB324.3.D66 1993
   635—dc20   92-21479
                                                                          CIP

Manufactured in the United States of America
First Edition/First Printing

Contents

Acknowledgments

We wish to thank the many people who helped us as we gathered material for this book. There were intensive gardeners in fourteen states who made themselves and their gardens available to us for questions and photographs. All of them were generous with their time; most of them spent a couple of hours patiently answering questions and showing us their gardens. Seldom did we give them much notice, yet all of them were very accommodating. Especially kind were Hank and Cecelia Bissell, John and Betsy Hibbard, Louise and Drew Langsner, Carolyn and Earl Lawrence, Betsy Millmann, Janney Munsell, Vic Sussman, Adam and Bonnie Tomash, and Ray Wolf, who welcomed us not only into their gardens but into their homes, sharing meals or offering accommodations during our travels.

Dr. Frank Eggert was extremely patient with our questions and gave us his time both at his home and at the University of Maine. Eliot Coleman put us on the trail of many of the gardeners with whom we have been in touch, and he made his unusual library available to us, for which we are most grateful. Leandre and Gretchen Poisson made a significant contribution to what we have to say about season-extending methods. Leona Collier at the Greensboro Free Library was sympathetic and helpful in obtaining for us the obscure books we needed quickly. Patti Nesbitt deserves special thanks for her enthusiasm and for helping us to locate a number of the gardeners we interviewed. Eleanor Adams was also helpful in contacting intensive gardeners, as were the Maine Organic Farmers and Gardeners Association, and the Boston Urban Gardeners.

Other gardeners whose help is very much appreciated and whose intensive gardens appear in photographs through this book are Bobbie Allshouse, Winnie Amato, Liz Blum, Tony Bok, George Crane, Alan Eaton at the University of New Hampshire, Barbara Eggert, David Emery, Galen Fisher, Irene Fuderer, Barbara Greenspun, Nancy Jo and Richard C. Harrison, K'uan Choi Heung and Shui-Ying Lam and the other gardeners at Unity Tower in Boston, Joe Howko, Paul Ladd, Eric Laser, Kenneth and Marjorie Lauer, Norm and Sherrie Lee, Luis Lopez, Hilde Maingay formerly at the New Alchemy Institute, Jim Markstein at Ramapo College, Dianne Mathews and Jeff Moyers at the Rodale experimental farms, Ray Nelson, Heather and Don Parker, Warren Pierce formerly at Carmel in the Valley, Jane Schmelk, Kathy Sheridan, Sam and Elizabeth Smith, Don Sunseri, Steve Tracy, Robin West of the Claymont Society, Charles Woodard at Goddard College, and Dr. Michael Wirth at New England College.

Edna Knapczyk was helpful in lending books, and Laurette Perron graciously translated some nineteenth-century French material. Virginia Richardson helped type. Ralph and Sally Fisher both assisted with proofreading.

Our special thanks are due to Deborra Doscher, for her advice and encouragement.

Introduction

Who doesn't wish to be more efficient? Practically everyone has too little time and too many things to do. For gardeners this either keeps you out of the garden when you wish you were there, or it prevents you from making the garden as beautiful and productive as you imagined it to be when you planned it. Like us, you are certain that if you could either get more time to work in the garden or simply find more effective methods, your garden would be a wonderful showplace.

Other gardeners lament the limits that nature places on their growing season. They know that it should be possible to squeeze a lot more lettuce, carrots, tomatoes, or other crops out of their limited garden space, but always get cut off by fall frosts. Perhaps you are a gardener who has always wanted to be the first in the neighborhood to have ripe tomatoes but never manage to get enough of a jump on the spring planting season.

There are other gardeners whose fondest desire is to produce the most at the least cost. These folks go to great lengths to find free fertilizer, mulch, and other recycled garden supplies but never seem to be able to get enough. The demand always seems to exceed the supply.

To all these gardeners getting better at gardening means getting more efficient. The efficient gardener aims to make the best use of time and resources while providing a bountiful harvest of vegetables over a long season. To do this requires that gardening efforts become more intensive, focusing on getting more from smaller amounts of space and with less work.

Intensive gardening has become very popular in recent years for just this reason. Building a rich soil and careful management assure that time, space, and materials are not wasted. Most efficient gardens have raised beds in which the soil is constantly in use by a succession of intermixed, closely spaced, and healthy plants. With the use of simple glass- or plastic-covered sun-capturing devices, the production and harvest continue on into the colder months.

An efficient intensive garden reduces the labor of weeding, water-

FIG. 1 Garden of Kenneth and Marjorie Lauer in Pennsylvania.

FIG. 2 Garden of Kenneth and Marjorie Lauer in Pennsylvania.

The ability to grow a great many vegetables in a small, compact area is one reason for gardening intensively.

FIG. 3 Excellent results are achieved with intensive methods in large gardens as well as small. Garden of Ray and Linda Nelson in Maine.

ing, and pest control, making these jobs less repetitive and more enjoyable. This kind of garden, with its compact size, lush growth, and careful management, can add beauty to any yard.

As gardeners ourselves, our lives have changed since portions of this book were first published in 1981 under the title *Intensive Gardening Round the Year.* The Doschers' garden has evolved from a home garden into a market garden, in which intensive techniques are used to produce high economic yields from each square foot. After fifteen years of gardening together in the

FIG. 4 *Garden of David Emery in Maine.*

same location, Tim Fisher and Kathleen Kolb have moved on to new gardens: Tim to a village lot where he has transformed the narrow south-facing side yard into a necessarily efficient garden; Kathleen to a smaller, more manageable raised-bed garden in a rural setting.

We also have young children and growing career pressures that make large demands on our time, so we have had to become more efficient gardeners by necessity. We are still enthusiastic about intensive gardening, for it feeds our ever-busier lives well. "Growing our own" still provides food of a quality that is nearly impossible to match, a habit of good eating that would be very difficult to break. Add to this the pleasure and pride we take from our gardens, and you see why we resist the temptation to let the garden go. Instead we have streamlined our gardening to create the same harvests with less work.

We grow vegetables using only natural fertilizers and pest controls. We find that an organic soil, rich in humus, is the most appropriate way for the home gardener to assure a successful garden. Using this approach, we all become soil builders rather than consumers, caretakers of a precious natural resource.

FIG. 5 *Boxed beds at the Rodale New Farm in Pennsylvania.*

In addition to our own ideas, this book contains the suggestions of numerous other intensive gardeners we have visited. Their ideas are creative and varied, making intensive gardening a pursuit that can respond to almost any difficult or unusual situation. These people have, more than anything else, proven to us that intensive gardens produce the best food in the least space with a minimum of effort.

We wish you a beautiful, healthful, and delicious garden.

FIG. 6 This simple greenhouse makes fresh green crops possible in the winter. Former garden of Timothy Fisher and Kathleen Kolb in Vermont.

FIG. 7 Garden at the Rodale Old Farm in Pennsylvania.

CHAPTER 1

The Garden Plan

A ny gardener will find it worthwhile to plan his or her garden, for a little attention given beforehand to location, soil, and varieties of vegetables to grow can save work and make the garden more enjoyable and productive. Planning is perhaps even more important in an intensive garden, where maximum production in a limited area relies on efficient coordination of the various aspects involved.

Efficient gardeners try to use the full growing season and the entire garden area. They also plan to use water, fertilizer, light, and labor as economically as possible. This takes a lot of coordination, which becomes easier with practice. You will find that after a couple of seasons, the different elements of an intensive garden, along with the other requirements of vegetable growing, will be sufficiently embedded in your consciousness for you to be able to manage it easily, with successively better results. Initially though, a plan is enormously helpful.

CULTURE

Intensive gardeners are prone to making statements about how they grow two to four times as many vegetables as they used to in the same amount of space. There are many variables in a garden situation, but, barring a raccoon invasion or similar natural calamity, you can expect to produce a lot more vegetables in an intensive garden of the same size. A well-planned scheme of successions and intercropping, calculated to make use of your entire growing season, will increase your yields. Keeping a record of planting, transplanting, and harvest times can help make even more efficient plans for next year's garden.

Larger yields are also achieved by a much denser vegetable cover on the beds than one sees in row cultivation. In row cultivation there is one row of plants between each path. In an intensive garden the equivalent of many rows of vegetables is planted between each path. The elimination of these paths allows more space in the garden for plants. Such a close and productive number of plants is supported in a small area as a result of the equally intensive soil preparation.

In an intensive garden one generally prepares only the soil in the beds and walks only in the paths. In row cultivation one prepares the soil in the whole garden, then proceeds to trample a path between each row of vegetables. One gardener we spoke with calls this "farming footprints." Not only is this a waste of effort, and quite likely of fuel and fertilizer, but the soil on both sides of the row becomes compacted, which is a serious impediment to healthy root growth.

Ideally plants are spaced at such a density that the leaf tips just touch, creating a canopy through which little soil is seen between the plants. While each plant has adequate sunlight and root space, this situation creates a living mulch that shades the soil, retains moisture, and inhibits weeds (see figure 1–1). This, of course, is a difficult state to maintain because the plants are always growing, but it is an optimal situation from which to gauge your compromises (see figures 1–2 and 1–3).

What must be remembered is that you are trying to maintain this optimal spacing throughout the growing season. This requires a coordinated plan. You can establish a living mulch

FIG. 1–1 Densely spaced plants create a living mulch. Garden of Sam and Elizabeth Smith in Massachusetts.

FIG. 1–2 Dense plantings can achieve higher yields. Garden of Sam and Elizabeth Smith in Massachusetts.

FIG. 1–3 Garden of Sam and Elizabeth Smith in Massachusetts.

quickly at the beginning of your growing season by using transplants and sprouted seed. This not only gives your plants a jump on the weeds but also gives you earlier harvests. When the plants in the beds begin to crowd one another, quicker-maturing ones can be thinned out. A good example would be broccoli interplanted with lettuce and timed so that the lettuce

would be ready to harvest just as the broccoli needed the space made available by the removal of the lettuce (see figure 1–4). If, after harvesting a crop, its growing space is not needed by a neighboring plant, a succession crop should be ready to fill the space.

As you make a plan, try to visualize your garden over the whole growing season. It is under a constant plant cover, but throughout the season the specific plants are changing, growing, and being harvested and replaced by new plants. The more coordinated your management of these transitions, the less abrupt they are and the more productive your garden will be.

FIG. 1–4 In this interplanting of broccoli and lettuce, the broccoli will be ready to harvest when the lettuce needs more space for continued growth. Garden at the Carmel Garden Project in Virginia.

LOCATION

An important decision is where to put your garden. If you have only one possibility, it will be an easy decision. If you have a choice, there is a lot to consider. Location is determined on the basis of soil, microclimate, and accessibility. You will also have to consider how your vegetable garden fits in with the other ways in which you use your property. Few locations will afford all the desired ingredients, but an awareness of them at least permits you to make selective compromises.

Soil

Soil is a basic criterion of location. Chapter 3, Healthy Soil, will help you identify the best garden soils as well as modify existing soils. You will be able to alter almost any soil situation enough to create a successful intensive garden, but if you have a choice, naturally choose the best. A soil test is very valuable for showing you the weak and strong points of your soil so that you will know what you do and don't need to add to it.

In urban areas and near highways, the soil should be tested for lead contamination from paints, car exhaust, and industrial pollutants. A vegetable garden should be at least 50 feet from a busy street and shielded from the road by a hedge or fence to lessen the effect of exhaust. There is also a danger that there may be lead in the soil where a lead-painted building once stood. Leafy vegetables particularly absorb lead from the air and soil, so a concern about lead poisoning may prove critical to your garden location.

Much of the work you do with your soil will consist of adding organic matter to it. Locating or making and storing these materials should be a part of your overall garden plan and schedule. A space may need to be provided for making compost. Leaves, which are useful in the garden all year, must be gathered in the fall and stored or composted. Manure is available all year, but in the spring you may be competing for it with your fellow gardeners, so a stored supply would be convenient.

The ability of a soil to hold or drain water can make it a desirable or an undesirable garden spot. A loam is generally considered ideal (see chapter 3). It neither drains too quickly (like sand) nor refuses to absorb water readily (like clay). Either extreme could result in drought or flood. The selection of a site that is slightly above the surrounding ground level, perhaps on a slight slope, gives you lower ground for excess water to drain off to (see figure 1–5).

Land with a slope is subject to potential erosion, particularly when tilling exposes its soil to the weather. It is quite possible that this land has lost much of its topsoil before you ever garden it, so you will have to give it special treatment if you garden there. Though a slight slope to your garden site is often beneficial in terms of water and frost drainage, a slope

FIG. 1–5 A garden site slightly above surrounding ground level will aid in water and frost drainage. Garden of Sam and Elizabeth Smith in Massachusetts.

of any severity requires you take adequate measures to prevent erosion. Suggestions for how to do this will be found in chapter 4.

Microclimate

Another factor in determining the location of your garden is the microclimate. We are all aware of climatic differences between different areas of the country and of the climatic zones shown on USDA maps. Your garden site, however, is part of a smaller zone that may not answer to the generalized description of the large zone indicated on the map. Your pocket zone, or microclimate, may be significantly warmer or colder, wetter or drier, than surrounding areas because of solar and wind exposure, water and air drainage, elevation, topography, or other more subtle considerations.

As oceans modify the larger climate, smaller bodies of water are modifiers of the microclimate. This is noticeable, for example, in the Finger Lakes region of New York State, where vineyards thrive on the hillsides that form the lake valley. Once you crest the hill and leave the valley, you enter a colder region no longer suited to grapes.

Living in the Northern Hemisphere, with the sun always to the south, a garden on a gradual south-facing slope is the ideal exposure. The sun will warm up this area earliest in the spring, and it will receive the longest periods of sunlight during the day. A southern slope also affords protection from the cold northwest winds.

We visited a southern New Hampshire garden on the south slope of a mountain. In many ways it was an unlikely garden site, consisting of little soil and lots of rocks. But dealing with only the relatively small area necessary for an intensive garden, its gardeners were able to add large quantities of organic matter to build a soil. They were more than compensated for their work by a microclimate they estimated to be comparable, because of their southern exposure and air drainage, to the general climate 50 miles to their south.

Even if you haven't ideal solar exposure, try at least to stay out of the shade. Trees can be cut down or pruned to allow more sunlight to reach the garden. In addition to shading the garden, tree roots are competing with the vegetables for moisture and soil nutrients. Some tree roots even emit toxins. Nevertheless, an intercropping of trees and vegetables can be successfully managed, as the photograph of vegetables in a Cape Cod peach orchard shows (see figure 1–6).

If your lot is hemmed in by buildings, put your garden on the north end of the lot to give it maxi-

FIG. 1–6 Intercropping trees or vines and vegetables can be successfully managed, as in this Cape Cod peach orchard.

FIG. 1-7 If your garden location is hemmed in by buildings, you can place the garden on the north side of the lot to give it maximum southern exposure. This garden benefits from wind protection and heat storage provided by the wall it's backed against. Garden of Ray Wolf in Pennsylvania.

mum southern exposure (see figure 1–7). An exception to this rule is that during midsummer, cool crops such as spinach and lettuce may prefer areas on the south end of the lot or under trees. If sunlight is unavailable elsewhere, you can still build window boxes or create a garden in a container on a porch or rooftop (see chapter 2).

Wind protection is significant in creating a milder microclimate more conducive to plant growth. The natural topography, a forest, a planted windbreak, hedges, fences, walls, and buildings all serve to modify the force of the wind. The windbreak both raises the temperature and protects plants from breakage caused by strong winds. A windbreak will cause snow to settle behind it, adding moisture to the garden, but it may mean you won't get into the garden as early in the spring. Windbreaks also slow down hot, drying summer winds. Bees don't like strong winds and will better pollinate plants that are sheltered by a windbreak.

Providing shelter from the wind is a feasible site modification in any location. A windbreak may also serve as an erosion control if laid out across a hillside. In a small yard there is a possible problem of the windbreak shading the garden. The roots of a living windbreak could compete with the garden for soil nutrients. There is also a potential competition for a limited garden space, though it would be hard to begrudge space to a living windbreak that consists of fruits, berries, and flowers. Such a windbreak can also attract and provide a habitat for birds and predatory insects that are a major control to destructive insects in the garden. (The windbreak, of course, can also harbor garden pests.) Though generally it takes a period of time to establish an effective living windbreak, a thick planting of tall annual plants can be grown in one season. A multiflora rose (*Rosa multiflora*) hedge becomes established in a few years (see figure 1–8). Multiflora roses can, however, become pernicious weeds. In all but the most severe climates, the extension service discourages *Rosa multiflora* in favor of *Rosa rugosa*, which is easier to control. Other possible windbreak shrubs are autumn olive, barberry, honeysuckle, euonymus, yew, and arborvitae. All these can also help attract birds to the garden.

A wooden fence provides a quick and effective windbreak. A stone or masonry wall is the most time-consuming and expensive to build. Traditionally, the south side of a masonry wall is the area for the earliest crops. In addition to the warmer temperature afforded by the

FIG. 1-8 A multiflora rose hedge becomes established in a few years. In milder climates, however, they can get out of control. Other possible wind-break shrubs are Rosa rugosa, autumn olive, barberry, honeysuckle, euonymous, yew, and arborvitae. These also help attract birds to the yard. Garden of Ray and Linda Nelson in Maine.

wind protection, the thermal mass of the masonry is warmed during the day by the sun, and this heat is gradually released during the night, creating a favorable microclimate. This is dramatically illustrated in cities, which usually have a warmer microclimate than the surrounding countryside because of the wind protection of the buildings and the enormous amounts of concrete and pavement acting as thermal mass (see figures 1–9 and 1–10). Heat also emanates from the concentrated burning of fossil fuels for heating, manufacturing, and transportation.

FIGS. 1-9 & 1-10 The microclimate in cities is usually warmer than that in the surrounding countryside due to the wind protection of buildings and the concrete and paving, which acts as a thermal mass. Shui-Ying Lam in community garden at Unity Tower, Boston, Massachusetts.

Despite the preceding advice, an ideal exposure is not essential. The garden the Fishers formerly tilled together was located on a northwest slope subject to very strong winds. It was very productive even in the short season of northeastern Vermont (see figure 1–11). In this location they benefited from good frost drainage, not to mention the view. Cold-air drainage was dramatically illustrated one year when the hillside garden enjoyed a four-month frost-free season, whereas valley gardens in the same town had a period of only forty days between frosts. The farther north you live, the more critical becomes your concern about frosts. A basic principle to bear in mind is that cold air sinks and hot air rises. Cold air behaves like a fluid, flowing from higher elevations and becoming trapped in low areas, where it can freeze a garden (see figure 1–12). A small difference in elevation can make a big difference in the length of your growing season.

Apart from the use of season-extending devices and covering your garden with sheets, plastic, or blankets on cold nights, if your summer garden is in a frost pocket, you have a problem. There are, however, a few things you can do to lessen the problem. The first thing to make sure of is that you are allowing as much airflow as possible to lower areas. Remembering that air moves much like water, it can be prevented from flowing to lower ground by a dense forest growth or hedge, a raised road or railway embankment, or a wall, all of which can act like a dam. Try to provide a break in this "dam" to allow the cold air to flow past your garden. Similarly, a garden situated directly below such a "break" in the frost "dam," will be subjected to more frost damage than will a garden just 50 feet to either side of the break.

In mild frost situations even the height of a raised bed can be a significant elevation

FIG. 1-11 *Despite an exposed location on a northwest slope, the hillside allows for a comparatively long growing season due to good frost drainage. Former garden of Timothy Fisher and Kathleen Kolb in Vermont.*

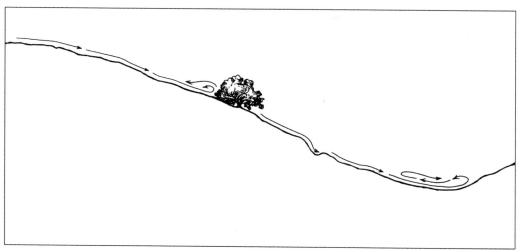

FIG. 1-12 *Frost drainage on a hillside. Cold air collects behind barriers and in ditches and low areas.*

difference to avoid frost damage. One year we had potatoes planted directly in the ground only 2 feet from an 8-inch raised bed of potatoes. The potatoes in the bed were unaffected by a frost that settled at ground level, killing the potato plants there. In certain situations the raised-bed advantage could be exploited by building much higher beds or even a miniplateau for the whole garden. On cold mornings one often notices that frost has settled in drainage ditches and stream beds. This situation could be duplicated in your garden by digging ditches specifically for the cold air to drain into or to promote its movement to lower areas.

Accessibility

Aside from considering soil and microclimate in your choice of a garden location, you should think about access. Whether by truck, tractor, trailer, car, or boat (see Floating Dinghy Garden, page 144), you will want to deliver loads of fertilizer, mulch and compost material, stakes, cold frames, and other needed materials directly to the garden with a minimum of hand moving. Being able to get to the garden easily yourself is also a consideration, whether you are growing a little salad for summer use or supplying a large vegetable stand. Generally the closer your garden is to your house, the better (see figure 1–13). This makes it convenient to go out and pick a few things for a meal or to work in it for short periods of time. On frosty nights it will be easier to run out and cover tender plants. You will be able to keep an eye on it, watching for marauding animals or vandals, and the mere proximity of the garden to the house will discourage some wild animals.

Even in regions with reliable rainfall, most gardens will benefit from watering during the dry periods and when seedlings are set out, so your location should include access to water.

Understandably, all the criteria of an ideal garden site rarely occur in one place. You will know which of the preceding considerations are most important to you, and you probably will add a few of your own. You may be left with a site that seems far short of ideal. Don't

FIG. 1-13 It is convenient for the garden to be close to the house so you can easily work for short periods, pick a few things for a meal, or cover plants on a frosty night. Garden of Heather and Don Parker in Maine.

let this deter you. The initial labor may be considerable, but the productivity of the garden will be commensurate with the work invested. Perhaps, too, you are a person who is challenged by the difficult spot to make it a place of beauty and usefulness. If so, you will enjoy the satisfaction of terracing, soil building, hedge planting, and fence making.

LAYOUT

Initial planning efforts are important in laying out an intensive garden as well as in deciding where to locate it. In some ways an intensive garden is architectural, for, unlike field gardening, intensive beds are relatively permanent; thus, without initial planning, you might be sorry later if the garden was not well planned.

Garden beds can be made modular—of uniform shape and size—to fit with the season-extending devices like cold frames and such things as reusable mulches and black plastic mulch. Uniform size allows for their interchangeability (see figure 1–14). To make the most efficient use of materials, the size of modular equipment will be affected by the standard dimensions of materials used in their construction. If it is necessary to irrigate your garden, you will need to lay out the beds to most efficiently use the irrigation plumbing and the water itself (see chapter 6 for more irrigation information).

Beds can also be made in free-form shapes for aesthetic purposes. You may choose to make a few modular and a few free-style beds, depending on how you hope to use the garden. We saw a beautiful intensively gardened yard in Chelsea, Vermont, where vegetables, dye plants, herbs, and flowers were all grown together, bearing more resemblance to flower garden beds than to anything else (see figure 1–15). Though most of the plants were useful

FIG. 1-14 Modular shaped beds allow for the interchange-ability of season-extending devices.

FIG. 1-15 An example of free-form beds in Chelsea, Vermont.

or edible, they were arranged for beauty, making a lovely curving border to the lawn. Another garden in the same area had vegetable beds of all sizes and shapes, designed strictly for the gardeners' enjoyment and delight, creating a swirling vegetable mosaic.

The size of the beds will be determined by several factors. Can you reach all parts of the bed from surrounding paths? This is important, for stepping into a bed damages plants and compacts the soil. Most people find a bed width of 3 to 5 feet to be comfortable. Some gardeners plan the width of the beds so that they can be straddled with a truck or other vehicle for easy unloading of organic matter (see figure 1–16). You may also choose to build the beds narrow enough to be able to straddle them yourself while weeding, digging, or cultivating (see figure 1–17). Other people plan the size of their beds so that they will be 100 square feet in area, or a multiple thereof. This helps the gardener who wishes to keep accurate records. It is also useful because recommended doses of soil amendments are usually measured per 100 square feet; thus, a 4-foot-wide bed would be 25 feet long. Beds should be

FIG. 1-16 (left) The width of garden beds can be planned so they can be straddled by a truck for easy unloading.

FIG. 1-17 (above) Garden beds can be narrow enough to be straddled while digging, weeding, and cultivating.

short enough to assure that cross-traffic won't be difficult. Sometimes a shorter bed is psychologically more satisfying than a longer bed, for the gardener then tends the whole bed in a short time rather than achieving only part of the job on the long bed. If you are planning beds boxed in with lumber, to conserve lumber bear in mind that standard-length lumber comes in multiples of 2 feet.

Make your paths wide enough to accommodate any carts, wheelbarrows, rotary cultivators, or lawn mowers you will use in the garden. We favor paths at least 2 feet wide. By late summer many plants will have become so large that foliage overflows into pathways, making them effectively narrower (see figure 1–18). If land is at a premium, however, paths can be much narrower (see figure 1–19). Some gardeners opt for paths 12 to 18 inches wide, which join into wider cross-paths that may be 3 or 4 feet wide. Some traditional French market gardeners had paths only 9 inches wide. In addition to saving space, narrower paths required far less manure, which the French gardeners banked up in the paths against the outside of their wooden frames to create additional warmth for the plants during cold weather. Those Frenchmen, however, were willing to carry the manure in baskets on their backs for delivery to the garden. If that appeals to you, it's your back. We still like wider paths.

If your lot size permits it and your terrain does not necessitate arranging your growing beds along the contour for erosion control, there is an advantage in situating your beds to run on a north/south axis. This allows the maximum amount of sun to fall on all the plants with minimal shading, as the sun moves across the sky from east to west. In any garden place the tallest plants to the north end of the garden to prevent their shading the other plants.

FIG. 1-18 By late summer many plants will have become so large that foliage overflows into pathways, making them effectively narrower. Garden of Eric Laser and Peggy Smith in Maine.

FIG. 1-19 The use of trellises is another way to economize on garden space. Garden at the Rodale New Farm in Pennsylvania.

In deciding how to lay out your garden beds, you may want to put beds that will have cold frames in the part of the garden closest to the house. When you go out to harvest from these in below-freezing or snowy weather, this may make the trip easier for both you and the produce.

In laying out your garden, space should be provided for whatever compost piles, manure, or mulch storage you expect to need. These may fit right in with the growing beds, or occupy odd corners left by charting your beds according to the compass, or be placed under the shade of nearby fruit trees. They should, however, satisfy the requirements of easy accessibility from both the path network within the garden and the vehicle access to the garden (see figure 1–20). Space should also be provided for storing season-extending and shading devices and trellises. After the time and expense of building these, it's a shame to let them deteriorate through careless storage.

Unfortunately, you must also plan your garden in relation to animal pests, and a fence is an important consideration. The height and material of your fence will be determined by the pests in your area. It is also sensible to have nets available to protect garden beds (espe-

FIG. 1-20 Space for compost piles should be provided for easy access to the garden. Garden at the former Carmel Garden Project in Virginia.

FIG. 1-21 (left) This whole bed is lined with chicken wire to keep out gophers. Garden of Galen Fisher in California.

FIG. 1-22 (above) Rather than fencing the whole garden, this gardener in Hope, New Zealand, uses a movable steel and chicken wire cover to keep pests out of his bed. Notice also the permanent cement sides to the bed and the irrigation pipe down the center.

cially berries) from birds. In one California garden gophers were such a severe menace that the whole bed, excavated to a depth of 2 feet, was lined with 1-inch-mesh chicken wire—an expensive proposition, but one that will work until the wire rusts away (see figure 1–21). A cheaper small-scale solution is setting plants in containers such as plastic five-gallon pails with holes cut in the bottom. This solution may also be advantageous in dry climates because it forces the roots to go deeper for water, making them less drought prone.

In an intensive garden you have a choice between fencing a particular bed or crop, or fencing the whole garden. If only one crop is being marauded, then it will be easier to fence only that crop (see figure 1–22). Often a framework around and/or over a bed to support fencing can also support growing plants, or plastic or blankets for frost protection (see figures 1–23 and 1–24). A snow fence can do double duty—for shading and for wind protection. A windbreak can also serve as a fence. More information on pest control will be found in chapter 6.

Having given consideration to a complete garden plan, you are ready to proceed with the actual building, planting, nurturing, and harvesting of your garden. We are confident that with this forethought, you can be an efficient and prolific gardener.

FIG. 1-23 This garden fence also serves as a tomato trellis. Garden of Kenneth and Marjorie Lauer in Pennsylvania.

FIG. 1-24 A cucumber trellis can be used to support fall protection. Garden of Bobbie Allhouse in Vermont.

CHAPTER 2

Healthy Soil

A rich, dynamic, and healthy soil is a key to the success of any garden. Any method of growing plants will produce good results if the soil is good. But with intensive gardening the density of cropping and constant use of the soil mean that a rich soil resource is absolutely critical. With it production and plant health can be virtually assured. Without it failure and disappointment are almost certain.

WHAT IS SOIL?

Obviously, if soil is so important, it is a good idea for every intensive gardener to understand what soil really is. Soil is an "ecosystem," a series of interacting groups of organisms and all the environmental factors that affect them. It is not only the particles of rock we call clay, silt, or sand, but all the decaying organic matter, animals, fungi, bacteria, and plants that inhabit this underground world. Factors we don't normally consider part of soil—air, water, sun, heat, and cold—are also integral to the function and life of the soil ecosystem.

Under natural conditions soil is constantly changing. To the naked eye this change is imperceptible. yet, when we look close enough, it becomes evident that the activity in the soil is as diverse and complex as any we can observe above ground.

At any one point varieties of processes are going on just below the surface of the ground, including weathering of rock. The action of air, water, cold, and heat are constantly working to pulverize rock material. This occurs both above the ground, where rock is exposed to the elements of weather, and below ground, where complicated chemical and physical actions break apart the bedrock well below the topsoil. But environmental factors are not the only ones that act to "weather" rock. Such plants as lichens, mosses, and liverworts produce

FIG. 2-1 A freshly built bed of soil. Any method of growing plants will produce good results if the soil is good.

acids as waste products. These acids dissolve rocks, causing small particles to fall off. Below ground, plant roots creep into rock crevices and expand, causing the rock to break apart. In rich organic soils tiny particles of rock are constantly being broken down by the action of organic acids produced by soil bacteria, fungi, and small animals.

Life within the soil ecosystem is extremely important (see figure 2–2). In fact, without the thousands of kinds of organisms inhabiting it, soil is nothing more than "dirt." The most obvious soil organisms are plants. Plant roots not only break apart rock into smaller particles, but they also excrete substances that in turn dissolve soil particles into mineral nutrients. Most important, all plant material ultimately becomes dead organic matter, which, if allowed to return into the soil, becomes the food source of microscopic soil life.

Dead organic matter is quickly attacked and is gradually consumed by thousands of bacteria, fungi, insects, and other tiny animals. In some fertile forest soils, the quantity of soil bacteria alone is estimated to weigh as much as 5,600 pounds per acre. In agricultural soils the quantity is lower, but it tips the scales at a quarter to a half ton per acre. Bacteria perform many important functions, including the decomposition of plant tissues into minerals, the fixing or absorption of nitrogen from the air, and the production of wastes, which become food for other soil organisms. Generally, soil bacteria are highly beneficial. Unfortunately, some are the sources of harmful crop diseases.

Fungi perform many of the same tasks as bacteria. Fungi such as mushrooms, which act to break down organic matter into mineral nutrients and humus, are called saprophytes. They attack even the most decay-resistant materials, tree bark, for instance, and recycle their components back into the soil. Fungi are also the janitors of the soil, working to clean up the waste products and bodies of dead bacteria.

Another group, actinomycetes, are half fungi, half bacterialike organisms that are pre-

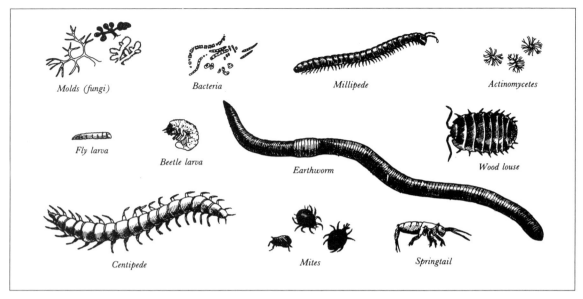

FIG. 2-2 Common soil organisms.

sent in all soils in small quantities. They do the same work as fungi but grow best in warmer environments. The compost pile is a favorite home for actinomycetes, for they thrive in the warmth created by heat-producing bacteria.

The natural cultivators of soil are invertebrate animals. These creatures, without skeletons or with external skeletons, are the most numerous and successful group of animals ever to exist on earth. Many of them spend all or part of their lives in the soil. Mites, ants, millipedes, centipedes, sow bugs, and many insects burrow through the soil in search of food. In the process they create minute channels that aid the passage of air, water, and plant roots. When these creatures die, their bodies serve as food for bacteria and fungi.

The most famous soil-cultivator is the earthworm. There are many species of earthworms, all of which are important to some degree in soil cultivation. Some types are prolific producers of "castings" (excrement rich in minerals and plant nutrients). Earthworms, like other soil organisms, feed almost exclusively upon dead organic matter.

Other wormlike animals that benefit soils are the nematodes. They are very small creatures, often microscopic, many of which are helpful in soil building and aeration. Not all nematodes are beneficial. Some are parasites on plant roots, and some are spreaders of fungal diseases, but these types are found in nonharmful quantities in healthy soils.

The smallest group of soil organisms, but by far the most noticeable, is the larger animals. Burrowing moles, mice, gophers, voles, squirrels, woodchucks, and others carry the cultivation process to the extreme. Their activity is of great benefit in mixing and aerating soils, but in gardens where plants lack deep and extensive root systems, animal tunnels are a nuisance and can do great damage to crops. Nonetheless, larger animals are an important part of the soil ecosystem, and in their natural environment do much to help build fertile soils.

The importance of the roles of all these creatures cannot be underestimated. They play an essential role, in combination with the processes and elements of the environment, in assuring the continued growth of the soil ecosystem. As a general rule, the more variety of organisms within a soil system, the better. This is because nature promotes diversity as a means of creating stability—survival of the system. In diverse systems there is such a multitude of organisms at work that if one disappears or is eliminated, its individual loss is not catastrophic to the whole system.

Diversity of life is what builds rich soils in which plants grow strong and healthy. A soil that has abundant organic matter, bacteria, fungi, and other animals, as well as plenty of air, water, light, and nutrients, cannot help but produce profuse plant growth.

WHAT MAKES
GOOD GARDEN SOIL?

Good garden soil contains all the same components as good natural soil in a virgin forest or prairie. The differences are that nature takes thousands of years to build rich, deep soils; the intensive gardener needs to create them in only a few years. Additionally, the intensive garden is covered much more densely with fast-growing plants than are most forest soils or even conventional garden soils. Thus, all the essential life and minerals in soil must be compressed into a smaller space than they might normally occupy.

Creating the proper conditions for a successful garden requires some manipulation of the natural soil. This is particularly true in areas where the activities of man have caused the natural topsoil to be eroded or depleted, leaving only a bare skin of rich organic matter on top of mineral subsoil, which is relatively lifeless. Achieving the proper conditions will benefit any garden, but they are even more important in intensive gardens.

Aeration

Plants and soil organisms need air to breathe. Plant roots absorb oxygen from the air and give off carbon dioxide; they will suffocate in the absence of air. (During photosynthesis above-ground portions of plants do the opposite; they absorb carbon dioxide and give off oxygen.) Soil animals, like any other creatures, must breathe oxygen. In dense or compacted soil, the tiny spaces between particles are too small to allow free flow of air, and plant growth and soil functions suffer.

Water Drainage

Much of the water that falls as rain percolates downward through pore spaces between larger soil particles. This "gravitational" water eventually flows into the underground water table. As it flows downward, it is replaced by fresh air from above. In heavy clay soils, which have no large spaces or pores, water does not drain quickly enough, and plants can literally drown during extended rainy periods.

Water Retention

Not all water flows downward as gravitational water. Some remains in the very tiny spaces between smaller soil particles or is captured through the spongelike action of humus. This is capillary water and is the source of moisture for most plant growth. A good soil is both well drained of gravitational water and has the ability to retain capillary water. Although sandy soils have good drainage, sand particles are relatively large and do not create enough of the small spaces necessary to hold capillary water. This makes sandy soils very drought susceptible.

Balanced Nutrients

Nutrients are the source of plant growth. They are mineral substances consumed by plants to help create all the various plant tissues. These mineral substances are found in all soils in varying amounts and forms.

Just as humans need a balanced diet containing essential proteins, fats, and carbohydrates, along with vitamins and minerals, plants require a balanced supply of nitrogen, potassium, phosphorus, calcium, sulfur, magnesium, and many other substances. Different plants have varying nutrient requirements, but it is generally true that if a soil has an overall balance of these nutrients, it will produce good crops. On the other hand, too little of an important plant nutrient will result in a deficiency leading to poor health and slowed growth. Too much of a plant nutrient can be equally harmful, resulting in poor utilization of other nutrients or even crop failure.

Balanced pH

"Potential hydrogen" (pH), is a measure of the acidity and alkalinity of any substance. It is measured on a scale of 0 to 14, with 0 being extremely acid and 14 extremely alkaline. Seven is the neutral point. Most garden plants grow best in soils with a pH of 6.0 to 7.0. Although specific plants like more acid or alkaline conditions, the best garden soil falls within this range (see figure 2–3). Phosphorus and many trace elements are most available to plants in slightly acid soil conditions. More acidic conditions cause certain plant nutrients to be tightly attached to the soil so that they cannot be absorbed by plant roots. In alkaline soils some nutrients are changed into substances unusable by plants.

Plentiful Humus and Soil Life

Humus is a substance consisting of fine particles of organic matter, the end product of decomposition. In comparison with fresh organic material, it is relatively resistant to further decomposition by bacteria and fungi. It is the most important component of good soil. The substance of humus is the decay-resistant portions of both plants and soil organisms.

Humus is porous and lets air and light into the soil. It tends to increase the number and size of pore spaces in heavy soils, thereby improving drainage and at the same time acting like a sponge to hold capillary water. Since humus is the product of organic decomposition, during which mineral nutrients are slowly released into the soil, efforts to increase humus almost always result in improved nutrient balance. Lastly, humus acts as a

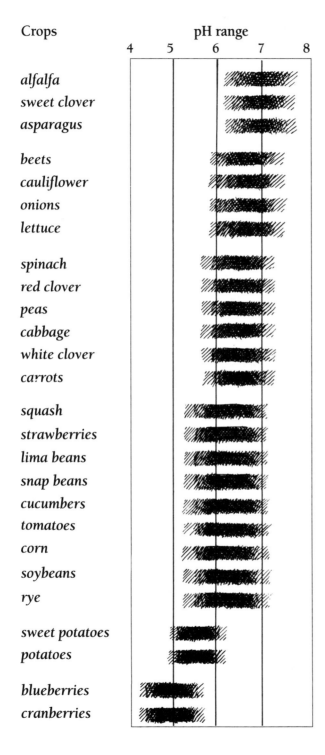

Crops

pH range

4	5	6	7	8

alfalfa

sweet clover

asparagus

beets

cauliflower

onions

lettuce

spinach

red clover

peas

cabbage

white clover

carrots

squash

strawberries

lima beans

snap beans

cucumbers

tomatoes

corn

soybeans

rye

sweet potatoes

potatoes

blueberries

cranberries

"buffer" to help hold pH close to neutral (or slightly acid), reducing the need for other actions to correct pH balance.

A full diversity of soil life is necessary to create humus, and the process of creating humus is just as important as the humus itself. The activity of microorganisms in breaking down organic substances releases not only the mineral nutrients needed by plants but creates an environment where other organisms can live, many of which have important roles to play in providing additional nutrients and minerals. This constant and gradual release of nutrients and minerals provides the most beneficial conditions for healthy plant growth.

The best intensive garden soils are built with the goal of achieving all of the above conditions. The soil that results is dark in color, loose in texture (it is easy to scoop up a handful without a digging tool), holds capillary water (stays damp just an inch or two below the surface), never has standing water on it (even after heavy rains), and rarely requires massive infusions of fertilizers or pH adjustment. The major requirement the soil makes of the gardener is to keep it fed with regular supplies of organic matter.

FIG. 2-3 *The pH preferences of common crops.*

BUILDING INTENSIVE
GARDEN SOIL

It is a lucky gardener who can begin an intensive garden in a place where the soil is so rich, dark, loose, and dynamic that no further soil building is necessary. Most of us are faced with the knowledge of what our soil should be and with the reality that it isn't even close to what we'd like it to be. After this realization comes the determination to "dig in" and start the laborious and time-consuming process of soil building.

Unfortunately, many gardeners make their first mistake right here. They rush out and buy soil amendments or hunt for the nearest source of manure without first taking the time to discover what it is their soil really needs. Although dumping quantities of high-priced organic amendments or fresh manure on a poor soil will probably not make it worse, it may not make it much better.

What every new gardener, and especially every new intensive gardener, should do first is take some time to examine the soil. You can learn quite a bit by simply observing soil and determining its strengths and weaknesses through a modest testing program. Then you can work to solve the problems in a direct way without also putting a lot of effort into improving conditions that are already good. For example, if a soil is poorly drained but high in humus and nutrients, adding lots of fresh manure or other organic matter may help, but the problem might be solved more easily by digging a drainage ditch and adding some sand. What is really needed is a way to get rid of the excess water.

The types of soil problems most often faced by the intensive gardener fall into the following four categories:

1. Poor soil texture (drainage and aeration)
2. Inadequate nutrient supply
3. Inadequate humus content
4. Unbalanced pH

All these problems can be solved with some planning, some understanding, and some manual labor. In most cases solutions need not involve spending large amounts of money on exotic soil amendments or fertilizers. Here's how to deal with the problems you are likely to find in each category.

1. Improving Soil Texture

Most of the bulk of soil is nothing more than minute bits of rock. They range in size from large grains of sand visible to the naked eye to microscopically small particles of silt and clay so tiny as to appear to form a solid mass. Each has a distinct and profound effect upon soil quality, which is commonly called soil texture.

During the past sixty years the Soil Conservation Service (SCS) of the U.S. Department of Agriculture has surveyed most of the nation, testing soils for their texture and other qualities. Soils have been classified into distinct categories and their individual characteristics described. Information on local soils is available to the public at any county office of the SCS.

It is useful, although not generally essential, for you to obtain this information before selecting a place to build an intensive garden. If you have a large plot of land, it can steer you away from spots that may look good on the surface but just below ground have impervious hardpan, high water table, bedrock, or heavy clay. On the other hand, if you already have a garden spot or only one choice of a place to put it, a soil survey is nothing more than interesting reading.

What a soil survey and your own inspection will tell you is the density and texture of your soil. It will probably fall into one of the following categories:

1. **Gravelly sand.** Extremely coarse particles, which make for a very well-drained but droughty soil that loses nutrients very quickly.

2. **Sandy loam.** Coarse particles, which are well drained, droughty in dry spells, lose nutrients quickly, and will not form clods when squeezed in the hand.

3. **Loams and silt loams.** Medium-grained soils, which are moderately well drained but have enough fine particles and organic matter to hold capillary water. These are the most fertile of natural soils and are usually found in river valleys or flat plains. These soils form clods when squeezed, but the clods break apart easily when handled.

4. **Clay loams.** Fine-grained soils, which are slow to drain but have moderate organic matter that keeps them from becoming too easily saturated. They can be very fertile, because fine-grained soils hold nutrients well. They form compact clods when squeezed in the hand but break apart easily when dropped.

5. **Heavy clay.** These are extremely fine-grained soils, which appear greasy when wet. They are often poorly drained and aerated. Heavy clays hold nutrients so tightly that plants often have trouble obtaining nourishment. They compact easily into bricklike masses, which can be broken up only by the use of tools or tillers. Dried clods can become as hard as rocks.

Obviously there are numerous variations and combinations of these basic types. Of the five the most desirable are loams and silt loams. They have an excellent combination of aeration, drainage, organic content, water retention, and nutrient-holding ability. But what do you do if you have a less desirable soil? The following rules of thumb should be your guide:

1. **Sandy soils.** Turning in any organic material will add to the water-holding capacity of the soil. The sandier the soil the more organic material it will take. It may require that 3 to 6 inches of material be added to the top few inches of soil for three to four years. The key is to create a sponge effect. Adding loam may help, but fine particles easily slip downward between grains of sand and can be lost to the subsoil. Building humus content will also help the soil hold nutrients.

2. **Clay soils.** If the soil is also poorly drained, look around first for the slope of the land, then dig a drainage trench (with gently sloping sides) 1 to 2 feet deep in a direction that will carry water away from your garden. Next, loosen the soil with a rototiller or garden fork to a depth of about 12 inches, or to the level where mineral subsoil begins. One to 4 inches of coarse sand can be added

over the entire bed to provide immediate loosening, but organic material is essential for long-term improvement (see figures 2–4, 2–5, and 2–6). Humus will increase the porosity of the soil over time, but it cannot create instant results. Adding too much organic material at one time can result in a long decomposition process that will tie up essential plant nutrients.

FIG. 2-5 Sand and compost are turned into an intensive bed with a spading fork. Note that this bed is only 2¹/₂ feet wide and can be straddled while working.

FIG. 2-4 Sand and compost are added to a bed of clay-type soils. The sand and compost are mixed into the top 6 to 8 inches. Note the finished bed in the foreground.

FIG. 2-6 Freshly prepared beds ready for planting. The ultimate objective is to produce a loose crumbly soil that forms easily broken clods when squeezed in the hand.

In either case these rules should be followed if possible: (1) Add well-composted or rotten material if planting is to follow within a month of soil preparation, and (2) if fresh material must be used, use it either in the fall when no further cropping is anticipated or when the soil is to be left fallow for longer than a month. The exception to this rule is when green manures are used in spring. With green manures allow at least three weeks between turning in and planting of crops.

Your ultimate objective is to produce a loose, crumbly-textured soil that forms easily broken clods when squeezed in the hand.

In most places topsoil is shallower than the 18-inch depth that is most desirable for intensive gardening. This can prove to be a problem if the subsoil below is hard clay or so densely compacted that it constricts root growth. But before undertaking a laborious effort to break up the subsoil consider the following (and refer to figure 2–7):

Earthworms spend most of their time in topsoil feeding on organic matter.

But when winter approaches they move downward to stay below the level of freezing

and during the cold weather "hibernate" at depths down to 6 feet. They are even able to penetrate through dense hardpan layers.

Topsoil—high in organic material

Loosened subsoil—mostly mineral matter

Unloosened subsoil— mineral matter (occasionally with an impervious "hardpan" layer)

Bedrock, glacial material —mostly rock.

FIG. 2-7 Earthworms are able assistants in loosening subsoils in most climates. Earthworms often make double digging or other laborious subsoil-loosening techniques unnecessary.

1. In climates where winter temperatures drop consistently below 0°F (–15°C), frost penetrates deep into the ground. In beds not covered by glazing or mulch, freezing is a major cause of subsoil loosening. This is a natural process, which can provide enough cracks and pores in subsoils to allow considerable root penetration. We observed this effect in an experiment conducted in our Hancock, N.H., garden, with beds that were double dug (double digging is a

method by which the topsoil is temporarily removed in small sections, allowing the subsoil to be loosened, resulting in loose soil to a depth of as much as 2 feet). Double-dug beds yielded no significant improvement over undug subsoil in other beds. In both cases the subsoil is a heavy clay about 16 to 18 inches below the surface.

2. In temperate climates earthworms burrow deep into the subsoil to avoid winter cold. During a recent fall we removed a full 10 inches of topsoil from a one-year-old bed. We then observed that at the interface between the humus-rich topsoil and mineral subsoil the density of earthworms was almost five per square foot. The worms were apparently moving downward into the subsoil as the soil temperatures dropped. Our intention had been to loosen the subsoil with the Rototiller, and in doing so we discovered an amazingly large number of earthworms even farther down. It is doubtful if we will ever bother to go through all the grief of double digging or tilling the subsoil again with this army of cultivators doing it for us.

3. If you have such an impervious subsoil that even worms don't work through it, or if you live in a moderate climate where freezing fails to penetrate the topsoil, consider loosening the subsoil. A number of subsoil loosening methods are described in chapter 4.

One last comment about soil texture. Once you have obtained the conditions you want, don't stop adding organic matter. It is possible to reduce the additions somewhat, but since humus does decay over time, adding no organic matter at all will eventually put you right back where you started.

2. Balancing and Adding Plant Nutrients

Water is the most important plant nutrient and accounts for 90 percent of the substance of nonwoody plants. Following water in importance are carbon, hydrogen, and oxygen, which plants obtain from air and water. These three are the building blocks of photosynthesis and constitute most of the solid material in plant tissue.

The mineral nutrients gardeners are most concerned about actually make up only a tiny percentage of the dry weight of plants. Even so they are critical to growth, flowering, and fruiting. Today thirteen nutrients have been proven to be necessary in plants, although it is likely that scientists will add more to this list in the future. They fall into two categories: macronutrients, which plants require in relatively large amounts, and micronutrients (trace minerals), which are used in very minute amounts.

The macronutrients are nitrogen, phosphorus, potassium, calcium, magnesium, and sulfur. Micronutrients are iron, boron, manganese, zinc, molybdenum, copper, and chloride.

It is not possible to determine accurately how much of any nutrient is present in soil without chemical testing. This can be done with moderately successful results using one of the better commercially available soil test kits (see figure 2–8). (It is not advisable to buy a very inexpensive test kit; the results you will get can be very inaccurate.) A more precise test

can be performed by sending sam-
ples to a professional laboratory or
the Cooperative Extension Service
lab in your state.

We recommend testing soil
regularly during the first few years of
intensive gardening. Nutrients are
depleted much more rapidly in
intensive beds, and knowing how
much of a nutrient is present is
essential to determining the amount
to add. Without testing you will be
using the "shotgun" approach, and it
is possible that a lot of your ammu-
nition will be wasted or that you may
not be adding the right nutrients.

FIG. 2-8 A good soil kit includes chemicals for testing for nitrate, phospate, potassium, pH, and humus.

Generally, as soil tilth improves and humus content increases, frequent soil testing
becomes less important. As mentioned earlier, nutrient levels tend to fluctuate less in organic
soils, since the decomposition process yields a continual supply of most nutrients.

Do not test soil immediately after adding fresh organic matter. The nutrient material in
fresh matter is attacked by soil life and consumed in their digestive systems for as long as a
month. Testing soil at this time would provide false results, which do not reflect the ultimate
availability of the nutrients once decomposition is complete.

Testing is best done in late spring, before planting or fertilizing, and in fall before
planting winter or cover crops. Some gardeners also test in midsummer, but this is not essential. Always be sure to follow the instructions that come with the soil testing kit to get
accurate results.

Of the macronutrients, nitrogen, phosphorus, and potassium (abbreviated NPK) must
be replenished regularly as part of the soil-building program. Calcium, magnesium, and sulfur are equally important to plant growth but are usually abundant in soils or need only
occasional replenishment.

NITROGEN. Nitrogen is the most plentiful component of air (about 78 percent), but in its
gaseous form it is inert and unusable by plants or animals. In its mineral forms (ammonia and
nitrates), it is a key element in the production of chlorophyll, the substance that is the basis of
photosynthesis. It is also necessary for the production of plant proteins and amino acids.
Because plants prefer to use nitrogen as nitrates, and nitrates are soluble in water, this important nutrient is often in short supply in garden soil. It can be present in adequate quantities in
the beginning of the gardening season, only to be leached away by rainwater and gradually
used up by densely cropped plants. To minimize this problem it is recommended that nitrogen be supplied to the soil in the form of organic matter. The slow decomposition of the
material releases nitrates over the course of many months, providing better and more consistent plant growth. If midseason nitrogen "boosting" is necessary, a liquid tea can be made

from compost, manure, fish emulsion, or certain soil amendments. Another approach is to "side-dress" with a mulch of compost, grass clippings, or other nitrogen-rich material.

For intensive gardens the best sources of nitrogen are rotted manure, compost, and leguminous green manures (see figures 2–9 and 2–10). These materials (except green manures) will provide the most nitrogen if they are stored under cover. Rainwater can rapidly diminish the fertilizer value of uncovered materials. You may choose to look into some of the products made from human sewage or the sludge from sewage treatment plants. They can provide substantial quantities of nitrogen and other nutrients, but you must be sure that they are tested and free of toxic metals and chemicals before you use them in the garden. Unless the material is frequently tested or certified safe, it is best to stay away from these substances. This is unfortunate, since using human waste would be a logical way to complete the nutrient cycle from soil to plant to human and back to the soil. Perhaps one day we will legislate that no

FIG. 2-9 Legumes are plants that host nitrogen-fixing bacteria on their roots. Using legumes as cover/green manure crops can add substantial amounts of nitrogen to the soil. These blackeyed peas have well-developed nitrogen nodules on the roots.

FIG. 2-10 Green manure crops hold nutrients during periods when beds are not in use, returning them to the soil after being turned under. This is a fall crop of hairy vetch.

industrial or toxic wastes can be dumped into our municipal sewers, and this resource will become safe for use in producing food. But until that day *be cautious!*

PHOSPHORUS. Phosphorus is used by plants in the form of phosphate (PO_4). It is important in the basic process of plant growth and cell division, and it is essential for healthy seedling growth, root growth, flowering, and fruit development.

Phosphate is water soluble, but in most soils it is greatly attracted to tiny soil particles and does not percolate out in rainwater. The major loss of phosphate comes primarily from its use by plants and the harvesting of fruits, which concentrate this nutrient.

The best way to add phosphorus to soil is through organic material. Most compost and manures contain a fair amount of phosphorus. If this proves to be inadequate, then it is economical to add phosphorus in the form of ground rock phosphate. Added in the rock form, the phosphate will gradually break down in the soil, making it unnecessary to add more for up to three years.

POTASSIUM. This nutrient is particularly important because it is a basic catalyst for many plant functions. It must be present for plants to manufacture sugars, proteins, and amino acids, even though it is usually not present in these substances. It is also critical to the flowering process. It is usually added to the soil in the form of potash, which is found in wood ashes, granite dust, or greensand. It is not plentiful in manures, except cow manure, and it leaches out quite quickly. For suburban gardeners one of the best sources of potassium can be freshly cut grass clippings. Potassium is concentrated in the leaves of plants, and grass is especially good for this. The clippings can be used as mulch, and the potassium will leach out of the leaves into the soil during rainstorms. Be cautious as to where you get your clippings. Avoid clippings from lawns that may have been treated with herbicides (weed killers), as these chemicals can be harmful to you and your garden.

CALCIUM. This plentiful element has many uses in plants, but its most notable use is in the formation of cell walls. As in animals, calcium provides strength to the skeletons of plants. In soils where limestone is the parent material, calcium is usually abundant and does not need to be added. In other places calcium is added during the occasional process of adjusting pH with the use of ground limestone.

Only rarely is this element a limiting factor in good plant growth. It is abundant and finds its way into the soil in many of the fertilizers used to provide nitrogen, phosphorus, and potassium.

MAGNESIUM. Magnesium is another component of chlorophyll and is part of the chemical structure of amino acids, vitamins, sugars, and plant fats. Sandy soils, particularly along the Atlantic Coast, appear to be severely deficient in magnesium. Most other soils are naturally rich in this element. Where it must be added, the best sources are raw rock phosphate and dolomitic limestone.

SULFUR. Sulfur is used by plants in the manufacture of vitamins, particularly the B vitamins. It is such a plentiful nutrient that only in extremely unusual circumstances is the addition of sulfur required. Perhaps one of the few positive effects of the burning of fossil fuels is the contribution it makes to preventing sulfur depletion in soils. Sulfur is a major contaminant in most fossil fuels, and when we burn them, sulfur dioxide is released into the atmosphere. It is then washed out as acid rain (in the form of sulfuric acid) and ends up back on the ground. Of course, if it lands on cars, houses, and other manufactured objects, it causes corrosion, and in streams and lakes it can seriously affect fish life. In soils an apparent effect is the lowering of pH. This assures that in most of the United States there is no deficiency of sulfur for plant growth.

Another component of acid rain and air pollution is nitrogen dioxide. When this compound is returned to earth as nitric acid, it apparently can have beneficial effects on some plants because it can provide essential nitrogen to plant foliage and roots.

Research by scientists at Oak Ridge National Laboratories and other institutions has shown that some plants are benefited by this bath of acidic compounds whereas others are damaged. Those that benefit may do so because of the increased nitrogen provided by nitric acid. Those that are damaged seem to suffer because of the leaching of plant nutrients from the leaves by strong acids. Ongoing research points to air pollution as a likely contributor to the major declines in forest productivity now being documented in parts of the United States and Europe.

Although there is little a gardener can do to directly take advantage of, or prevent the effects of acid rain, one thing is to keep a close watch on soil pH. Areas with strongly acidic rainfall and sandy soils can experience significant drops in soil pH over the course of a few years. (The solutions are described in the previous section on soil pH.)

The major plant nutrients, their sources, and some basic information on nutrient deficiency symptoms that can be observed in the garden are displayed in the accompanying table (pp. 32–33).

The micronutrients are a perfect example of the fine-tuning of nature. They are absolutely essential in tiny, almost unmeasurable amounts (parts per million), yet in larger quantities they can become harmful and even toxic. Most soils contain ample amounts of the seven trace nutrients, but certain conditions can cause them either to be used up or to become unavailable. Therefore, although you cannot easily supplement your garden's micronutrient supply, it is important to know the proper conditions for making it useful.

IRON. Unless iron is present, chlorophyll cannot be created in plant leaves. It is also an important component of certain plant enzymes. Most soils contain sufficient iron for healthy plant growth, but high alkalinity (pH over 7.8) can cause it to become tightly bound to the soil. Adding more iron would not solve the problem; only lowering the pH will. Iron is commonly added to soils with the application of greensand or glauconite.

BORON. A crucial and widely used nutrient, boron has at least sixteen different functions in plants, from being essential to flowering and seed germination to assisting in nitrogen metabolism. This is one of the micronutrients that is used up quickly by plants, and a deficiency will be noticeable as a dieback of tender young leaf and bud growth. Boron shortage can also be caused by liming, since it is adequately available to plants only in acid soils (another good reason for maintaining soil pH at 6.0 to 7.0). Oddly, scientists report that boron deficiency, whether caused by liming or plant uptake, is common only in humid climates east of the

Mississippi and particularly in the Northeast. Fortunately, in the process of adding other nutrients and organic matter, you will also be adding boron, so it will be very rare that a special addition of boron will be needed. The common sources of boron are animal manures, alfalfa green manure, rock lime (in small quantities), and granite dust.

MANGANESE. This element is another key component in the creation of chlorophyll. Plants exhibit manganese deficiency when young leaves are light green but show a network of dark green veins. Although manganese is plentiful in virtually all soils, it can become unavailable in alkaline conditions (above pH 8.5). In very acid conditions so much manganese can be absorbed that it becomes toxic to plants. Proper pH adjustment is the way to solve manganese problems.

ZINC. Plants use zinc to produce starches, which are the key to both healthy root and leaf growth. Without it roots grow abnormally and leaves develop a mottled color and white streaking. Zinc-deficient potatoes and squash will often show brown spots on their leaves. Another symptom of zinc deficiency is a noticeable shortening of stems, and plants seem to be miniaturized.

There is usually a great deal of this nutrient in soils, but it becomes less and less available as pH rises above 5.5. This means that in alkaline conditions zinc deficiency is quite frequent. On the other hand, high levels of zinc in soil become toxic when pH drops below 5.5. Once again, a slightly acid soil condition proves best for nutrient availability. If zinc deficiency still exists, continued application of manures or raw rock phosphate will generally solve the problem.

MOLYBDENUM. Vitamins and plant proteins are created with the aid of this nutrient. Additionally, plants need molybdenum in order to take in and use nitrates. A deficiency is almost indistinguishable from nitrogen deficiency except in the cabbage family, where it is indicated by narrower than normal leaves. Shortages of molybdenum are rare but can occur in acid soils.

COPPER. Copper is highly toxic in more than minute quantities, and it is impossible to add a correct amount of it directly to soil without sophisticated equipment. It is used by plant roots during nitrogen absorption, and a deficiency is difficult to detect, except in onions, where the skins fail to develop their characteristic brown color.

Clay and loam soils generally have adequate copper, but as organic content increases, copper becomes tightly bound to soil. This has led some scientists to expect copper deficiency in highly organic soils, but this has not been confirmed. If you wish to add very small amounts of copper without danger of overdose, wood shavings, sawdust, and grass clippings are recommended sources.

CHLORINE. Most of us know chlorine as being a highly toxic gas. In the gaseous form it can kill almost any organism, yet when combined with sodium to form sodium chloride, it becomes common table salt. In this form chlorine is essential to life, and plants must have it in order to release oxygen during photosynthesis. A deficiency will produce stubby roots and wilting of plants in conditions when they would normally not wilt. An excess of salt is equally damaging, since high sodium levels are toxic to most plants. Salt is highly water soluble and tends to wash downward in soil. Fortunately, chlorine is added to soil in rainfall, and some

Major Plant Nutrients

Nutrient	Sources	Deficiency Symptoms	Notes
Nitrogen	Rotted animal manure (best if protected from rain) (very good)	Foliage is yellow-green instead of normal dark green. In older plants yellowing occurs first in older leaves.	Fresh manures are fairly high in nitrogen, but since they are also very high in undecomposed organic matter, when added to the soil, organisms that attack this material may also consume all the nitrogen as well. This is only a temporary problem, because when the decomposition nears completion, the nitrogen is again available for plants. It does mean that fresh manures or fresh organic matter should not be applied just before planting or turned into the soil during the growing season.
	Compost (good)	Size of leaves is reduced.	
	Legume green manure crops (good)	Edges of leaves turn yellow or brown.	
	Nonlegume green manure crops (good)		
	Fish meal or emulsion (good)		
	Blood meal (very good, but expensive)		
	Cottonseed meal (very good)		
	Grass clippings (good if fresh)		Sewage sludges may be high in nitrogen, but in some cases are also contaminated with industrial wastes, heavy metals, or other toxic substances. Unless sewage material has been certified free of toxic material *do not use it* in your vegetable garden.
	Fresh animal manure (fair to good, but can cause problems) *see Notes*		
	Leaves (fair to good)		
	Sewage sludge and miscellaneous soil amendments (poor to very good) *see Notes*		
Phosphorus	Soft or hard rock phosphate (very good)	Stems turn purple or leaf veins turn purple (most commonly seen in tomatoes planted in cold soils).	When pH is less than 4 or over 8.5, phosphorus becomes bound to the soil and cannot be used by plants.
	Colloidal phosphate (very good)	Retarded maturity	Rock sources of P contain a large amount of the nutrient, which becomes available to plants over time, though only a small percentage is immediately available. They need not be applied every year. Rock phosphate is usually necessary every three to four years.
	Compost (good)	Poor yields (especially common in early spring plantings of cabbage family plants)	
	Rotted animal manures (good)		
	Fresh animal manures (fair)		
	Bone meal (very good, but expensive) *see Notes*		Bone meal is also alkaline and should not be added to soils where alkalinity is a problem.

Major Plant Nutrients *(continued)*

Nutrient	Sources	Deficiency Symptoms	Notes
Potassium	Granite dust (very good) Compost (fair) Greensand (very good) Wood ashes (very good) Seaweed (good) Cottonseed meal (fair) Alfalfa green manure (very good) Sul-po-mag (a soil amendment)	Lowered resistance to disease Low yields Mottled, speckled, or curled leaves (especially older leaves)	Potassium is concentrated in the leaves of plants, but is readily leached out by water. If green manures or grass clippings are to be used as a mulch to supply potassium, they must be protected from rain until used. Wood ashes must also be protected from rain. They are also alkaline. Be sure not to burn colored newspaper or plastics with your wood if you plan to use it in the garden. Colored inks and plastics may contain lead and other toxic substances.
Calcium	Rock lime or dolomitic limestone (best) Wood ashes (good) Compost (good) Bone meal (good) Shells (good)	Deformed terminal leaves, buds, and branches Poor plant structure (weak stems, etc.) Celery black heart, lettuce tip burn, internal browning of cabbage, cavity spot in carrots, blossom end rot.	Calcium is lost by water leaching downward through the soil. Lime can be added by turning it into the top few inches of the soil in the fall. It can also be added with compost or manure and helps speed up the decomposition process. Rock lime should be used rather than hydrated lime. It is less subject to leaching and need be applied only every few years.
Magnesium	Dolomitic limestone or rock lime (good) Rock phosphate (fair) Compost (good) Manures (good) Sul-po-mag (a soil amendment)	Lack of green color in leaves between the veins. Occurs first in older leaves.	Magnesium is generally plentiful except in sandy soils. In most cases occasional liming provides all the necessary magnesium. Epsom salts can be used as a foliar spray (in low concentrations) to combat Mg deficiency. (Consult your extension agent for recommendations.)
Sulfur	Acid rain (unavoidable in the eastern U.S.) Aluminum sulfate (not recommended) Sul-po-mag (a soil amendment)	Similar symptoms to nitrogen deficiency, but on younger leaves.	Sulfur is almost never in short supply.

plants can absorb it directly from the air, so a deficiency is probably possible only in garden beds and greenhouses which are constantly under glass.

When gardeners who use chemical fertilizers need to add nutrients to the soil, they have a simple procedure to follow. They find out how many pounds per acre of NPK are in the soil and then add the appropriate chemical fertilizer to meet the need. Perhaps this simple process is what leads so many gardeners to the nonorganic method despite the losses in long-term soil texture, humus content, and overall fertility.

For an intensive organic gardener, the task of determining how much of a given nutrient to add to soil is more complex but not necessarily more difficult. By using the procedure outlined below, you should be able to add enough (but not too much) of the essential macronutrients along with a little dose of the micronutrients.

(a) *Conduct a soil test.* Your results will tell you if you have low, medium, or high levels of unusable (soluble) nitrogen, phosphorus, and potassium. These levels are roughly equivalent to the following levels of nutrients:

	high	*medium*	*low*
Nitrogen	200 lbs/acre .5 lb/100 sq ft	125 lbs/acre .3 lb/100 sq ft	50 lbs/acre .1 lb/100 sq ft
Phosphorus	250 lbs/acre .6 lb/100 sq ft	175 lbs/acre .4 lb/100 sq ft	85 lbs/acre .2 lb/100 sq ft
Potassium	200 lbs/acre .5 lb/100 sq ft	125 lbs/acre .3 lb/100 sq ft	65 lbs/acre .15 lb/100 sq ft

(b) *Determine how much NPK you want in each garden bed depending upon what you plan to grow.* Heavy feeders prefer high levels of all three nutrients. (Heavy feeders are plants like cucumbers, tomatoes, melons, eggplant, squash, and most greens.) Light feeders (root crops) prefer medium nitrogen and medium to high phosphorus and potassium. Legumes prefer medium nitrogen and medium to medium high phosphorus and potassium.

(c) *Figure how much of a particular source of nutrients you must add to obtain the desired level.* This is not difficult. First, take the desired level of nutrients, and then subtract from the figures (in lbs/100 sq ft) the amount you already have present (as determined by the soil test). The result will be the amount you must add in fertilizer. Next, consult the chart on NPK percentages in common organic fertilizers (page 37). For example, since fresh cow manure has approximately .4 percent nitrogen, it will have .4 lb nitrogen per 100 lbs manure and bedding. If your soil test showed you that your soil has low nitrogen (.1 lb/100 sq ft), and you want nitrogen (.5 lb/100 sq ft), you will need .4 lb of nitrogen per 100 sq ft of garden space. Since cow manure has .4 lb/100 pounds, you should add 100 lbs of the manure per 100 sq ft of garden space. This same process could be performed for any of the sources of nitrogen, phosphorus, or potassium. Fortunately, you will be adding all three in the same 100 pounds of manure, so your actual manual labor in handling the material will be limited to the manure and any possible supplements you may need if the manure does not contain enough of other desired nutrients.

This process is not exact. The problem comes not in the calculations but in the fact that no two piles of manure or compost contain the same amounts of nutrients. Homegrown organic fertilizers vary considerably in their nutrient content, depending upon how they are stored, what the animals may have been fed, the type of bedding used, or the source of materials used in composting. To solve this problem, if you are concerned that you may not be adding enough of a nutrient or that you are adding too much, conduct a soil test about three weeks after adding the material. If the results are not satisfactory, you can supplement, using commercial organic fertilizers which have a guaranteed analysis.

Some last words of caution. If you err on the side of excess, you will probably not have much of a problem with phosphorus or potassium. On the other hand, excess nitrogen causes many problems and should be avoided.

If you hate doing calculations, you can console yourself in the knowledge that as your soil improves, the need for them will diminish. On the other hand, you can always use the "shotgun" method and just hope for the best.

3. Building Soil Humus

Soil humus is so valuable to intensive gardening that it is essential to understand its function in promoting healthy plant growth before going into how to build it.

We have already discussed the important role of humus in providing water retention and drainage as well as aeration. But there is an even more important job humus performs known as "cation" (pronounced "cat–i–en") exchange. It is a complex process, which is crucial to organic gardening methods, even though most gardeners and farmers know little about it. Without becoming too technical, here is an explanation of how it works.

As you will recall from high school science, every substance is composed of molecules, which are combinations of incredibly small particles called atoms. Atoms themselves are made up of even smaller particles, known as protons, neutrons, and electrons (see figure 2–11). These pieces are arranged in a way that resembles a miniature solar system: protons and neutrons combined together to form a nucleus or "sun" and electrons that orbit around the nucleus like "planets." Electrons are negatively charged (–) and the nucleus is positively charged (+). (Neutrons have a neutral charge or no charge.) Since opposites attract, electrons are normally kept in their orbits around the nucleus (each atom has an equal number of protons and electrons so as to keep this balance). When atoms combine together, however, to form molecules, quite often an electron "escapes" or is removed for use elsewhere by other molecules. This results in a molecule or "ion" with a missing negative charge so that its net charge is positive (see figure 2–12). The molecule that captures the extra electron then has a net negative charge. The positive molecules are called "cations" and the negative molecules "anions." Since they are opposite charges, the ions themselves are often attracted to each other.

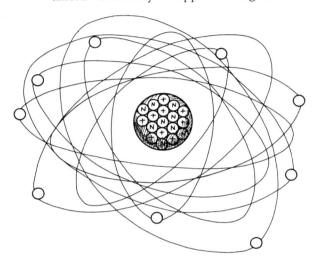

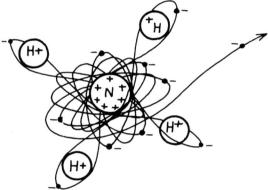

The nitrogen atom has seven of its own electrons. The hydrogen atoms have one each. NH₄ has ten, and one is set free.

FIG. 2-11 *An atom contains a positively charged nucleus and orbiting, negatively charged electrons. There are an equal number of protons and neutrons in the nucleus, and the number of electrons orbiting around the nucleus is generally equal to the number of protons.*

FIG. 2-12 *An example of an ion with a positive charge, a cation. When the atoms of nitrogen (N) and hydrogen (H) combined to form a molecule of NH₄, one electron was set "free," leaving a net positive charge.*

This becomes important when we discover that some of the important nutrients used by plants are found as ions in the soil. Both cations and anions are found in the soil. Soil particles themselves are negatively charged, and therefore only the cations are attracted to the soil and seek to attach themselves to the soil particles. Their ability to do this is determined by the number of attachment "sites" that a particle has. The more surface area a particle has, the more cation sites it has (see figure 2–13).

Now comes the crucial action. Plant roots and rootlets weave their way through the soil in search of nutrients, many of which are found as cations. When a rootlet comes near a particle of soil that is holding a number of desired cations, the plant gives off a hydrogen ion with a positive charge (H^+). H^+ ions always take priority over all other cations in electrical attraction, and so the H^+ ions "bump" loose the nutrient cations and take their place on the soil particles. The nutrient cations are then absorbed by the plant roots and taken upward for use in growth and photosynthesis (see figure 2–14).

Nutrients that are absorbed in this way are ammonium ($NH4^+$), potassium (K^+), calcium (Ca^{++}, magnesium (Mg^+), and most micronutrients.

Other nutrients are not found as cations and do not attach themselves to soil particles

NPK Percentages in Common Organic Materials

Manures*	N	P	K
Cow	.4	.3	.44
Horse	.65–.76	.3–.6	.5–.65
Pig	.3	.3–.4	.45
Sheep and goats	.65	.46	.23
Chicken	1.1–1.8	1.0	.5
Turkey	1.3	.7	.5
Rabbit	2.0	1.0	.5

Commercially Available Materials	N	P	K
Blood meal	9.0–15.00	1.0–1.3	.7–1.0
Bone meal (steamed)	1.0–4.0	20.0–30.0	0–.2
Bone meal (raw)	3.0–4.0	20.0–24.0	1.0–2.0
Cottonseed meal	6.5–8.0	2.0–3.0	1.2
Fish emulsion	5.0	2.4	2.0–3.0
Fish meal	8.0–10.5	4.0–9.0	0
Hoof and horn meal	7.0–15.0	0–2.0	12.0
Kelp meal	1.0	0	5.0–6.7
Greensand	0	1.5	3.0–5.0
Granite dust	0	0	0
Hard rock phosphate	0	25.0–33.0	0
Soft rock phosphate	0	15.0–20.0	

Collectible and Grow-Your-Own Materials	N	P	K
Alfalfa green manure	3.0–4.0	na	na
Alfalfa hay	1.5–2.5	.3–.5	1.5–2.1
Winter rye green manure	1.7–2.3	.18	1.05
Seaweed	.5–3.3	.1–2.0	1.0–5.0
Kentucky bluegrass	.66–1.2	.19–.4	.71–1.6
Oak leaves	.8	.35	.2–.3
Red clover hay	2.0–3.2	.25–.5	1.28–2.0
Sawdust and wood chips	.2	.1	.2
Coffee grounds	2.1	.3	.3
Wood ashes (unleached)	0	1.0–2.0	4.0–10.0
Wood ashes (leached)	0	1.0–1.5	1.0–3.0
White clover green manure	.5	.15	.60
Sewage sludge	.74–6.0	.33–4.0	0–.24
Timothy hay	1.25	.55	1.0
Cow peas (green forage)	.45–3.0	.12–.25	.45–1.45
Oats green manure	1.3–1.4	.17	1.09

*NPK levels in rotted manures can be slightly higher if kept under cover from rain. If manures are leached, nitrogen and potassium levels will be lower than the values shown.

SOURCES:

John Jeavons. *How to Grow More Vegetables* (Berkeley, Cal.: Ten Speed Press, 1979).

J. I. Rodale. *Encyclopedia of Organic Gardening* (Emmaus, Pa.: Rodale Press, 1959).

J. I. Rodale. *How to Grow Vegetables & Fruits by the Organic Method* (Emmaus, Pa.: Rodale Press, 1961).

"Sources of Compost" by Fred J. Jisbet in *Country Journal*, July 1979, p. 53.

NOTE: Compost varies widely in its NPK content, depending upon the materials that are used to produce it. Even so, unless the compost is kept under cover, it will have very little fertilizer value.

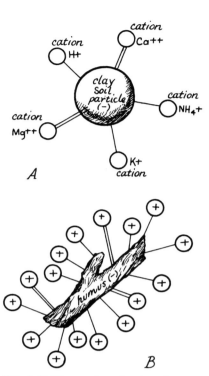

FIG. 2-13 *The number of cations that a soil particle can "hold" is a factor of its surface area; a particle of clay holding on to a number of positively charged cations is shown in A; a particle of humus, even though its actual size may be no larger, has more surface area, and thus more cation receptor sites, as shown in B.*

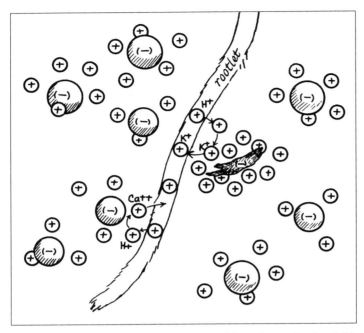

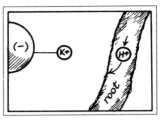

1. H⁺ ion in the root is moving downward and toward the soil

FIG. 2-14 Rootlets in the soil are surrounded by soil particles that hold cations. When the plant needs a nutrient cation, it releases an H⁺ ion, which "bumps" a cation off a soil particle so that it can be absorbed by the plant.

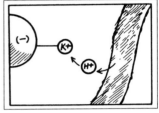

2. H⁺ is released by the root.

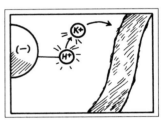

3. K⁺ ion is bumped by the H⁺ ion.

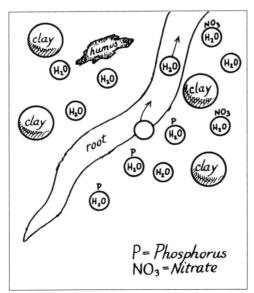

P = *Phosphorus*
NO₃ = *Nitrate*

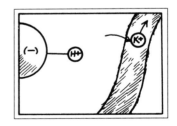

4. K⁺ ion is absorbed by the root for use by the plant.

FIG. 2-15 Nutrients that are not found as cations, and thus not absorbed by plants through cation exchange (Figure 2-14), are usually anions. Anions are usually water soluble and are absorbed by plants when they take in water. (Nitrates and phosphates are examples of water soluble anions.)

the same way. These nutrients are usually negatively charged (anions) and are absorbed by plant roots when the roots take in water (see figure 2–15). Both nitrates (NO_3^-) and phosphates are water soluble anions and are absorbed in this way. (Phosphates, however, have the ability to bind themselves to the soil, while nitrates do not.) Anions, like nitrates, are dependent upon water for their movement in the soil and because of this can be easily washed downward out of the reach of plant roots by rainwater. This fact in itself is one of the major reasons why chemical nitrates are such a water pollution problem in the United States. Chemical fertilizers are very high in soluble nitrates, in fact so high that not all of them can be absorbed by plant roots before they are washed downward in the soil. The nitrates then find their way into the underground water table or into streams and lakes. Once in surface waters, the nutrient becomes food for another plant, algae, which eventually clog the water and die from overpopulation. This is called eutrophication and is one of the most serious and widespread forms of water pollution.

What does all this have to do with humus? Humus is important to all this because it is the most effective holder of nutrients in the soil. Humus particles are very porous; they have lots of surface area, which means they have plenty of sites for cations to attach to. Humus is even more effective than soil particles at providing cation exchange sites. This means that a humus-rich soil is capable of providing considerably better cation exchange than almost any mineral soil (see figures 2–16, 2–17, 2–18).

Humus also acts like a sponge to hold gravitational and capillary water. Since anion

FIG. 2-16 Composting organic material before adding it to soil breaks down most substances into humus. Garden of Eric Laser and Peggy Smith in Maine.

FIG. 2-17 A freshly built, properly constructed compost pile will rise to a temperature of up to 160° F. This steaming pile is a few days old, and was built entirely of garden wastes and mulch hay. Note the covered, finished compost pile in the background.

Fig. 2-18 Compost piles on a small farm in eastern Massachusetts.

nutrients are soluble and are absorbed by plants in water, humus acts to prevent loss of these nutrients through leaching or erosion.

Finally, we should recall that many of the nutrients in the soil being held for use by plants came from the humus-building process in the first place. Humus is certainly a versatile performer. It supplies the nutrients, prepares them for use, and serves them to plants in the needed amounts at a gradual rate. What more could we ask for?

Most of today's agricultural soils are deficient in humus and have less than a 5 percent humus content, although a well-managed farm or garden soil can have as much as 10 percent humus. Organic farming and gardening associations most often establish that for proper organic growing conditions a 5 percent humus content is the minimum. But, as with nutrients, more is not always better. Muck soils formed in swampy areas build up a humus content of 10 to 40 percent, and peat bogs range from 40 percent to 100 percent humus. In both of these cases drainage is poor, most nutrients are used up quickly or leached out, and soil microbial activity is low. If these wet soils can be drained and loosened, they can often be very productive, but without a rich soil flora and fauna, they are almost useless as an agricultural resource. This illustrates an important point about humus. Although humus alone is an important measure of soil fertility, it is valuable only where conditions are dynamic and where there are also adequate nutrients.

Humus is by nature a rich, dark color. If you have a soil that has this dark chocolate coloration, you probably have a good humus content. The exception is in soils with excess manganese, which take on a dark color even if humus is not present. Of course humus-rich soils also have a spongelike texture, which distinguishes them immediately from manganese soils.

In your soil-building program you should use the following rules of thumb:

1. Keep soil humus content above 5 percent. This can be accurately determined only by a soil test, which is best done by sending a soil sample to a reliable testing lab. If you are working to improve humus content by using regular additions of organic material, it will be necessary only to have this test made once every few years to check your progress. If you are confident that you already have a humus-rich soil or that your soil-building program is making steady progress, the humus test is probably not essential.

2. Avoid excessive cultivation. It adds oxygen to the soil, speeding up the humus decay process.

3. Provide a constant supply of fresh humus. The action of soil organisms both produces and destroys soil humus. Any biologically active soil must have regular infusions of new humus to replace what is lost to this microbial action as well as from erosion by wind and rain.

4. Always add well-decomposed organic matter. Any addition of organic matter into soil produces an increase of microbial activity. This increase is generally desirable because its ultimate result is the release of nutrients into the soil. But the more fresh (undecomposed) material you add, the greater the risk you face that all that soil life will increase too much and consume large quantities of humus as well. Add to this risk the fact that microbial activity increases with soil temperature, and we find that in some warm climates (and perhaps in warm microclimates like covered beds and under cloches), the addition of fresh organic matter will spur so much soil activity that the result can be a net decrease in humus. This is exemplified by the soil structure of tropical regions. Temperatures are so warm that soil activity remains high all year. This produces a condition where any organic matter that falls to the ground is rapidly decomposed and its nutrients recycled into plants. As a result, tropical soils tend to be very low in humus content and have very shallow topsoils. The lush natural vegetation of the tropics is well suited to this condition, but whenever these soils have been used for agriculture, they are rapidly depleted and quickly become infertile.

Obviously it is not always possible to add only composted or well-rotted material to your beds. The use of fresh material, however, should be kept to a minimum, especially in beds that are under lights or cloches, where soil life activity is especially high. The best practice is to add organic matter in the form of rotted manure (two months minimum in warm climates, three to four months minimum in cooler climates like the Northeast), compost, decomposed leaves, or various hays that have been allowed to spoil for a year or longer (see figure 2–19).

5. Don't depend upon green manures to improve humus content in a short time. Many people have erroneously assumed that constant use of green manures will rapidly improve soil texture and humus content. This is not necessarily true.

Green manures have benefits in providing and conserving nutrients. Winter cover crops will capture soil nutrients and hold them over the winter, preventing them from being leached away by melting snow or spring rains. Leguminous green manures can obtain large quantities of nitrogen from the air and, when turned under, provide this nutrient for use by following crops. But there is considerable question about the efficacy of green manure crops for adding to humus content. Some experts believe that the increased biological activity caused by adding green organic matter to soil results in a possible net

FIG. 2-19 *At the end of the summer growing season the hay mulch in the paths of this intensive garden can be dug into the soil to add to its humus content.*

loss of humus under certain conditions (particularly heat and high humidity).

From our own experience we believe that green manures have a role to play in helping to build soil humus if they are used in combination with the addition of other organic matter and if they are used in the spring and fall when temperatures are lower. This means that although the green manure crop can be planted or grown at any time you choose, the best time to turn the crop into the soil is either in the early spring or fall. Our own unscientific testing seems to indicate that there is no appreciable difference in humus content of soils between beds that received both green manure and compost and those that received only compost. On the other hand, beds that received only green manure had a noticeably poorer texture after two years compared with those that received compost. Nutrient levels in all the beds were comparable, yet production in the composted beds appeared to be better. The added benefit of the green manure was in eliminating the need to add as much fertilizer, not in quickly improved soil texture.

Of course, if you have more patience than we do and are willing to wait a few years before the humus levels of your soil build up, you can rely more heavily upon green manures. If used in the right way, many gardeners have indicated that they can slowly improve humus content using only winter cover crops and a rotation of leguminous green manures.

6. Once you have reached a satisfactory humus level, you can reduce your organic matter additions. While building organic matter in our soils, we have regularly added 3 to 6 inches of rotted manure or compost to each bed every year. In beds covered by season-extending devices, we have added slightly more, but in

regular applications between crops. Once our beds become established, however, we have found that cutting back to 1 to 2 inches or organic material is sufficient to maintain quality in summer beds, and 2 to 4 inches is sufficient in glazed beds. In calculating this figure we have included turning under spoiled and decomposed mulches.

Lastly, if you subscribe to the "no-till" method of gardening, we suspect you will find our method extremely labor intensive. There is no doubt that the most laborious part of intensive gardening is soil building. It certainly was for the early French intensive gardeners, who had not only to mix the soil by hand but also to carry the manure on their backs! (See Appendix A.) But we believe that the results are worth the effort. After building a good soil, you will want to go back to the no-till/heavy mulch method. We describe in chapter 4 the no-till methods used by some of the gardeners we visited while preparing this book.

4. Balancing pH

Potential hydrogen or pH, discussed earlier in this chapter, is a measure of the existence of H^+ ions in the soil. Since in any soil H^+ ions take top priority for cation attachment sites, an excess of H^+ ions results in fewer spaces for nutrient cations to attach themselves. This condition is commonly referred to as "acid." On the other hand, if there is an excess of OH^- ions (hydroxyl ions) in the soil, it produces what is known as an alkaline condition. In alkaline soils OH^- ions combine with whatever cations are available (usually nutrients), taking them away from exchange sites and locking them up.

This means that in either an acid or alkaline soil nutrients become unavailable to plant roots. In acid soils they are being bumped out of exchange sites by the abundance of H^+ ions, and in alkaline soils they are being "stolen" by OH^- ions. Obviously the way to solve this problem is to have a balanced amount of each or a neutral soil where neither of these ions gains control.

As indicated earlier, the desirable pH level for most plants is 6.5 to 7.0 (see figure 2–20). There are exceptions, and they fall mostly into the category of acid-loving plants like strawberries, blueberries, and potatoes. Some plants, like beets, seem to prefer a slightly alkaline soil, pH 7.0–8.0. A quick check of the pH chart that comes with most soil test kits or in any basic gardening book can give you specifics on individual plant species.

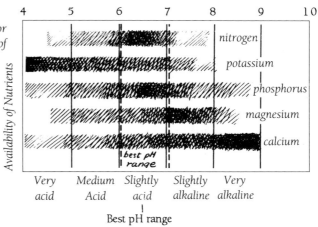

FIG. 2-20 The availability of nutrients for use by plants is a factor of the pH level of the soil.

You should be especially careful always to have proper soil pH. If your soil varies considerably from the neutral point, you can have serious problems. Aluminum becomes available as a cation as soil pH rises above 8.0 and becomes toxic at levels not much higher. Aluminum is normally found in all soils but is usually bound tightly to soil particles and cannot be taken up by plant roots. The cation form, however, is taken up by plants.

At very low pH (below 5), not only are most macronutrients less available, but some trace nutrients (iron and manganese in particular) become too available and can cause imbalances in plant metabolism (see figure 2–21).

Many gardeners feel they can determine the soil pH by looking around to see which weeds are most common in their garden. Weeds are often a good indicator of pH levels because each species has a specific pH preference. On the other hand, we have seen situations where weeds are very inaccurate indicators of pH because of other complex soil conditions. This being the case, it is wise to keep the soil test kit handy and use it regularly to test for soil pH. We usually test once in the spring, before adding fertilizer or other organic matter, then again shortly before planting. Adjustments can be made easily at these times, but they are more difficult once crops are established. We test again in the fall before planting our winter vegetables or cover crops.[1]

FIG. 2-21 *These tomatoes were grown in soil watered exclusively with solutions at the pH shown on the labels. Notice that the plants grew best when the pH was 7.0, or neutral. All the plants in this experiment received the same amount of nutrients in the watering solution.*

The frequent addition of well-decomposed organic matter has what is known as a "buffering" effect upon soil pH. A buffered soil tends to stay at a stable pH because the constant decomposition of organic matter released both acidic and alkaline compounds in roughly equal amounts. This means that as your soil texture and humus content improve, it becomes less and less common that pH adjustments are necessary—pH will tend to stabilize at around 6.5 to 7.0. Of course, if you are adding a very acidic organic substance like pine needles or peat moss, this buffering effect can be negated.

You can use the following rules to guide your efforts in balancing pH:

1. If acidity is your problem (as in most of the eastern United States), you must add an alkaline substance to the soil. There are a few to choose from: rock lime; wood ashes (unleached); bone meal.

---

[1]For more information about weeds, consult "Weeds as Indicators of Soil Conditions" by Dr. Stuart Hill, McDonald College, McGill University, Montreal, Quebec.

Rock lime is the most commonly used pH conditioner. The amount you use depends upon the size of the particles in your soil. Clay soils are more difficult to adjust because there are more particles and thus more places for H^+ ions to "hide." The following amounts of ground dolomitic limestone are recommended:

Light sandy soil	5 lbs/100 sq ft will raise pH one point
Sandy loam	7 lbs/100 sq ft will raise pH one point
Good humus-rich loam	10 lbs/100 sq ft will raise pH one point
Heavy clay	12–15 lbs/100 sq ft will raise pH one point

Wood ashes (from hardwoods) are also an alkaline substance containing significant amounts of calcium, potassium, and magnesium. In general, one pound of wood ashes will have the same liming value of two-thirds pound of ground limestone. The nutrients in wood ashes are more soluble than these in lime and will have a rapid, but not long-lasting, effect on soil pH. Rain will quickly leach out these minerals if you don't store your wood ashes under cover, before use.

Use caution in applying ashes. They are mildly caustic and can cause adverse skin reactions in some people. Avoid getting them on plant leaves, as some plants will be damaged. It is also important to use only ashes from wood and not from burned trash, magazines, plastics, or coal. These products might contain hazardous materials like toxic metals and other compounds.

It is also wise to use wood ashes only as an occasional fertilizer because wood ashes can be high in trace metals, such as cadmium, which build up in the soil. If you use ashes in the vegetable garden, use them either in small amounts each year or in larger amounts every few years.

2. If your soil is alkaline, the traditional solution has been to add sulfur. Sulfur mixes with hydrogen and oxygen to form sulfuric acid, and this lowers pH. Unfortunately, most sulfur for pH adjustment is provided using calcium sulfate (gypsum), which adds more calcium to soils tending to have more than enough calcium already. Another traditional solution has been to add borax, but excess boron can easily kill many plants. Ammonium sulfate is another chemical used by nonorganic growers.

The preferable way to reduce alkalinity is through the addition of acidic organic matter. Cottonseed meal, acid peat moss, or decomposed oak leaves will gradually reduce pH to acceptable levels. Pine needles can be used for some crops like strawberries or blueberries, but many vegetables find the tannins and acids of pine needles to be toxic.

Humic acids in compost and other acids found in fresh animal manures tend to neutralize pH as well. Fifty pounds of fresh manure (with minimal bedding), or 2 cubic feet spread over 100 square feet of loose loamy soil, will generally lower pH one point.

CONCLUSION

If we consider "efficiency" in the garden to mean getting the most production with the least effort, the place to put that effort is into soil building. The best soils produce the best vegetables. It is certainly more efficient to build good soil than it is to struggle with the weed, pest, and nutrient problems that attend poorly managed soil.

An additional benefit is that recent scientific research is beginning to show what good organic gardeners have long suspected: Food grown on rich organic soils can be higher in nutritional value and more healthful than that grown on chemically boosted mineral soils. Evidently the balance of trace minerals and the more consistent growth cycle are capable of producing crops with small, but measurable, increases of vitamins and minerals necessary in the human diet. Of course, organic gardeners always claim that their produce tastes better, too, but this is a claim too subjective to verify.

Recent attention to biological pest control and "integrated pest management" has looked into the role that certain plant hormones have upon insect pests. It appears that under stressful conditions, (drought, nutrient deficiency, poor soil texture), plants either fail to produce some insect-repelling hormones or instead produce excesses of compounds that attract pests. This information may help to explain the observation of many organic gardeners that pests somehow seem to prefer the least-healthy plants, leaving the robust individuals alone or less ravaged. In the rich organic soils of the intensive garden, stressful conditions are minimized. Our own experience seems to confirm this notion. As our soil has improved over the years, certain pest problems have become noticeably less severe, and some pests that rampage through neighbors' gardens are "endangered species" in ours.

There's one more thing soil building can do for efficiency. It can be an efficient way to get some exercise without putting on your jogging shoes. Let's face it—soil building is just plain physical exercise. If you look at it as drudgery, it will be; if you consider it a pleasant alternative to daily workouts or the same old jog around the block, it can be a pleasant and rewarding opportunity.

FURTHER READINGS:

Alther, R., and R. Raymond. *Improving Garden Soil with Green Manures* (Charlotte, Vt.: Garden Way, 1974). *A short booklet with practical suggestions.*

Buckman, H. O., and N. C. Brady. *The Nature and Properties of Soils* (New York: Macmillan, 1969). *A widely used college textbook on agricultural soils.*

Campbell, Stu. *Let It Rot!* (Charlotte, Vt.: Garden Way, 1975). *A how-to book on home composting.*

Coleman, Eliot. *The New Organic Grower* (Chelsea, Vt.: Chelsea Green, 1989). Eliot Coleman is one of the most expert organic market gardeners in America. His discussion of soil is practical and readable.

Farb, Peter. *Living Earth* (New York: Harper Colophon, 1959). *A readable look at soil biology.*

Forth, H. D., and L. M. Turk. *Fundamentals of Soil Science* (New York: Wiley, 1972). *A basic textbook.*

Gershuny, Grace. *The Soul of Soil* (Cooperative Extension Service, University of Vermont, 1983). *An excellent guide to managing soils using ecological principles.*

Golueke, Clarence. *Composting: A Study of the Process and Its Principles* (Emmaus, Pa.: Rodale, 1972). *For advanced readers.*

Howard, Sir Albert. *The Soil and Health* (New York: Schocken, 1972). *A worldwide view of the importance of soil health and humus to agriculture, by a major pioneer in organic methods.*

Hyams, Edward. *Soil and Civilization* (New York: Harper Colophon, 1952, 1976). *A history of the relationship between human civilizations and their use and abuse of the soil.*

Janick, J., R. Schery, F. Woods, and V. Ruttan. *Plant Science: An Introduction to World Crops* (San Francisco: W. H. Freeman and Co., 1974). *Contains a very good chapter on soil science and its relation to plant growth and health.*

Koepf, H. H. *Compost: What It Is, How It Is Made, What It Does* (Biodynamic Farming and Gardening Association, 1966).

Logsdon, Gene. *Gardener's Guide to Better Soil* (Emmaus, Pa.: Rodale, 1975).

Martin, Deborah L., and Gershuny, Grace, editors. *Rodale Book of Composting* (Emmaus, Pa.: Rodale Press, 1992). An excellent source of information on composting and fertilizer values of compost.

Ogden, Shepherd. *Step by Step Organic Gardening* (New York: Harper Collins, 1992). A good general guide to organic gardening with a detailed discussion of soil building.

Organic Fertilizers: Which Ones and How to Use Them. The Staff of *Organic Gardening* magazine (Emmaus, Pa.: Rodale, 1973). *Provides good information on a wide variety of fertilizers and their application.*

Parnes, Robert. *Organic and Inorganic Fertilizers* (Woods End Agricultural Institute, Mt. Vernon, Maine, 1986). *Perhaps the best existing discussion of the values of organic and inorganic fertilizers in building good soils and crop productivity. Highly recommended.*

Putnam, Cynthia, editor. *Easy Composting* (Ortho Books, 1992). Detailed sets of instructions for numerous methods of building compost.

Soil. U.S. Department of Agriculture, Yearbook of Agriculture, 1957.

CHAPTER 3

Building Intensive Garden Beds

While visiting intensive gardens in the eastern United States, we were impressed with the diversity of methods successfully used to prepare garden beds. The gardeners we met had adapted intensive techniques creatively for many individual locations and needs. In recognition of this diversity, we will describe a variety of these gardens, with the hope that you can gain from them as you evolve a method suited to your situation and personality.

PERMANENT BEDS

The growing beds in most intensive gardens are permanent, meaning that they are in the same place every year. The obvious advantage to this is that the majority of the work in establishing a garden is done the first year. Thereafter, preparing the bed is a much smaller chore. The gardener adds his compost, etc., to the same bed areas each year rather than broadcasting it across an entire garden, including areas to be used for paths. Thus he takes advantage of all the work and organic matter put into the bed the previous season.

The garden that Tim Fisher and Kathleen Kolb had in northern Vermont was composed of permanent beds. These beds were boxed in with wooden sides. Boxed-in beds were chosen for the following reasons: (1) The board sides made efficient use of the deep-dug area because no growing space is lost to the sloping sides typical of beds without sides. (2) Board sides prevent erosion of beds. (3) They look tidy. (4) By clearly separating the path and garden-bed areas, the board sides made an easy barrier to remind their small children to walk only in the paths, not in the bed. (5) The boards, by extending 2 inches below

FIG. 3-1 The Allhouse's garden in northeastern Vermont has permanent grass paths between the garden beds.

the level of the paths, provide a barrier that prevents weeds from encroaching onto the beds from the paths.

The bed sides were made of 1-by-10-inch or 2-by-10-inch lumber nailed together at the corners, making 10-inch tall frames. Tim and Kathleen found it convenient to have two standard sizes of beds, 3 feet by 7 feet and 3 feet by 16 feet. As discussed in chapter 1, there are a number of considerations in deciding what size beds to build, the most important being that beds much wider than 4 feet become hard to reach across.

A mixture of grass and clover was grown in the paths, which were mown as part of the surrounding lawn. In addition to being attractive, the grass paths prevent erosion and create a soft ground cover between the beds that is neither muddy nor dried out (see figure 3–1).

The beds themselves were dug by hand. Sod, weeds (and pernicious weed rhizomes), and many rocks were removed from the soil in excavating the bed area to a 2-foot depth. Then wood ashes, compost, manure, and rock phosphate were mixed with the loosened soil. Though this was done fairly casually, the average addition was a wheelbarrow load of manure and one of compost per 20 square feet, and a few shovels full of ashes and rock phosphate. For certain crops not nearly so much was added, whereas others get a higher share (see chapter 5 for more detailed fertilizer information). The box sides were placed on the bed area and filled with the fortified soil to create small, level plateaus of rich, aerated earth. Though it initially requires a lot of work to establish these beds, they need little maintenance during the growing season and were given only a cursory turning, with the addition of organic matter and necessary fertilizer, each subsequent spring. Some people will find such deep soil preparation unnecessary, but in this situation it was worthwhile, if only because some of the rocks removed took up nearly half the area of the smaller beds (3 feet by 7 feet).

A big work saver in establishing a new bed is to lay salvaged sheets of corrugated metal roofing over the area where the bed will be. This is done a full year before digging the bed. The next spring the soil under the roofing will be free of weeds and sod, and will allow very easy digging.

Because Tim and Kathleen had scrap hardwood boards available, they used them to box in their beds. Some people have expressed a concern that wood sides on beds harbor slugs. Though none of the gardeners with boxed beds whom we visited have had problems with this, it is definitely a possibility. The wood sides last well for about seven years. After fifteen years gardening in the same location the oldest bed sides had to be replaced. As the old sides rot, they replaced them with permanent concrete sides, which proved to be the best solution for them.

After some experimentation Tim Fisher found that the best method of making concrete sides for garden beds was to cast them in place (see figure 3–2). He used an outer form and an inner form, and poured the concrete between them. The forms, made of 2-by-4-inch lumber, had a slight taper to them, making concrete sides that are 2 inches wide at the top and 4 inches wide at the base. The taper makes it much easier to remove the form in one piece because as it slides upward over the hardened cement, the fit becomes looser. Tim has only one set of forms, which he moved from bed to bed as he casts the concrete, so easy removal and reuse is important. He had some trouble separating the inner form from the concrete, so he stapled a scrap of polyethylene sheeting around both ends of the inner form. This made a slick surface, which separates readily from the concrete. The diagram (figure 3–3) shows the dimensions of the forms Tim used for making beds 7 feet long by 3 feet wide. If your beds are a different size, you would use different dimensions, but the principle is the same.

Tim removed a 6-inch strip of the soil down to the level of the path all around the perimeter of the raised bed. He then put the forms in place, measuring the forms across their diagonals to assure the corners were square. To make the garden beds level (to avoid any rain or soil runoff), he used a carpenter's level, raising the low side or sides of the form until all sides are level. Scrap boards or two-by-fours placed flush with the inside edges of the forms kept the forms in the level position and prevented the liquid concrete from flowing under the forms. The result is that the beds were 6 inches high at the low end and 8 to 10 inches high at the high end. To strengthen the concrete, Tim placed a length of re-bar (steel reinforcement bar available at building supply stores) all the way around inside the

FIG. 3-2 Cast-in-place concrete makes permanent sides to these garden beds. The bed in the foreground shows the forms in place ready to be filled with concrete.

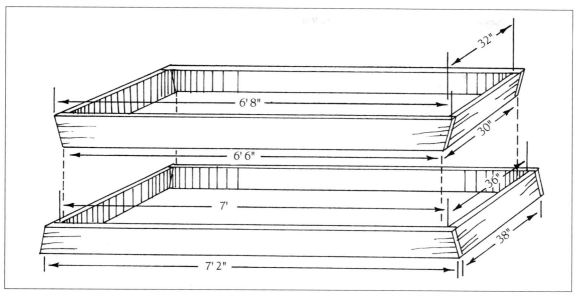

Fig. 3-3 This diagram shows the dimensions of the inner and outer forms on cast-in-place concrete garden bed sides. The dimensions shown make a three-by-seven-foot garden bed.

forms. He wired the ends of the re-bar together and put small rocks under it to assure that the re-bar was embedded in the main body of the concrete. Then he mixed one part portland cement to four parts sandy gravel and poured it between the forms. He allowed at least twenty-four hours for the mixture to harden before he removed the forms. The setting up of the forms and mixing and pouring the concrete took two or three hours per bed. Materials cost about $5.00 per bed.

After the forms were removed, Tim dug a ditch 2 inches deep and 3 inches wide around the perimeter of the concrete. He poured concrete into this trench, troweling the top surface smooth and level with the surrounding path. The purpose of this strip of concrete is to keep rhizomic weeds, such as witch grass, from invading under the sides of the beds. This concrete also improves the appearance of the garden. The lawn mower can never quite mow up to the edge of the bed, so this strip prevents grass that would require hand trimming from growing there.

SHIFTING BEDS

Intensive beds do not need to be permanent to be successful. Betsy Hibbard in Pennsylvania alternates her beds and paths each year. She uses a garden fork to form six parallel beds. Throughout the season the paths between beds are sheet-composted with leaves, grass clippings, or similar coverings. The following spring soil from the beds is forked on top of the composted paths to form new beds, and paths remain were the previous year's beds were. The new paths are sheet-composted to become beds the following year.

At the former New Alchemy Institute on Cape Cod, a similar method was practiced on a much larger scale. Four-foot-wide beds were laid out with 1-foot-wide paths between them.

The paths were dug out to a depth of 6 to 12 inches, and the dug-out soil was spread on the beds. The New Alchemists then sheet-composted, gradually filling the paths through the season with any available organic matter. Gardener Hilde Maingay pointed out that this method is more efficient because compost materials are moved only once, and garden weeds and wastes can simply be thrown into the paths as one weeds or harvests. Also, their garden was designed as a prototype for a suburban situation, where there are seldom enough materials at one time to make a full compost pile, and where neighbors may complain that a compost pile is ugly. Other advantages are that nutrient leaching occurs where you want it to occur in the garden; the water-holding capacity of the soil in the beds is noticeably improved; the sheet composting replaces the need to mulch the paths and sides of beds; and the beds remain more moist than with mulch. In this system the paths could be flooded for irrigation, in which case the water would be enriched with nutrients from the paths.

Hilde mentioned that it requires careful maneuvering to deliver and distribute this organic matter to the narrow paths. In the *Journal of the New Alchemists, No.4*, she writes:

> *Sheet composting still does not completely replace the regular compost pile. In a well-built, balanced pile the heat created during the first decomposition process can kill grubs, eggs, and some pathogenic organisms. In the next steps of the breakdown process, the action of fungi produces antibiotics and growth hormones in higher concentration than possible in regular soil. . . . At the end of the growing season all the beds were moved a third of their width by digging up part of the beds and putting dirt on top of the sheet compost filled pathways. At the same time new pathways were created.*

After four years the beds will have shifted to their original locations (see figure 3–4). With the great quantity of organic matter composting in the paths, Hilde said they had no worries about compacting paths that would next year be part of the beds. The vitality we saw in the garden certainly suggests no such problems.

First year

Second year

Third year

Fourth year

FIG. 3-4 *Sheet composting in the paths between garden beds means that the beds move one-third of their width every year.*

TILTH AND CULTIVATION METHODS

There is debate among intensive gardeners whether it is best to dig beds by hand, use a Rototiller, or do no tilling at all. We have seen good gardens in which all three methods have been used.

The gardening techniques used by the late Alan Chadwick have been popularized in America by John Jeavons in his book *How to Grow More Vegetables.* Chadwick's method relies on hand digging to supply tilth. The garden beds are cultivated by double digging, an old technique for preparing garden soil that is common in ornamental horticulture (see figures 3–5, and 3–6). The method generally is first to skim vegetation off the growing bed with a sharp spade and set it aside. A trench is dug across the bed one "spit" (the height of a spade's blade) deep, and the soil is removed. Next, a spading fork is pushed into the soil at the bottom of the trench and worked and twisted around so that the soil is thoroughly loosened without being removed. Then the weeds or plant residues that had been skimmed off are put into the trench. They are covered with soil removed in the process of opening the adjacent trench. In opening the second trench, the digging becomes "double slide digging," for the soil is cut in chunks and tossed (or "slid") onto the layer of vegetation in such a way that the soil retains its natural stratification, top on top and bottom on bottom. Though loosened, the soil basically holds together without crumbling. After this basic preparation compost and manure are added in a separate process, being turned into the top inches of the bed.

FIG. 3-5 Double-digging was used to form the beds of the late Alan Chadwick's gardens in Virginia (Carmel in the Valley).

1. Skim vegetation from the bed surface and open a trench as deep as your shovel.

2. Loosen the subsoil in the trench.

FIG. 3-6 Double digging.

3. Put the skimmed vegetation in the trench.

4. Fill the first trench as you open the next one, continuing in the same manner.

Chadwick's methods (as described by John Jeavons) were followed successfully by many of the gardeners we visited. The gardens founded by Alan Chadwick at Carmel in the Valley in Virginia were an inspiration to many gardeners. (Unfortunately, since his death, these gardens no longer exist.) We have found, however, that except for places with severe hardpan or no winter-frost heaving of the soil, the tremendous amount of work involved in double digging and subsoiling is unnecessary and no more productive than other methods of building garden beds. It is more important for the top soil to be fertile than to spend a lot of time subsoiling, particularly if it means you get only half the garden planted.

Machine Tilling

Many intensive gardeners find that a Rototiller is an invaluable tool. Many other gardeners who now use hand tilling or no tilling found a Rototiller helpful when originally establishing their beds. All the commercial intensive gardeners we visited relied upon some rototilling or the use of larger machinery, finding hand tilling too time-consuming to be profitable. They relied upon green manure crops as part of their fertility program and found a Rototiller indispensable for tilling these crops into the soil.

In Paul Doscher's southern New Hampshire garden, he uses a Rototiller both to form and cultivate beds. To form the beds he uses a rear-tined tiller and furrowing tool (see figure 3–7). First, he tills the entire garden area to as deep a level as possible, usually 6 to 8 inches. Then he attaches the furrower to the tiller and runs it across the area wherever paths will be located. The furrower pushes the soil up onto surrounding areas, forming instant beds after only one or two passes. He then levels the beds with a rake.

The Doschers have also used the tiller in subsoiling. First, with a cultivating fork and shovel, they pull aside the topsoil from a bed already built or a new bed area. The soil is raked into long mounds on either side of the bed, revealing the subsoil. They then run the

FIG. 3-7 *Paul and Debbie Doscher use a rear-tined tiller and furrowing tool to build their beds.*

tiller down into the subsoil, loosening it and turning it to a depth of 8 to 10 inches. Next, the topsoil is pushed back over the subsoil, with care not to mix the two layers. The bed is finally reformed and allowed to settle for a few days before planting.

Adam Tomash in Maine uses a walking tractor with furrower attachment to deep-dig his market garden in preparation for carrots. He makes a preliminary pass with the furrower where the wide-row carrot plantings will be, leaving approximately 6-inch-deep trenches in the wake of the furrower and ridges of earth between the trenches. Adam often adds compost to these trenches. He next offsets the position of his furrower on the walking tractor by half the track width of the tractor. With the furrower off-set he digs new trenches where the ridges of earth were, pushing both the ridges and the soil from the new trenches on top of the original trench. By this method Adam builds narrow raised beds, which are loosened and enriched to a depth of approximately 12 inches. As determined by the 24-inch width of his walking tractor, the raised beds are about 12 inches wide.

George Crane, a commercial vegetable grower in Vermont, had a bed-forming attachment built to his specifications and mounted it on the three-point hitch behind his tractor. The tractor straddled one 4-foot-wide bed with its wheels, forming the paths between beds. George's bed-forming system was coordinated with the machinery he used for planting, surface cultivating, spraying, and harvesting. Although George's bed former was designed for a commercial scale, a home gardener could build this on a smaller scale for use behind a garden tractor or walking tractor and save a lot of work in the garden.

Before making the beds, the soil was cultivated. The final cultivation involved rotovating (a rotovator is a wide Rototiller that attaches to the rear of a tractor) the full area with a thirty-six-tine, 60-inch-wide (the same width as the tractor) rotovator to a depth of 12 inches. To permit rotovating to this depth, the field must be free of rocks. To minimize soil compaction George used a lightweight tractor for rotovating and bed forming.

The bed-forming frame works as follows (see figure 3–8). A disk is mounted behind and just inside each rear tractor tire. Each disk (from a heavy-duty disk harrow) is adjustable in angle and depth, but usually is mounted at an angle of about 45 degrees to the direction the tractor is moving in. The disks scoop into the loose soil, forming the sides of the bed and pushing soil toward hardwood forming boards (also adjusted at about 45 degrees), which spread the soil across the bed. Behind the forming boards a hardwood flattening board

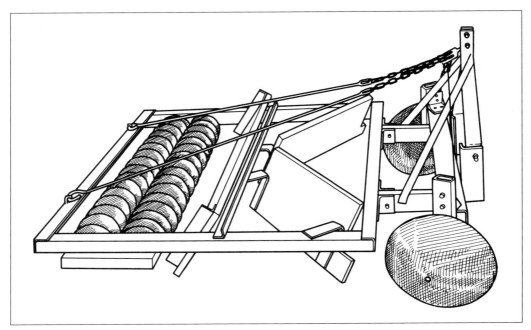

FIG. 3-8 A tractor-drawn bed-former.

stretches the width of the frame to smooth the bed surface. At the back of the frame, forty small disks give the soil a final pulverization to break up any small clumps and leave a fine seedbed.

The height of the beds can be adjusted by the three-point hitch and the individual parts. George normally made the surface of his beds about 8 inches above the tractor-wheel path. The soil in the beds was loose to a depth that usually enabled him to push his arm into the soil up to his elbow.

Minimal Tilling

Many gardeners find a Rototiller valuable for preparing the seedbed and controlling early weeds. The soil should not be tilled, however, any more than is necessary. Tilling destroys the soil's structure, and a gardener should be trying to improve this structure.

A loose, rich soil can be built and maintained with no tilling by either hand or machine. We visited the very productive garden of David Emery in Maine, which has been managed organically for twenty-five years. He adds up to a foot of mulch to the garden each year, but he never tills (see figure 3–9). When he wants to plant, he simply pulls apart enough mulch to allow him to scratch the soil with his finger and drop in the seed.

To establish raised beds, Janney Munsell, also of Maine, used a Rototiller on her garden area (see figure 3–10). Then, on the loose soil, she laid out bottomless boxes to contain her raised beds and shoveled the loose topsoil from the paths into the beds, filling the boxes to the top. Once the beds were set up, she didn't till the beds again. To maintain the beds she adds mulch and organic matter to the surface each spring and fall. The soil looked beautiful, and so did her vegetables.

FIG. 3-9 David Emery's no-till garden in Maine.

Carolyn and Earl Lawrence have a hard clay soil on their southern Virginia farm. Through chisel plowing, surface disking, manuring, cover cropping, green manuring, and strict crop rotation, they have developed it into a viable organic vegetable farm.

Of special interest to us was that with little work and no tilling, they were able to produce a soil in their kitchen garden as good or better than that in their commercial farm. Furthermore, they estimated that the soil improvement accomplished in a single growing season in the kitchen garden was comparable to three to five years' work on the farm soil.

To do this the Lawrences laid baled hay, solidly, one-bale deep across their new garden area (see figure 3–11). They then spread 5- or 6-inch-deep strips of compost across the top of the bales and planted their seeds directly in these compost strips. The vegetables grew prolifically atop the bales, which decompose down to a depth of 2½ to 3 inches over their growing season (see figure

FIG. 3-10 Janney Munsell in her garden in Maine.

Fig. 3-11 Earl and Carolyn Lawrence create a garden area on their hard clay earth in Virginia by spreading baled hay solidly across the area, one bale deep.

3–12). The Lawrences have an ample supply of hay bales on their farm because the price of hay fell so low in some years that they chose to return the hay to the soil rather than sell it at no profit. This practice makes sense for their kitchen garden, though it would not be appropriate, nor would they have an adequate supply of hay, on the farm scale. Obviously, many people won't have the number of hay bales necessary to cover their whole garden, but in difficult soil conditions it could be tried on individual garden beds.

The Lawrence family is trying a similar technique in a smaller area, which their son plans to use for tulip propagation. One course of hay bales was laid around the new garden space, forming a low wall, and the enclosed area was filled with compost materials that break down into a rich growing medium.

WET SOILS

If your garden is too wet, your soil preparation may correct the problem. Often the addition of organic matter and sand may be all that is necessary. One Vermont gardener, in a wet location where water saturated his beds late into spring, found it advantageous to do his basic bed preparation in the fall. He raked each bed up into a rough-surfaced peaked ridge to shed water and left it that way through the winter. In spring he raked the bed flat, and it was ready to plant.

Poor drainage on a clay soil was the primary reason that Winnie Amato of Medina, Ohio, chose to establish her raised-bed garden. Her combination of raised beds and trenched paths has eliminated her drainage problems. In fact, she has turned her clay into such a rich worm-filled soil that she has won first prize for her vegetables at the county fair.

To prepare her garden Winnie Amato tilled the entire area and laid out 4-foot wooden frames about 8 inches high on the tilled area. She allowed for paths about 2 feet wide between the beds. The path areas were dug into trenches, depositing the soil from the trenches into the boxed beds, and the trenches were filled with corncobs, a waste product in her corn-growing area (see figure 3–13). Lawn cuttings were also added to the paths as the

FIG. 3-12 After only one year, the baled hay in the Lawrence's garden decomposed to form this black humus, which is scraped aside in this photo to show the clay underneath.

FIG. 3-13 To solve poor drainage in her clay soil, Winnie Amato in Ohio trenched her paths and filled them with waste corn cobs.

season progressed. The corn-cob-filled trenches acted as a drainage area for the beds, eventually decomposing into a humus. The clay in the garden was mixed with sand, compost, and chicken manure to make a healthy loam. With her beds established, Winnie pointed out that she no longer rototills the garden and is able to work the garden earlier in the spring.

The conventional agricultural soil-drainage method is either ditching or installing a buried drain-tile network to carry excess water to lower ground. This method is rather expensive and time-consuming, but it is effective and should be considered where simpler methods don't work.

FIG. 3-14 Terracing is common in places with a hillside agricultural tradition. In these terraced beds in southern Italy, citrus trees are covered with a protective netting.

EROSION

Erosion is a serious concern to any gardener trying to build a rich soil and to any citizen who recognizes the necessity of maintaining soil fertility for the survival of future generations.

    In parts of the world with hillside agricultural traditions, such as the Mediterranean, much of Asia, and the Andes, permanent stone-wall terracing is a standard erosion control without which agriculture could not have survived (see figure 3–14). In severe terrain the example of these cultures is well worth following. In addition to stone, retaining walls can be

FIG. 3-15 Tony Bok's terraced beds in Maine.

made of planks, railroad ties, logs, concrete blocks, and bricks, or they can be formed of an earthen berm maintained in a permanent ground cover.

The intensive gardener has the option of either terracing a large garden area or terracing each bed individually. Even on moderate slopes your garden beds should follow the contour of the land, each bed acting as a dam that prevents precious soil from washing down the hill.

In order to counter erosion on his hillside farm in Maine, Tony Bok has adopted a system of terraced beds stretching across the steep slope of his commercial vegetable garden (see figure 3–15). To establish the beds he rototilled the garden area and marked out 4-foot-wide beds with 2-foot-wide paths. He raked the dirt uphill out of each path, building up the low side of the bed above until it was level. He always raked uphill to counter the effect of soil washed down the hill through erosion.

Ray Nelson of nearby Friendship, Maine, has also established terraced beds along the contours of his hillside garden (see figure 3–16). He has refined this method by keeping his paths planted in a permanent sod to assist further in controlling erosion. He mulched extensively for the same reason. As he said, "I try to do as little damage to the natural world as I can, and do as nature does. Nature doesn't leave soil bare." Ray also laid rocks along the lower edge of the beds to stabilize them.

Cover crops and mulching are valuable practices, which, among their other benefits, help to hold the soil in garden beds. Cover crops can be seeded just before or after a bed is harvested. Mulches are useful both during and after the growing season.

FIG. 3-16 Ray Nelson contours his beds across the hillside and leaves his paths in permanent sod to control erosion.

PATHS

The treatment of paths between garden beds is important to most gardeners even where erosion is not a problem. Most people garden for pleasure in addition to food. A muddy or hard and dry path is not pleasant to work on. Permanent grass and/or legume paths are attractive, pleasant to work on, and hold the soil. As always, legumes may improve the soil in which they are grown as well as provide the other benefits of a ground cover. Sod paths, however, must be mown regularly, and, particularly with unboxed-in beds, the edges of the paths must be maintained to prevent them from encroaching into the beds (see figure 3–17).

Sheet composting and mulches are also satisfactory path treatments. With unboxed beds many gardeners like to mulch the sloping sides of the beds in addition to the paths. Common mulching materials are hay, grass clippings, leaves, wood chips, etc. (see figure 3–18). Newspaper is often used as a mulch, but it is usually held down by another mulch material, such as straw, hay, bark, or wood chips to keep it from blowing away. Organic mulches must be replenished frequently because they decompose and weeds begin to grow through them, but, of course, all that rotted mulch is enriching the garden soil.

More permanent paths can be made of paving materials such as concrete, brick, or stone. These materials will also absorb solar heat during the day, radiating that stored heat to the surrounding soil and air at night.

Weeds growing in the paths are not necessarily bad; after all, some weeds are an effective ground cover, and just because they are self-sowing does not make them undesirable.

FIG. 3-17 Cement sides keep grass from encroaching into this garden bed in Richmond, New Zealand.

We even know of some gardeners who "eat out of the paths." Many edible weeds, such as amaranth, chickweed, dandelion, sourgrass, and purslane, grow wild in the paths. But path weeds can get out of control if their roots encroach into the beds. If they are not kept cut, the weeds go to seed, sowing more weeds in the beds, where they may overwhelm, or at least retard, the domesticated vegetables. Many weeds not only spread their seeds, but also creep and spread by root division. Eventually, even edible weeds like purslane and sheep sorrel can become a major nuisance if not rooted out.

FIG. 3-18 A garden path mulched with wood chips in Janney Munsell's Maine garden.

CHAPTER 4

Planting

A s an efficient gardener, in addition to all your other skills, it will help to be a visionary. Your planting, transplanting, and successions all benefit from your being able to envision the garden throughout the growing season. Using that vision, you can then anticipate when to start new plants so that they will be ready to fill their niche in the garden cycle when it becomes available. This includes having transplants ready as soon as the weather warms enough to plant in the spring, having replacement plants ready as crops are harvested, and having cool weather plants started for the fall.

SPROUTING SEED

Using sprouted seed is an obvious way to extend your growing season by a few days. It also helps to assure that you will get a plant from each seed, because you can discard the seeds that didn't germinate before planting. Most seeds need a fairly warm temperature to germinate, but once sprouted, they will grow in less ideal circumstances. A simple sprouting technique is to lay your seeds on a moist paper towel, roll the towel up, and place it in a plastic bag to retain moisture. Place it in a warm area. A spot near a heating vent or radiator works well; some people use an electric heating mat that maintains a soil temperature around 75°–80° F. Check the seeds frequently. If left too long unattended, the seed can rot from over moisture or grow into large sprouts that are hard to plant. When the seeds sprout, you can plant them in a flat or in the garden. It is more difficult to plant sprouted seeds than dry seeds because, being wet, they tend to clump together, and you have to be careful not to break the radicals (seed roots). Even if you don't go to the trouble of sprouting seeds, you can speed up the germination of most seeds simply by soaking them in water overnight before planting.

PROPAGATION SPACES

When starting seedlings for transplants, we recommend starting them in flats in a propagation space. You can use a box (like a coldframe with a transparent top) or a plastic tent and set it up in a greenhouse, on a windowsill, or under plant-growth lights (see figure 4–1). Within the propagation space the environment retains added heat and moisture, which are conducive to good seedling growth. A more sophisticated propagation chamber is an insulated box with fluorescent lights over the flats and a heat coil on the bottom to provide heat. When using a warm propagation space, there is no need to pre-sprout the seeds.

FIG. 4-1 *This simple propagating tent is made of plastic and is heated by an electric cable.*

TRANSPLANTS

Transplants are an important aspect of your intensive garden. Not only will they help you to establish a living mulch on your growing beds quickly, but they are also a way to use space efficiently (see figure 4–2). For instance, you may be accustomed to planting a row of lettuce seeds, then thinning the seedlings to stand 12 inches apart. If your row is 15 feet long, this will give you fifteen lettuce plants, which occupy that space for a full six or seven weeks. If, however, you grew fifteen lettuce plants in a flat for their first four weeks, they would take up considerably less space, and in the meantime you could get a full crop of radishes from your 15-foot row.

Many people start long-season vegetables, such as tomatoes and eggplant, indoors so that their fruit will ripen before the cool fall weather. You can keep peppers and tomatoes over the winter in pots, transplanting already-bearing plants in the spring (see figure 4–3). Suckers and cuttings can be taken from an overwintered tomato, which will grow and produce fruit faster than seedlings will. By starting early and transplanting some faster-maturing vegetables, such as lettuce and broccoli, you can eat them much earlier than you would otherwise. It is important to transplant seedlings carefully, avoiding disturbance to the roots and

FIG. 4-2 Transplants help to quickly establish a growing bed, using space more efficiently. In short growing seasons they are an essential step in raising long-season vegetables such as eggplant and tomatoes.

FIG. 4-3 This cherry tomato plant, kept over the winter on a windowsill in a five-gallon bucket, was already bearing tomatoes by the time it was transplanted outside in the spring.

main stem; otherwise, their growth will be slowed down, eliminating any advance on the season you had been hoping to make.

The gardener with a long season and plenty of room may see little reason to spend time transplanting, yet the time spent on this may be saved on weeding and watering. The advantage in terms of weed control is that the soil can be turned and raked to eliminate all weeds just before transplanting. This gives the seedlings of your crop a good head start over the next batch of weeds, which will come later. By the time the weeds germinate (some will always still be there no matter how often you cultivate), the crop will usually be well established. It will also start to form the desired living mulch to help conserve water (see figures 4–4 and 4–5).

To grow good seedlings in flats requires a moist, loose soil. A good soil for flats is made up of equal parts of compost, garden loam, and sand. A mixture of equal parts of purchased potting soil and peat moss, plus 10 percent vermiculite is often preferable because it is a sterile medium, and thus you won't have to worry about soil-transmitted diseases affecting the seedlings. In order to minimize transplant shock and encourage growth, you should occasionally fertilize flats with manure tea or fish emulsion. Plants started inside should be gradually acclimatized before transplanting outside or they will suffer shock from the temperature extremes and changes, the intensity of outdoor light, and wind. To acclimatize, or harden, these plants, place them outside on warm days, but bring them in again before nightfall. This can be done easily in a cold frame, which would be open during the day and closed

FIG. 4-4 These broccoli transplants will be far ahead of any weeds that sprout now. Carmel Garden Project in Virginia.

FIG. 4-5 Broccoli transplants and nicotiana at the Carmel Garden Project in Virginia.

at night. Gradually increase their exposure to the weather to include any day, warm nights, and eventually all the time. When they are used to the outdoor temperature (usually about four to five days), they are hardy enough to be transplanted. Transplants that are started in individual pots, or in flats divided into many cells, do better than plants that are grown in an undivided flat. Separating plants in an undivided flat from their neighbors always means some torn and cut roots. To minimize this stress use a sharp knife to cut through the soil between seedlings in an undivided flat about a week before you plan to put them in the garden.

Transplanting is best done in late afternoon or on a cloudy day to avoid sunscald. Depending on the weather, you may want to construct simple shields of mulch or paper around new transplants to protect them from the sun or wind. Always water seedlings promptly upon transplanting, and give them special attention until they become established.

SUCCESSION PLANTING

Succession planting means that when one crop is harvested, there will be a succeeding crop planted to take its place. The purpose of this is to keep the garden in continual production, thus giving the greatest yields per area. Whether planting seeds or seedlings, a productive intensive schedule will include succession planting. Because different vegetables are suited to different seasons and conditions, succession planting can take advantage of these differences by starting cool weather crops in the spring, followed by warm crops in midsummer, and cool crops again in the fall. With quick-maturing vegetables you may fit several successions into a single season. Even when growing long-season vegetables that require the full season to mature, it is a good practice to succeed them with a winter cover crop such as winter rye (see figure 4–6). The cover crop will hold the soil, preventing erosion during the winter, and it can be tilled in as green manure in the spring.

In Maine Tony Bok maintains a weekly schedule in his commercial lettuce garden. Every week seeds are started in flats in a greenhouse, where they remain for two weeks, after which individual plants are transplanted into larger flats with more space. When the plants are four weeks old, they are planted in the garden beds. Each week he begins this process again and so has a constant supply of young lettuce plants to

FIG. 4-6 A cover crop of winter rye.

FIG. 4-7 Succession lettuce plantings in the garden of Sam and Elizabeth Smith in Maine.

take the place of those harvested from the garden. Though dealing with only one crop, this example illustrates how succession planting can help you to utilize your entire growing area to the maximum. The growing season is stretched to include four weeks' growth inside the greenhouse before it is warm enough for outdoor planting, and it could be extended at the end of the season with the use of cold frames.

Succession planting is often combined with intercropping (growing two or more crops together). If possible, you should include crop-rotation principles in your succession planting.

CROP ROTATIONS

Different vegetables take different nutrients in varying amounts from the soil, whereas some plants also enrich the soil's store of nutrients. In order to maintain a balance of nutrients in the soil, it is necessary to rotate crops, that is, grow different plants from year to year in each of your garden beds.

Some deep-rooted plants are capable of loosening the soil; others, such as alfalfa and buckwheat, even bring up mineral nutrients from the subsoil. If these plants are green manured or composted, the nutrients will become available as the roots and foliage decompose.

In planning rotations, vegetables are usually divided into groups according to the quantity of nutrients they take from the soil. The group called heavy feeders such as tomatoes, corn, and cucumbers, draw larger quantities of macronutrients (particularly nitrogen)

Feeding Requirements of Common Vegetables.

(LF=light feeder, HF=heavy feeder.)

Artichoke, Jerusalem	*HF*
Artichoke, regular	*HF*
Asparagus	*HF*
Beans, all types	*LF*
Beets	*LF*
Broccoli	*HF*
Brussels sprouts	*HF*
Cabbage, all types	*HF*
Carrots	*LF*
Cauliflower	*HF*
Celery	*HF*
Chard	*HF*
Collards	*HF*
Corn	*HF*
Cucumbers	*HF*
Eggplant	*HF*
Garlic	*LF*
Horseradish	*LF*
Kale	*HF*
Kohlrabi	*LF*
Leeks	*LF*
Lettuce	*HF*
Melons	*HF*
Mustard	*HF*
Okra	*HF*
Onions	*LF*
Parsley	*HF*
Parsnips	*LF*
Peas	*LF*
Peppers	*HF*
Potatoes, Irish	*LF*
Potatoes, sweet	*HF*
Pumpkins	*HF*
Radishes	*LF*
Rhubarb	*HF*
Rutabagas	*LF*
Salsify	*LF*
Spinach, New Zealand	*HF*
Spinach, regular	*HF*
Squash, all types	*HF*
Sunflowers	*HF*
Tomatoes	*HF*
Watermelon	*HF*

FIG. 4-8

from the soil to grow large quantities of foliate or larger fruits. Light feeders, generally legumes or root crops, withdraw fewer nutrients and are usually plants of less physical mass (see figure 4–8).

Legumes are classed as light feeders because bacterial nodules that live on the roots of leguminous plants have the ability to convert nitrogen in the air into a form usable by the plants. The roots of the legumes then absorb this nitrogen from the bacteria. Vegetable legumes like peas or green beans are not usually carried through a long enough life cycle in the garden to contribute a significant amount of nitrogen to the soil as a whole. For legumes to add nitrogen to the soil, they should be grown to maturity and then plowed into the soil. In addition to their ability to fix nitrogen, deep-rooted legumes such as clover and alfalfa are able to bring calcium and phosphorus up from deeper levels in the soil.

Nonleguminous light feeders are mostly root crops, including turnips, parsnips, carrots, radishes, and beets. Heavy feeders include corn, potatoes, eggplant, peppers, squash, melons, the cabbage family (especially cauliflower), lettuce, spinach, chard, and celery. A useful rotation possible in an intensive garden would be a heavy feeder such as corn, followed by legumes such as soybeans, followed by a light feeder such as carrots.

Your rotation should make certain that a bed planted in heavy feeders will be followed in succession by light feeders. This succession can occur in one growing season or from one year to the next. If you grow grains, they should be incorporated into the rotation, too, as well as cover and green-manure crops. If you have a limited supply of organic fertilizer, such as manure, then including a leguminous cover crop (clover, alfalfa, vetch, etc.) in your rotation will be very important.

Although crop rotation aids in maintaining a healthy soil balance, it won't satisfy all your soil needs. you will need to continue other soil maintenance practices, too.

Diseases and insects that cause crop damage are usually partial to a specific genus or species and can often remain over winter in the soil. Used as a sanitary measure, crop rotation can minimize the damage they do. If the same crop or crop family (for example, any of the many members of the cabbage tribe) is planted in the same soil two or more years in a row, then your disease problems and pest population will increase, and your problems are likely to get worse each year. The idea is to starve out diseases and harmful insects by depriving them of their chosen host plants. The severity of this problem will vary with your location and situation, but if you play it safe by rotating your crops, you can expect healthier plants and soil.

INTERCROPPING

The importance of intercropping, or the practice of growing two or more crops together, in the intensive garden is to obtain the maximum of individual plants within each bed while avoiding the ill effects of overcrowding (see figures 4–9 and 4–10). The best vegetables to interplant are those that make opposite or complementary demands upon the soil, water supply, and available sunlight, or those that supply each other with particular advantages such as support or shade.

A heavy-feeding vegetable and a light-feeding one, planted next to each other, can offer the soil balancing effects of crop rotation at once rather than over a period of time. Of course, sequential crop rotation will still be important in the intercropped garden to combat disease and pest problems.

Theoretically, the optimum planting scheme for interplanting is a grid on which every

FIG. 4-9 Intercropping of lettuce and broccoli. By the time the broccoli needs additional space, the lettuce will have been harvested. Garden of Paul and Debbie Doscher.

FIG. 4-10 Intercropping of celery, lettuce, and beets in the garden of Drew and Louise Langsner in North Carolina.

other plant is a heavy or light feeder. This works very well when the sizes of plants grown together are relatively close, such as lettuce and carrots. John Jeavons, writing about his California gardening experience, has evidently had good results using such a grid plan based on hexagons. But one has to be pragmatic. In New England, where we try to grow the majority of our year's vegetables in the few summer months (the same months during which most other outdoor endeavors must be accomplished), we tend to choose a simpler system. Alternating rows, bands, or blocks of heavy- and light-feeding vegetables make a very satisfactory intercropping layout. Some of our favorite intercrops are lettuce with onions, beets with carrots, beets with beans, and corn with white clover.

Though the principle of intercropping heavy and light feeders is sound, it has to be accompanied by knowledge of the individual vegetables involved. For instance, it sounds great to grow squash and perhaps beets together, but squash has a tendency to take over everything in sight, covering paths and shading all competition; what began as an intercrop ends as a squash patch with a few shaded, stunted beets. The moral of this is to give squash plenty of room or its plant neighbors will soon discover what unfair competition is all about. We usually plant squash in beds at the edge of the garden and encourage them to spread away from the rest of the garden. One way to deal with unruly squash is to buy seed for the bush varieties, which are productive and much tamer than other varieties. A good choice to interplant with squash is pole beans, so long as the beans have started up their poles before the squash starts covering the countryside.

It is well known that Native Americans grew corn, squash, and beans together. This is a logical combination, in which the beans supply their own nitrogen, leaving the squash and corn to consume the nutrients available in the soil. The beans and squash grow in the space between the corn, which would otherwise be uncovered soil and subject to erosion. Their leaves shade the soil, lessening water evaporation, and the beans' taproots use nutrients and water that the corn and squash cannot reach. The beans should get plenty of sunlight while the corn is still relatively small, though they may be shaded somewhat by the time the corn grows fairly large. Ideally, the beans should be harvested before the corn, when shading would not be a problem.

This method sounds great and in many cases is, particularly with a bush-type bean; however, with all the right intentions, we have also seen garden disasters—cases in which the corn growth outpaced the beans altogether, resulting in zero beans. The problems can be worked out with practice, observing and adjusting planting times and spacing in relation to one another.

In some situations sturdy, tall plants are planted with climbing plants to serve as a living trellis for the climbers. Corn and sunflowers are often planted to support pole beans or cucumbers. Some gardeners are great proponents of this idea, but it takes careful timing, spacing, and planting. Take the same corn and beans interplanting example again, using only pole beans instead of bush beans. It works very well for some gardeners, but we have also seen the pole beans get ahead of the corn, which continued to grow, but was so strangled and shaded that it produced few good ears. By the time the beans were ready to pick, they had grown into such a corn-intertwined jungle that many of them could not be reached at all. As you see, one has to think through an interplanting to its possible conclusions. For some crops it may be more practical to follow a more traditional crop rotation.

Shading can work both for you or against you, too, when you're interplanting. Shade-tolerant (or cool-weather crops in midsummer) plants will thrive in the shade of a taller plant. For example, lettuce planted on the east side of a trellis of pole beans will be shaded only during the afternoon, protecting the lettuce from the hottest part of the day. In another situation the shade of a tall plant can be detrimental to the shorter plant. In general, if an undercrop is being forced to grow abnormally tall and spindly, or fails to develop its normal green coloring, you have left the shading crop in the garden too long or planted it too densely. Cucumbers are often suggested as a good midsummer understory crop because they like both heat and some shade. But heat is relative; in northeastern Vermont our summer is cool enough that we find cucumbers need the full sunlight to prosper.

A limited water supply may be another reason for intercropping. An assortment of vegetables at different stages of maturity will not all require their peak amounts of water at the same time, so water needs per bed will be more balanced.

Intercropping is probably most useful to the intensive gardener when coordinated with succession planting. In this situation the intercropped vegetables are timed to be at different stages of development by planting or transplanting at different times. For example, you might transplant lettuce with cauliflower or broccoli into alternate rows in a bed. The faster-growing lettuce is harvested first, leaving more room for the brassicas to mature. In many ways an overlapping succession like this is the easiest way to manage intercropping. Because the peak growth of the plants growing together does not coincide, direct competition can usually be avoided. Seed packets give information about the number of days to maturity of the given vegetable. Use this information to schedule successions.

Difficulties with succession intercropping come when the timing is not coordinated. If two intercrops are coming to maturity at the same time, both may need more space, though neither is ready to harvest. All you can do is let them remain crowded and get inferior produce or thin them out and get less food than you anticipated. You will know next time to schedule the planting times of the two plants farther apart or to allow more space between plants.

Besides all these other possible benefits, interplanting can mean a wider variety of plant growth and habitat for spiders and insect predators, which can be a valuable control of destructive insect populations in your garden. Nature creates complex interrelationships among living organisms. This diversity gives natural systems a flexibility that enables them to recover amazingly from natural disasters and the insults of humanity. Imitating this diversity and complexity in your garden is certainly an important step toward growing food in a way that complements and respects the process of nature.

COMPANION PLANTING

Companion planting, like intercropping, is based upon using the natural interactions of plants for the benefit of the gardener. Companion planting includes intercropping but carries these principles further, dealing with plant interactions that are much subtler, more variable, and more controversial.

Plants have been found to like, dislike, or respond indifferently toward neighboring plants (see figure 4–11). These relationships may have a direct bearing upon how well various plants will grow. For example, leeks and celery are both supposed to suffer ill effects from being planted together. In other relationships one species may benefit or suffer, while its companion appears unaffected.

Companion planting is also used to attract or discourage insects. Nature has endowed many plants with mechanisms designed to ensure survival, and pest attacks are an important threat to a species' ability to survive. Using plants that have developed an ability to repel certain insects is a logical way to promote a healthy garden environment. It is important to remember, however, that many of nature's mechanisms are very subtle, and what works in one situation may not work in another. Variances in soil, climate, nutrients, plant varieties, and different periods of their life cycle all affect the ability of plants to resist pests.

Few gardeners have consistent experiences with companion planting as a pest deterrent. The most commonly used plants for this purpose seem to be marigolds, nasturtiums, and members of the onion family.

A root excretion produced by both French and African marigolds has been proven to be toxic to soil nematodes. Apparently it is most effective when the plants are green-manured, but it also works while the plants are growing. Many gardeners grow marigolds because they believe that the odor is an effective repellent for bean beetles, whiteflies, and aphids. Where

How to Use the Chart

This chart is designed to be a handy reference for garden planning. As you are preparing to lay out your intensive garden, some quick glances at the chart can indicate which plants may work well as companions and which may not.

Use it like the mileage chart on a road map. Simply find the name of the plant you are concerned with, and look across its row and down its column to identify its possible relationship to the other plants on the chart.

The Symbols

●   Indicates that two plants may be mutual companions. It is possible that they will both benefit from being planted next to each other.

➡   Indicates that one plant may like the other, but only one of the two may clearly benefit from the relationship, i.e., beans are reported to benefit from being planted near carrots so the arrow points toward carrots.

☂   Indicates one of the two plants may deter or repel a particular insect pest. In most cases this symbol is associated with a plant that repels a pest from another crop.

✖   Indicates these plants are antagonists. Placing these plants together may be detrimental to either or both of them. In general antagonists should not follow each other in succession planting either.

The blank spaces on the chart indicate that either no companion/antagonist relationship has been suggested between the two plants involved or that no one has yet studied the relationship. If you have experience with pairs that are not shown on the chart, you can add your information in the blank spaces.

For more detailed information on companion planting relationships, consult one of the following books:

Companion Plants and How to Use Them by Helen Philbrick and Richard Gregg (Greenwich, Ct.; Devon-Adair Company, 1966).

Secrets of Companion Planting for Successful Gardening by Louise Riotte (Charlotte, Vt.; Garden Way, 1975).

How to Grow More Vegetables by John Jeavons (Berkeley, Calif.; Ten Speed Press, 1979).

Getting the Most from Your Garden by the Editors of *Organic Gardening* magazine (Emmaus, Pa.; Rodale Press, 1980).

4-11 Chart of companion plants compiled by Paul Doscher from various sources. Copyright © 1978 by Solar Survival.

FIG. 4-12 Where marigolds are planted generously throughout the garden, most gardeners report few insect problems.

marigolds are planted generously throughout the garden, most gardeners report few insect problems (see figure 4–12). Additional scientific research shows that marigolds may also be useful in controlling fusarium and verticillium bacteria in the soil.

Nasturtiums are supposed to deter whiteflies, aphids, and squash bugs. Some people report that this is true, whereas others have watched their squash plants wither into skeletons surrounded by mounds of luxuriant nasturtiums. Alas, that is the state of companion planting at this point—we know far too little to practice it effectively on a consistent basis.

Garlic and onions are renowned for discouraging garden pests and are interplanted with members of the cabbage family in the hope that they will repel cabbage worms (the larvae of a small white butterfly). Some experts speculate that this is an effective measure only when the larval stage coincides with the time of the onions' flowering.

There is, however, evidence that certain substances in onion skins have a suppressive effect on some soil-borne parasites and diseases. We like to grow nicotiana (flowering tobacco) in our greenhouse. The plant's sticky stalk, leaves and flowers attract and then trap flying pests like aphids.

Many plants require insect pollination for fruit development. Honey bees are generally credited with performing much of the pollination of garden crops, but many other insects do this also. Certainly any flower that serves to attract large numbers of bees will be a benefit to insect-pollinated, fruiting garden plants such as melon, squash, cucumbers, tomatoes, peppers, and the like. Many flowering herbs are planted in gardens for this purpose, including borage, coriander, and catnip (see figures 4–13 and 4–14). In general there is value in planting any kinds of flowers near the vegetable garden as they attract a variety of beneficial insects. And who can argue with their beauty?

Companion planting, it is claimed, can also enhance the flavor of vegetables. This is

FIG. 4-13 When a vegetable plant dies in his
Maine garden, Tony Bok replaces it with a flower.

hard to substantiate, for taste is a difficult
thing to evaluate objectively. In general the
advice for this kind of companion planting
is to follow a scheme of planting together
what you like to eat and cook together.

   In spite of all the "ifs" involved in this
account of companion planting for pest control and flavor improvement, we have
confidence in the principles of the idea. Still,
it is hardly a complete area of study, and
there is not enough knowledge to ensure
success. Just as in any planting scheme you
use, keeping a record of what you grow, and
where, when, and with what other plants
you grow it will turn out to be your most
valuable garden-planning resource.

FIG. 4-14 Flowers like borage attract bees and
help to ensure pollination of fruiting vegetables
such as squashes, cucumbers, and peppers. Garden
of Bobbie Allhouse in Vermont.

SPACING

Spacing between plants is one of the most important aspects in which intensive culture differs from row or field culture. Spacing will vary according to your climate and the sizes that plants usually attain in that climate. Obviously this will take experience and time to know. You will probably adjust the spacings recommended here by your experience. For instance, you may plant eggplant 18 inches apart and find that in your situation they don't fill the full 18 inches. In the Northeast, where the weather is often moist, close planting can cause rot at ground level in lettuce, for example. If you have a damp or cool garden, this is something to be aware of.

    The general goal in spacing is that the leaf tips of neighboring plants, when mature, will just touch. Spacing tables given here will approximate the space needed by one mature plant. These are only guidelines, as spacing will vary considerably with soil, climate, and vegetables.

    If you are growing two intercrops that will be maturing at the same time, you can determine their spacing by adding the individual spacings together and dividing by two. Things can be spaced closer if you plan to use interplanted, overlapping successions. This is because the intercropped vegetables in a bed, say, of lettuce and cauliflower, will be planned to reach maturity at different times. Thus, although full spaces must be left for one of the plants, the other will be less than full size, so less space need be allowed. The larger plant will, as has been discussed before, be harvested, allowing space for the younger plants to grow to maturity (see figure 4–15). This cycle can be continued by transplanting small seedlings into the spaces where the first maturing plants were harvested; these will grow, and when the second crop is taken off the bed, the third one will fill in again. This sort of coordination takes careful planning to succeed, and factors of weather could change the most well-laid plans. Only experience will be able to tell you how best this may be done in your situation.

Your spacing may also vary depending upon how you will use or harvest your crop. For example, we often broadcast lettuce in a bed and tear off handfuls of leaves when we need them for a salad. When marketing lettuce, however, we use the same 10- to 12-inch spacing popular with commercial growers because the wide spacing produces shapely plants that can

FIG. 4-15 This mature cabbage should be harvested to give the growing lettuce more room.

be cut and sold as heads. In general market gardeners favor slightly larger spacing for any crop where the whole plant appearance is important in pleasing their customers.

To determine spacing for vegetables not included in the following chart, a general spacing guide is to follow the recommendations found on the seed packet for distance between plants in the row and then space plants that distance apart in every direction, ignoring the recommended distances *between* rows.

Suggested Spacing Between the Centers of Mature Plants

Plant	Inches	Plant	Inches
Asparagus	12	Mustard greens	6
Beans, bush	6–8	Onions	3–6
Beans, pole	4–6 plants per pole, 18 inches apart	Parsley	4–5
		Parsnips	3–4
Beets	3–6	Peas, bush	3–4
Broccoli	14–18	Peas, climbing[†]	3–4
Brussels sprouts	14–16	Peppers	10–16
Cabbage, Chinese	10–12	Potatoes	10–14
Cabbage, early	15–18	Pumpkin	24–30
Cabbage, late	24–30	Radishes	1–2
Carrots*	2–3	Rhubarb	6–8
Cauliflower	12–18	Rutabagas	6
Celery	6–10	Salsify	2–4
Chard	6–8	Scallions	1
Corn	12–18	Spinach, New Zealand	10–12
Cucumbers	8–12	Spinach, regular	4–6
Eggplant	14–18	Squash, summer and zucchini	20–36
Garlic	3–4		
Kale	12–18	Squash, winter	26–30
Kohlrabi	4–8	Sunflowers	12–24
Leeks	3–6	Tomatoes	18–24
Lettuce, head	12	Turnips	2–4
Lettuce, leaf	10–12	Watermelon	20–24
Melons	12–18		

* Carrots are easiest planted in rows 3–4 inches apart and thinned to 2 inches apart within the row.

[†] Peas planted in rows on either side of a trellis

SEED SELECTION

Choosing seed suited to the climate and season you will be gardening in can make a big difference and help you to utilize fringe ends of the season. The ideal, of course, is to get varieties of vegetables that will mature from seed within the length of your growing season. This is impossible with some vegetables in many places, such as tomatoes, peppers, and eggplant in New England. This will make it necessary for you to start plants indoors or in season-extending devices before your growing season has actually begun. Of course it is easy to get seedlings from a nursery if you find raising them yourself difficult or unnecessary. The advantage of starting your own is that you have a much wider choice among varieties in buying seeds than in buying plants.

On the other end of things, you can expect to get more than one crop of quick-growing vegetables like spinach, peas, and lettuce. Some varieties of these grow best in the cool of spring and fall but dislike the heat or dryness of summer, even other varieties may be much more tolerant of summer weather. Selecting which variety to plant during different stages of the growing season can go a long way toward giving you a continuous supply of these fresh vegetables.

You can economize on space in your garden by choosing seed for compact varieties, when available, of the vegetables you plan to grow. Some compact types are probably developed more as novelties than for food production, so read the catalog or seed packet carefully. Look for phrases such as "productive" or "prolific" to avoid nonproductive varieties.

If you have never grown vegetables in your area before, it would be helpful to ask neighboring gardeners what varieties they have had success with. It may also be to your advantage to purchase your seed from seed companies located in a similar climate to yours. A seed that grows to maturity in fifty days in one climate may grow more quickly or slowly in your location. Unfortunately, since most seed companies don't grow their own seed and may buy them from a grower in a very different climate, the information on the seed packet regarding length of time to maturity may not be completely accurate.

A last consideration is whether you hope to save your own seed. If this is so, the seed you select initially will have to be open-pollinated rather than hybrid, as hybrid seed does not generally produce a plant true to its parent.

CHAPTER 5

Efficient Management

A great advantage of intensive techniques is the opportunity to manage the garden efficiently. The reduced size, permanent beds, and living mulch provided by dense planting all act to reduce the repetition associated with regular garden chores. In this chapter we will discuss some of the ways intensive gardeners make more efficient use of their time during the "heat" of the growing season. In particular there are ways to boost crop yields with supplementary fertilization, eliminate weeds with easy mulching techniques, control pests without using synthetic chemical pesticides, and use water-efficient devices for keeping things from drying out.

These efficiency improvements will reduce the amount of time you'll spend in the hot sun, sweating and laboring with hoe in hand. As a bonus, these more effective weed-control techniques can produce a more beautiful garden as well. They will also help you minimize the health risks associated with chemical pest and weed controls.

FERTILIZING DURING
THE GROWING SEASON

Most intensive gardeners rely upon a rich soil preparation to provide the nutrients needed by their vegetables and flowers. In addition to the fertilizer added to the soil before planting, many gardeners use a top dressing of compost or a liquid fertilizer during the growing season. Your bed preparation provides a generalized, longer-term fertility throughout the bed, and liquid fertilizers can be applied to a specific plant or area for its immediate use.

Top dressing or liquid fertilizing is particularly important to supply nitrogen. Nitrogen, in the form of nitrate, is water soluble and will either be taken up by plants or leached downward through the soil. This means that in many gardens, plants become nitrogen deficient around mid-to-late summer. It shows up as the yellowing of older leaves. If allowed to go unchecked, nitrogen deficiency will result in the necrosis (death) of these leaves and may reduce plant yields. The solution is to keep a close watch on your plants and fertilize at the first sign of a problem, or have a routine program of top dressing to prevent it entirely.

You can use bagged organic fertilizers that are high in nitrogen (leather meal, cottonseed meal, cow manure) or your own compost. If you plan to use your own compost, be sure to keep it out of the rain, or the nitrogen content will be significantly diminished.

Common liquid fertilizers are fish emulsion or a "tea" made of manure and water. All liquid fertilizers are applied with lots of water to ensure that they penetrate through the surface soil down to the plant roots. When using fish emulsion, be sure to follow the directions supplied with the concentrate so as not to overfertilize. It's also a good idea to wear rubber gloves when handling fish emulsion, as the odor is penetrating and will stay on your hands despite the most vigorous cleaning.

Manure tea is made by taking a couple of shovelfuls of fresh or unleached manure, placing it in a cloth bag or cheesecloth, and then submersing it in a large bucket or garbage can full of water. Let it set a day or two before using so as much of the nitrogen as possible is dissolved into the water.

A liquid seaweed fertilizer is used by some gardeners as a foliar spray. The diluted mixture is sprayed directly onto the plant leaves, where nutrients are absorbed by the plant, giving it a quick "spurt." The benefits of foliar spraying are minor compared to the benefits of feeding plants via the roots, so don't depend on sprays to overcome or prevent significant soil deficiencies. Perhaps the greatest benefits documented for seaweed sprays are in the addition of trace elements and the growth hormones called cytokinins. Some researchers have reported increased yields in certain crops after seaweed applications. Others indicate that tomatoes sprayed with seaweed are more resistant to foliar diseases. Some have even shown that seaweed imparts a bit of frost protection to tender plants, allowing them to survive down to 2 or 3 degrees below freezing.

While adding these fertilizers two or three times during the growing season may seem like a lot of work, it really pays off. After all the preparation work you put into the garden, it would be a shame to get less than the maximum production. Plants grown in close proximity to one another can either compete for scarce nutrients or feast on an adequate supply and assist one another in outcompeting the weeds. Mid-season fertilization assures the latter.

USING MULCHES IN BEDS

Mulches have already been mentioned as a great way to treat garden paths. The idea of a living mulch created by growing plants themselves for weed control and moisture retention is covered in chapter 4. The next type of mulching to consider is that which is used in the growing bed to control weeds and conserve moisture before the plants can do the job.

These mulches can be either organic, such as hay, wood chips, seaweed, leaves or grass clippings, or inert, such as plastic, metal, or rocks (see figures 5–1, 5–2, and 5–3). Each has its advantages and disadvantages.

FIG. 5-1 Hay used as mulch in Paul and Debbie Doscher's New Hampshire garden.

FIG. 5-2 Grass used as mulch in the garden of Norman and Sherrie Lee in New York.

FIG. 5-3 Newspaper mulch in the garden of Heather and Don Parker in Maine.

The nicest feature of an organic mulch is that by decomposing it adds organic matter and nutrients to the soil. On the other hand, because it decays, you must replenish the mulch or it ceases to be an effective weed control. Some mulches, particularly hay, can also introduce weed seeds into your garden. One gardener told us that because of weed seed in hay he now leaves the hay outside for a year to rot prior to using it: "When it's slimy and black, it's ready to go." The only problem is that by that time much of the nutrient value is also gone.

A thick layer of mulch acts to insulate the soil from the extremes of air temperature. In midsummer it keeps the soil from baking, and throughout the growing season it functions as a moderator between day and night temperatures. But on the negative side, a thick mulch, by preventing the soil from warming up, can also retard a vegetable's growth in the spring, particularly in northern climates. In this situation it is better not to mulch until later in the season (usually midsummer) when the soil is fully warmed.

A black polyethylene plastic covering for vegetable beds is popular with both commercial and home gardeners (see figure 5–4). After the bed has been prepared, but before planting, the polyethylene is rolled down the length of the bed. It should be held in place by burying the edges under the soil, and in windy locations a few rocks can be placed on top to prevent billowing.

Next the gardener cuts slits or holes in the plastic and inserts a transplant into the soil. A very easy way to make these holes has been demonstrated by commercial growers, who use a 4-foot-long piece of 4-inch PVC drainpipe. The pipe is cut to length, one end "sharpened" with a file, and then used to punch a neat 4-inch hole through the plastic. To plant from seed larger holes are needed, and this technique works very well.

FIG. 5-4 A black polyethylene mulch used on raised beds on the vegetable farm of Howard Prusack in Vermont.

The plant growing through the plastic suffers no competition from weeds, and the black color acts to warm the soil in the beds. This heat can be an advantage or disadvantage, depending on the crops being grown. The best crops for this treatment are tomatoes, cucumbers, squash, peppers, eggplant, and melons, all of which enjoy the extra soil warmth.

Unless one is careful to create a depression in the middle of the bed or around each plant, much of the rainwater will wash off the bed (see figure 5–5). One technique for letting water in is to wait until after a rainfall, then poke a hole through the plastic at the point where puddles are formed.

Recently some commercial growers have taken to using clear plastic as a bed mulch. This is even more successful at increasing early spring soil temperatures and improving seed germination; however, it also allows light to the soil and encourages weed growth unless chemical herbicides are applied prior to laying the plastic. Thus, it is not a method that can be successfully employed by organic gardeners.

"IRT," a dark-green semitransparent plastic, allows infrared light (heat) to pass through to the soil for warming. Because it allows very little other visible light to penetrate to the soil, weed growth is substantially suppressed. This material, while more expensive than black plastic, is very effective at warming cool spring soils. If you remove it immediately after completing a harvest of melons, tomatoes, or other crop, it can also be reused a second season.

Many gardeners object to plastic mulches on aesthetic grounds or because they contribute nothing to the soil as do organic mulches. Though some gardeners are able to get several years' use out of a sheet of polyethylene, it does deteriorate with age, leaving pieces of this inorganic material in the soil. The best way to avoid this is to remove the material after the gardening season.

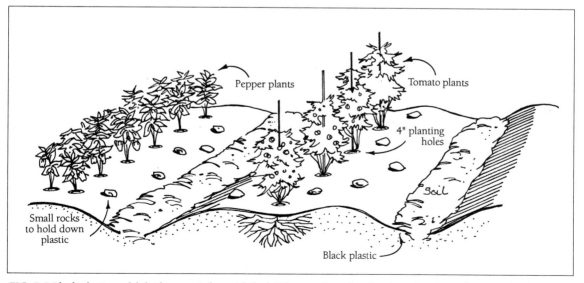

FIG. 5-5 Black plastic mulch laid over a 3-foot-wide bed. Edges are buried under the soil in the paths. Note the depression in the center of the bed, allowing rainwater to enter the soil rather than run off into the paths. Four-inch holes were punched through the plastic using a piece of plastic drain pipe.

Some plastics have been intentionally designed to deteriorate after a certain period of time. These "self-destructing" materials are supposed to break down either from exposure to sunlight or from decomposition resulting from the action of microorganisms. Research has shown, however, that these plastics do not fully decompose very quickly, if at all, and the result is a garden filled with small pieces of plastic that may take years to disappear.

Additionally we question the environmental soundness of using nonrenewable petro-chemicals to create a mulching material of such limited durability. But it is hard not to be seduced by the weed-free garden and early harvests made possible by plastic. Some sheet-plastic mulches are available with a longer life expectancy than that of polyethylene, but they are also more expensive. An example is the "landscape fabric," a woven material that is pene-trable by rainfall but prevents weed growth. Landscape fabric must be covered by an organic mulch, however, or it will eventually deteriorate from the ultraviolet rays in sunlight.

Salvaged steel roofing with holes cut out for plants to grow can be used to the same effect, and some gardeners have even used old pieces of carpet and horsehair carpet under-layment.

Stone mulches are another possibility (see figure 5–6). The stones, like other mulches displace weeds and retain moisture. Their big advantage is that the rocks absorb the sun's heat during the day, keeping the soil warmer through the night. Jeff Moyer at the Rodale Experimental Farm in Emmaus, Pennsylvania, told us that their stone mulch makes the soil warmer by a couple of degrees, extending their season in both spring and fall. The disadvan-

tage with stone mulches is they are a lot of work to establish, and once established, are relatively permanent, limiting your alternatives. There is also a considerable weeding problem between the stones. If you can obtain surplus or broken roofing or floor slate, you can make a more easily movable rock mulch, in which the square-cut pieces fit together well, lessening the weed problem.

Boards can also be used as mulch between plants. They will eventually rot, though not in a single growing season. A problem with boards, though, is that unless they are well sealed or painted, they will warp because they are exposed to the sun's warmth on one side and the soil's

FIG. 5-6 Stone mulches absorb the sun's heat during the day, keeping the soil warmer through the night. Garden at the Rodale Old Farm in Pennsylvania.

moisture on the other. As this makes them curl at the edges, they become less effective at preventing weed growth. They also become good hiding places for pests like slugs and squash bugs.

FIG. 5-8 *Tires absorb the sun's heat, making them a good mulch for these heat-loving tomatoes. Garden of Sam and Elizabeth Smith in Massachusetts.*

FIG. 5-7 *Wood chips are used as mulch in this garden with permanent wood-sided beds. To prevent weed penetration, a thick layer (about 5 sheets) of newspaper was laid down first and then covered with 2 inches of chips.*

Old car tires are popular mulches around large, warmth-loving vegetables like tomatoes and eggplant. In addition to mulching the tires give wind protection to the young plants and absorb the sun's heat (see figure 5–8). Often the inside of the tire is filled with stones to store this heat. The tire interior can be filled with rich soil to make a mini-raised bed.

WEEDS AND WEED CONTROL

Because it's difficult to mulch every square foot of the garden, weed control is an integral part of intensive gardening. Even though the use of living mulches and careful bed preparation will make weeding less of a problem than in conventional gardens, some weeding will still be necessary. Fortunately when weeds do spring up, they are easy to pull from the loose soil in the beds.

Some gardeners use a tiller between crops to cut down weeds, whereas others think that tilling only turns up dormant weed seeds, which proceed to sprout near the soil surface. The best and most efficient way to get weeds under control is by shallow cultivation with a Dutch hoe, or scuffle hoe (see figure 5–9). The idea is to cut the weeds off just below the soil surface with the sharp edge of the hoe. This avoids bringing new seeds to the surface and prevents the weeds from regrowing from the roots. It is a particularly effective technique and has the potential to significantly reduce the time limit spent reweeding between plants that cannot make a living mulch (onions, leeks, etc.).

In areas surrounding your garden, it is worthwhile to keep weeds mowed to prevent them from going to seed and sowing themselves in your beds. Winter mulches and cover crops should lessen the number of weeds in garden beds in spring, though cover crops (for example, buckwheat and rye), if allowed to go to seed, can themselves become a nuisance.

Finally, though weeds cannot be allowed to dominate the vegetables, a few weeds do little harm; they can serve as a living mulch until vegetables grow large enough to fill that role. If you remove them or cut them down before they go to seed, you can use the weed foliage as a dry organic mulch on the soil surface. A variation on this idea is the use of Dutch white clover as a living mulch between rows of taller plants like corn, tomatoes, or squash. This can work nicely because the clover is low growing and can be left in the ground at the end of the season as a cover crop. In spring it is tilled under to provide organic matter and nitrogen to the new crops.

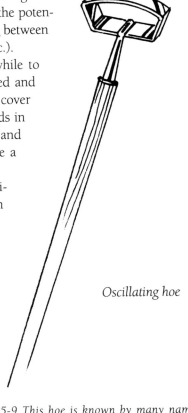

Oscillating hoe

FIG. 5-9 *This hoe is known by many names: Dutch hoe, stirrup hoe, oscillating hoe, and scuffle hoe. Regardless of its name, it is an essential tool for efficient weeding. It can be drawn through the soil surface in either a forward or backward motion.*

It is important to distinguish between weeds that are a problem and those that are not. Weeds like lamb's-quarter, pigweed, and wild mustard, which produce from seed, can be brought under control by mowing and minimizing soil cultivation. When they do sprout, they are relatively easy to uproot or cut down with a Dutch hoe. There are other weeds, however, that are not so easily dealt with. Weeds such as witch grass (quack grass) and milkweed, which proliferate from the roots or have very deep roots or rhizomes, can be a real nuisance. The best thing to do is learn to recognize the plants and pick out the vital roots, runners, or rhizomes while digging the bed. Time spent doing this is well repaid when it comes to weeding, because tough grasses that are firmly locked into a deep underground root system will be nearly impossible to pull out effectively. Once the root system is established, rototilling may multiply the problem by chopping and distributing the living roots, so it is best to take care of this problem beforehand.

IRRIGATION

Providing adequate water to your garden is essential. The rule of thumb used by most gardeners is that you need an inch of rain a week to maintain maximum productivity. Such regular rainfall has never occurred in our garden, which means that supplementary watering is a must.

The two most common alternative methods are overhead sprinkling and drip irrigation. Almost every gardener owns a sprinkler, and many use it for watering the garden, but this can cause significant problems. First, most sprinklers provide an uneven distribution of water across the area they cover. This means that some crops get too much and some too little. Second, overhead watering wastes a lot of water. In some hot, dry climates, as much as half the water can actually evaporate into the air before it ever reaches the ground. Third, and most important to the organic gardener, overhead watering is very conducive to the development and spread of diseases.

Most plant foliage diseases (rusts, leaf spots, etc.) are waterborne and spread primarily when the foliage is damp; consequently, by sprinkling the garden you create the ideal environment for disease. If you have to sprinkle, the best time to do it is in the early morning, stopping by midday. This will give plants the water they need for photosynthesis during the day and will allow the foliage to dry before evening.

Our advice on sprinklers is to use them for watering the seedbed and the lawn. For midseason watering use some variation on the drip system. Drip irrigation uses hoses or water lines that emit small amounts of water directly to the soil surface. This makes sure that the soil is damp for good plant growth, whereas the foliage stays dry. Another benefit is that drip systems do not waste water; very little is lost to evaporation.

There are dozens of drip systems on the market today. You can spend as little as $20 or as much as $1,000 installing this type of irrigation. Fortunately most of these systems are reusable for many years with little maintenance. Any system, however, will rapidly become plugged if you use water that is not filtered. Your ordinary tap water or well water will be fine, but if you use collected rainwater or pond water, be sure to install a filter in your line before the drip hoses.

For their very large garden, the Doschers have used a drip system that uses an inexpensive drip tube called "Twin-Wall" (Chapin Co., Watertown, New York). This drip line is a tube within a tube (see figure 5–10). Both tubes have minute holes punched in them, which allow for an even flow of water to the ground. The water enters the inner tube and then flows into the outer tube through the holes. From the outer tube the water drips to the ground. Using this system has resulted in greatly improved yields, reduced water consumption from the Doschers' dug well, and less time spent moving sprinklers around the garden.

If you use mulch in the garden, it is a good idea to lay out your drip lines prior to planting. Then you can cover them with black plastic or mulch. This will also increase the life of the drip hoses, as the ultraviolet rays of the sun will not hit them, causing the plastic components to degrade.

Know when to irrigate. Have a rain gauge in the garden and keep records of the rainfall. Although it might be nice to have 1 inch of rain every week, it's certainly not essential in the rich soil of an intensive garden. If your rainfall drops much below ½ inch per week, it would be wise to irrigate. Alternatively, you can regularly check the soil. If you cannot find damp, dark soil within 1 to 2 inches of the surface, it's time to irrigate. When you irrigate, do it thoroughly. One thorough watering is preferable to numerous ones of shorter duration.

Cultivation can affect the need to water. If you do not constantly break up the surface of the soil, evaporation will be reduced. This is simply a function of surface area. After a rainfall the soil surface is matted down by the impact of raindrops. This reduces the total surface area available for evaporation. If you then go in and cultivate the soil, you make the surface "rougher" and increase the area for evaporation dramatically. The use of Dutch hoes and other tools that have a knifelike action to cut off weeds just below the soil surface can help reduce this problem because they leave a smoother surface behind.

Fig. 5-10 The Chapin "Twin-Wall" irrigation system, like other drip-type systems, places water at the root zone where it is needed. Twin-Wall is very economical compared to systems that use soaker hose or emitters. Some of the special tools needed to install it are shown here and are available from Chapin at a very modest cost.

Finally, try to avoid using very cold water to irrigate. The water you put into the root zone should ideally be the same temperature as the soil. Cold water will cool the roots, slowing down the rate at which they can absorb water. The foliage will still demand as much water as before, but the roots will not be able to provide it. This is not to say that you shouldn't irrigate if your plants are wilting and you have no warm water; obviously, any water is better than none.

A drip-irrigation system can help warm the water because the flow rate is very slow. This allows the sun to warm the water as it travels through the hose to the garden. Another way to provide warmer water is to put a large drum or garbage can out in the garden and fill it with water. After a few hours of sunshine, the water temperature will be as warm or warmer than the air. Then you can use a watering can or siphon to irrigate your plants.

PESTS

Pests are inevitable in a garden sooner or later. We tend to take a somewhat philosophical view toward this problem. As one gardener we visited claimed, "If a vegetable isn't good enough for a bug, it isn't good enough for me." As far as insect pests go, the health of your plants is the best defense. A certain percentage of chewed and sucked leaves or flowers are normal in any garden and do little harm. They should not be considered a problem unless yields are considerably lessened because of it.

Garden crops can tolerate a certain amount of pest damage without much decline in production, provided the crops are healthy and vigorous. Recognizing when pests are simply a nuisance versus when they represent a true threat to production is essential to efficient gardening.

From a biologist's point of view, pests are considered parasites. But parasites only become a real problem when they become so numerous as to seriously injure their host. Of course, parasites that totally destroy their host are not likely to survive themselves, and many pests do only minor damage to your garden crops.

Understanding this ecological principle may not solve your immediate problem, but we think it's a good reflection of the extent to which humans ought (or ought not) to exert control in the area. It is backed up by many gardeners we have talked to, who plant a little more than they need and expect to lose some plants. Still, this is no comfort when you find an unreasonable onslaught of pesky eaters in your garden. It happens to every gardener at one time or another.

PEST-CONTROL TECHNIQUES

There are plenty of pest- and disease-control chemicals on the market. There is also a long list of chemicals once believed to be safe that are no longer legal to sell because of documented environmental and human health hazards. Another problem with chemical controls is the often-cited phenomenon of "pest resistance," which occurs as succeeding generations of insects develop a genetically improved ability to withstand the chemical killer.

Add these problems to the well-known hazard to the gardener posed by accidental misuse or uninformed abuse of toxic chemicals, and many people decide to avoid their use altogether. Does this mean that the organic gardener who shuns synthetic chemicals is doomed to lose his or her crops to hordes of rampaging insects? Perhaps, if no action is taken to control the problem. But fortunately there are numerous nonchemical alternatives for controlling insects that can work very effectively for the home gardener (see table 5–1).

The most important thing to remember about insects is that "control" is really an illusion. There is really no way to completely control an insect population. Rather, you can "manage" it to keep it at levels below which crops are not unacceptably damaged. Of course, a good manager knows what he or she is managing, and a good reference book on insect pest identification is a must for the serious organic gardener. It will tell you which bugs to ignore, which to encourage, and which to watch carefully.

TABLE 5-1   **Organic Insect and Disease Control Strategies**

Control	Insect or Disease Controlled	Potential Hazards
Planning	A great variety of pests can be avoided by not planting suscepti-ble crops. This is true, for example, with early spring brassicas, which are susceptible to infestation by root mag-gots. Strawberries are damaged by white grubs found in newly tilled grassy areas and can be avoided by preparing the soil a season ahead of time. It is also a good idea to select dis-ease-resistant plants. Some varieties, like butternut squash, which resists vine borers, can be insect-resistant as well.	none
Repellents	Reflective aluminum mulches can repel aphids from squash plants and leafhoppers from *young* beans.	damage to tender seedlings caused by intense reflection
Sanitation	Many diseases are easily controlled by removing infected twigs and foliage immediately. These should then be burned or buried. Destruction of crop residues in the fall is essential to keeping insect populations low. Bury, compost, or burn all residues. This will control EUROPEAN CORN BORERS, CABBAGEWORMS, CABBAGE LOOPERS, DIAMONDBACK MOTHS, MEXICAN BEAN BEETLES, and MITES.	none

Barriers:
  collars
  (FIG. 5–11)
	Control damage from CUTWORMS.	none

soil shields (FIG. 5–12)	Control some damage from CABBAGE ROOT MAGGOTS. Use black tar-paper squares, cut 6 inches across. Place around plant stem immediately after transplanting by slitting the paper.	none, if you remove them after you no longer need them
insect covers (FIG. 5–13)	The use of polyethylene "slitted row covers," spun-bonded polyester (Reemay and other brands), can effectively exclude many pests from your crops. Research results have shown they are effective against ROOT MAGGOTS, FLEA BEE-TLES, CARROT FLIES, LEAF MINERS, COLORADO POTATO BEETLES, and CUCUMBER BEETLES.	potential overheating and exclusion of pollinating insects
Traps: scent traps	Generally do not control pests, but are used to monitor popula-tions. An example is the JAPANESE BEETLE TRAP, which research shows is an effective beetle catcher; however, further research shows it can actually attract more beetles than it catches, so its overall impact may be nonbeneficial.	may attract more pests than they catch
visual traps	Some bugs are attracted to certain colors. A good example is the red, sticky balls used to attract and capture APPLE MAG-GOT FLIES (see figure 5–14). Also effective are yellow sticky boards (school-bus yellow, coated with "Tanglefoot") for attracting and catching WHITEFLIES.	none
sonic repelling devices	Ultrasonic devices advertised for repelling or killing pests have not been shown to be effective in unbiased laboratory research.	unknown

FIG. 5-11 A collar used to protect young transplants from cutworms. It can be made from metal, plastic, tar paper, cardboard, or discarded frozen juice cans.

FIG. 5-12 Black tar-paper squares can provide a degree of protection against cabbage root maggots. Some plants, however, will still be infested.

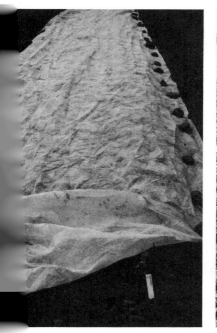

Fig. 5-14 A bright red painted wooden ball coated with "Tanglefoot"® acts as a visual lure to apple maggot flies. They land on the trap and cannot escape. Three spheres per dwarf tree will provide reasonable protection.

Fig. 5-13 Both spun bonded polyester (left) and slitted row covers (right) are very effective insect barriers. They give the added benefit of helping warm the soil in the spring.

TABLE 5-1   **Organic Insect and Disease Control Strategies** (continued)

Control	Insect or Disease Controlled	Potential Hazards
Traps: *(cont.)* light traps	"Bug Poppers" are a common sight in many parts of the country. They are generally not recommended by researchers because while they can attract and kill TOMATO and TOBACCO HORNWORM MOTHS, and other HARMFUL MOTHS, they destroy many more harmless or beneficial insects.	kill many beneficial insects
dark traps	Many insects "hide" in certain places when not feeding. SQUASH BUGS will hide under boards in the evening and can be captured in the morning before they become active. SLUGS will hide under boards or in any other moist, dark location during the day and can be collected. You can bait the slugs with something sweet under the boards.	none
Predators and Parasites	The best strategy to encourage predators and parasites of garden pests is to have a good variety of flowering plants in or near your vegetable garden. Most of the predators and parasites are native insects that benefit from having nectar sources nearby. Minimizing any use of pesticide sprays is also important, as most predators are *more* susceptible to pesticides than are the pests they feed on. Don't depend on purchased LADYBUGS as they may not remain in the garden long enough to supply any significant control. They do work for APHID control in greenhouses, however. An increasing number of "insectaries" are selling predatory and parasitic insects to commercial and home growers. Garden supply catalogs generally buy beneficial insects from these suppliers for shipment direct to customers. For example, Gardens Alive (5100 Schenley Place, Lawrenceburg, IN 47025) sells LADYBUGS, SPINED SOLDIER BUGS, LACEWINGS, TRICHOGRAMMA WASPS, and other insects in small quantities. Successful use of these natural controls requires careful adherence to instructions. Gardeners should experiment with their use before investing any significant amount of money in larger orders. Attracting BIRDS to the garden can provide some control. For example, our observation of bluebirds shows that they feed a great many small caterpillars to their newly hatched young. Providing houses for swallows, bluebirds, wrens, and chickadees may not provide a major amount of bug control, but it will provide a lot of enjoyment. BENEFICIAL NEMATODES are now sold by many mail-order garden suppliers. These tiny organisms prey on nearly two dozen soil-dwelling pests including CUTWORMS, ROOT MAGGOTS, WIREWORMS, WHITE GRUBS, etc. Nematodes can be very effective if applied correctly, but they are presently too expensive for large-scale use by commercial growers.	none

TABLE 5-1   **Organic Insect and Disease Control Strategies** (continued)

Control	Insect or Disease Controlled	Potential Hazards
Nonchemical Pesticides:		
soaps	Soaps have long been known to be an effective control for APHIDS, MEALY BUGS, WHITEFLIES, and other soft-bodied insects. It is essential to spray them at the recommended concentration to avoid plant tissue damage. Among the most effective is "Safers" brand insecticidal soap.	phytotoxicity (damage to plant leaves)
BT (*Bacillus thuringiensis*)	Sold as various brand-name products (Dipel and Thuricide are two), BT is very effective at killing CATERPILLARS. It kills by paralyzing the gut, and the bug dies by starving, or as the bacteria spread throughout its tissue.	none
milky spore (*Bacillus popilliae*)	Infects the larvae of JAPANESE BEETLES and JUNE BUGS. Can be very effective in controlling these pests. Does not work well in northern climates where the soils are cooler.	none
"bug juice"	Some gardeners claim success in grinding up certain insect pests, mixing them in water, and then spraying them on the affected plants. There may be some scientific validity to this because some insects carry parasites that could be spread this way, but there is no guarantee that the method is effective.	unknown
Botanical Insecticides:		
nicotine	A contact poison produced from tobacco family plants, nicotine is effective on numerous pests including APHIDS, LEAFHOPPERS, THRIPS, SQUASH BUG NYMPHS, and ASPARAGUS BEETLE NYMPHS.	very toxic to humans, broken down by sun and water in one day
pyrethrum	Well known for many years as a very effective "knockdown" agent, pyrethrum is found in many household pesticides. It is effective against APHIDS, ASPARAGUS BEETLES, CABBAGE LOOPERS, CABBAGEWORMS, COLORADO POTATO BEETLES, CORN EARWORMS, DIAMONDBACK MOTHS, EUROPEAN CORN BORERS, FALL ARMYWORMS, LEAFHOPPERS, MEXICAN BEAN BEETLES, STINKBUGS, TARNISHED PLANT BUGS, and CUCUMBER BEETLES. Pyrethrum is commonly available and may be found mixed with the compound Piperonyl butoxide, a synthetic compound that increases pyrethrum's effectiveness. Straight pyrethrum is rapidly broken down by sunlight and warm temperatures.	moderate toxicity to mammals and humans; kills many nontarget insects, including beneficials
rotenone	A compound produced by at least sixty-eight plants, rotenone acts as both a contact killer and stomach poison and kills *many* pests. This is one of the most commonly used "organic" pesticides, but it should be used with considerable caution	*very* toxic to fish; known to be toxic to humans when breathed; toxic to many beneficial insects

TABLE 5-1   **Organic Insect and Disease Control Strategies** (continued)

Control	Insect or Disease Controlled	Potential Hazards
Botanical Insecticides: *(cont.)*		
ryania	Produced from a South American shrub, ryania is effective as both a contact and stomach poison on EUROPEAN CORN BORERS, CODLING MOTHS, and CRANBERRY FRUIT-WORMS.	less toxic to humans than rotenone; breaks down more slowly than rotenone and pyrethrum; very selective, so it's not harmful to beneficial insects
sabidilla	Derived from South American lilies, this compound is effective against PLANT LICE, LEAFHOPPERS, CHINCH BUGS, SQUASH BUGS, HARLEQUIN BUGS, LYGUS BUGS, and STRIPED CUCUMBER BEETLES.	irritating to throat and nose; less toxic to humans than rotenone
neem extract	Derived from the neem tree, this extract has been found to be very effective at controlling a number of insects. It acts as a growth regulator but is relative harmless to predatory insects. Neem is now manufactured and sold as Margosan-O. Unfortunately, because of rigorous and expensive government-testing requirements, it has only been registered for use by professional pesticide applicators. It may soon be available for home gardeners.	low toxicity to mammals and humans
Oil Sprays	Horticultural spray oil (an example is "Sunspray CRJ"), is a new variation on the traditional dormant oil used to control insects on dormant fruit trees. These "ultrafine" oils are not damaging to plant leaves (phytotoxic) and can be used to control APHIDS, ARMYWORMS, MITES, BEETLE LARVAE, CORN EARWORMS, LEAFMINERS, LEAFHOPPERS, THRIPS, WHITEFLIES, and some CATERPILLARS.	none known
Companion Planting	Planting certain plants to repel insects from other plants has long been advocated. Although scientific research has documented that plant residues from some plants (for example, marigolds) can be toxic to certain insects, very little good scientific evidence exists to verify any other pest control benefits (see chapter 4).	none

The information in table 5–1 is not intended to be an all-inclusive listing of either the possible methods of controlling pests or the pests each method can control. It contains only those strategies that have been proven effective by scientific research unless otherwise stated. Portions are excerpted from a publication by entomologist Dr. Alan Eaton, entitled "Pest Control for Organic Vegetable Growers," published by the University of New Hampshire Cooperative Extension Service, Durham, NH 03824 (1986). For a copy of this publication, send a self-addressed, stamped envelope and $1.00 to the above address.

Efficiency in pest control means only "managing" bugs when they need it. You will save yourself a lot of money and time controlling pests if you spend a little time getting to know your bugs.

Spraying with pesticides, even botanicals, should be considered a last resort for most pest-management problems because almost all botanical pesticide sprays are "nonspecific," meaning they kill a broad spectrum of insects. Included on the list of those killed will be many beneficials. To avoid the accidental destruction of beneficials, spray only when the pest is active or at levels that could cause damage. Never spray during midday, when bees and other wasps are most active.

Why are botanicals considered okay and synthetics are not? Most organic growers feel that whereas synthetics are relatively long-lived (they have residual effectiveness), botanicals are not. Both pyrethrum and rotenone, for example, are rapidly destroyed by light, heat, and moisture. Research indicates that either of these sprayed in the morning will be almost completely "deactivated" by the evening. This means that there will be no residual impact on beneficials after the pests are killed. It also means that there is little residual effect on the pests, either, and so you have to target your pests carefully to hit as many as possible with the initial spraying.

Obviously, botanicals are a trade-off. Although they have a minimal environmental impact after the day of spraying, they don't control as well as the synthetic compounds do. And even though they can be targeted to avoid killing beneficials, they will certainly destroy some. You should also treat botanicals with considerable respect because they can be toxic to animals and humans if mishandled.

Finally, be sure to read the labels on any pesticides you use. Mix and apply them strictly according to the instructions. Misuse of pesticides, including botanicals, is not only dangerous to you and the environment, but it is also a violation of federal law.

ANIMAL PESTS

Animals, too, can do a lot of illicit nibbling in your garden. When this occurs, the first thing to do is check your fences; mending or reinforcing them if necessary. Of course, a fence is not foolproof, not when it takes a 12-foot-high one to discourage deer. A dog in your garden can inhibit the activities of four-legged vegetarians. A light at night may work, too, or some kind of noisemaker. Often, though, these are short-term deterrents, as the offending animals readily adapt and become accustomed to the light and noise. Dried blood was used by some gardeners we've talked to, sprinkled around the area under attack. Another idea suggested by a gardener is loose chicken wire laid horizontally in its characteristically lumpy furls along the ground to entangle raccoons attempting a garden raid.

Our best suggestion, however, is electric fencing. The Doschers have been using this method for about ten years and report that when the fence is operating, they have never lost an ear of corn to raccoons. Electric fencing has even successfully kept the masked marauders out of the peach trees full of ripening fruit. What about woodchucks? It works for them, too.

TABLE 5-2   **Organic Pest Control for Specific Crops**

This table is a quick reference for nonchemical methods of controlling pests on specific crops. For more detailed information on the pests or methods, consult a good reference book on organic pest control.

Selected Recommendations for the Most Common Troublesome Pests

Crop	Pest	Control Methods
Beans	Mexican bean beetle (MXBB)	Handpick when they first appear. Remove eggs (orange clusters) and larvae from undersides of leaves. Destroy plants as soon as crop is harvested. Introduce *Pediobius foveolatus* (Pedio wasp) as soon as you see MXBB larvae. Spray with rotenone or pyrethrum. Introduce spined soldier bugs.
Brassicas (cabbage, broccoli, etc.)	cutworms	Use collars. Handpick during night hours. Dig out caterpillars from base of damaged plants. Introduce beneficial nematodes.
	cabbage root maggot	Plant in late June (time varies with climate) after most maggot flies have completed their life cycle. Cover plants with spun-bonded polyester row cover (Reemay or other) to prevent flies from getting to the crop. Use tar-paper shields (see table 5–1). Introduce beneficial nematodes.
	cabbage looper	Use *Bacillus thuringiensis* (BT); as a second choice, use pyrethrum or rotenone.
Carrots	parsleyworm (larva of the black swallow-tail butterfly)	Use BT. Cover plants with spun-bonded row cover.
	carrot rust fly (maggot)	Cover with spun-bonded row cover. Rotate crops annually. Wait to plant until midsummer, when fly numbers are reduced. Introduce beneficial nematodes.
Cucumbers and melons	whitefly	(see Squash)
	striped cucumber beetle	(see Squash)
Lettuce	earwigs	These monsters inhabit the cool, damp leaves of maturing lettuce. They do minimal damage and are difficult to control. Pyrethrum and soaps can be effective if sprayed directly on the insect. Insecticidal soaps can achieve some control.
	six-spotted leafhopper	This pest spreads the virus of *aster yellows* to lettuce, carrots, asters, and celery. Prevent infestation by using polyester row covers Control by spraying with pyrethrum, or apply horticultural oil.

TABLE 5-2   **Organic Pest Control for Specific Crops** (continued)

Crop	Pest	Control Methods
Onions	onion maggot	Plant onions scattered around the garden rather than in one group. Each maggot requires more than one onion to mature, so separating the plants will defeat them. Introduce beneficial nematodes.
	onion thrips	These tiny, almost-invisible insects produce whitened, weakened stems. Can be controlled with soap sprays if spray penetrates into leaf crevices. Pyrethrum is a very effective control. Apply horticultural oil.
Peas	aphids	Use soap sprays or pyrethrum.
Peppers	tarnished plant bug (TPB)	Spray pyrethrum onto plants when temperature is cool. As temperature increases, the bugs will fly to avoid the spray. TPB is a pest of many crops. Control is similar for all.
	tomato hornworm (see tomatoes)	(see Tomatoes)
Potatoes and Eggplant	Colorado potato beetle (CPB)	Rotate planting sites. Handpick when first adults appear; then remove orange egg masses from under leaves. Use spun-bonded polyester row cover in early part of the season. Spray with rotenone or pyrethrum. BT (var. San Diego) (trade name "M-One") is effective against young larvae.
	three-lined potato beetle	Handpick. Spray with pyrethrum or rotenone.
	white grubs and wire-worms	Rotate crops every year. Do not plant potatoes where grass grew the year before. Introduce beneficial nematodes.
Spinach, Beets, and Chard	leaf miner	Plant early, before pest becomes active; eliminate small white clusters of eggs from underside of leaves when they appear. Cover with spun-bonded row covers to keep out adult insects. Apply horticultural oil
	blister beetle	Handpick as soon as they appear. Dust or spray sabadilla.
Squash	squash vine borer	Use resistant varieties such as butternut; avoid nonresistant varieties like zucchini. Spray rotenone to control adult moths beginning around late June or early July; weekly spraying is necessary. Destroy vines *immediately* after first fall frost.

TABLE 5-2   **Organic Pest Control for Specific Crops** (continued)

Crop	Pest	Control Methods
Squash (continued)	aphids	Use soap sprays. Use reflective aluminum mulch. Cover with spun-bonded polyester. Apply horticultural oil.
	whitefly	(same as for aphids)
	striped or spotted cucumber beetle	*These insects transmit bacterial wilt and must be controlled immediately.* Protect plants with row covers, which must be removed when flowers appear. Use rotenone or rotenone/pyrethrum-mixture sprays.
	squash bugs	Handpick (but be prepared for the obnoxious odor). Destroy crop residues. Use sabadilla or pyrethrum/rotenone mixture on young insects. Try row covers (polyester).
Sweet Corn	European corn borer	Because moths lay eggs early, delay planting as long as possible. Spray corn with BT as first tassels appear, then again after each rain for about three weeks. BT (var. Kurstake) is available as pelletized granules for use on sweet corn and is more effective than spraying. Rotenone or pyrethrum can be effective if timed to catch the caterpillars before they bore into the stalk. If you see the tassel fall over, look for an entrance hole; then split the stalk with a fingernail a few inches below the hole. You will most likely find the borer and be able to remove and destroy it.
	corn ear worm	Spray BT as soon as the corn silk appears and up until harvest. Once a week is adequate unless there are frequent rains. Mineral oil can be applied to the stalk at the tip each year. Wait until the silk has wilted and begun to turn dry. Apply horticultural oil.
Tomatoes	whitefly	Grow or buy only insect-free plants. Soap sprays can be effective Pyrethrum is effective. Apply horticultural oil
	cutworms	(see Brassicas)
	hornworms	These ugly beasties can be easily controlled with BT or rotenone as young larvae; larger larvae are more difficult to control with BT.

FURTHER READINGS:

Organic Pest Control, Editors of Organic Gardening Magazine, Rodale Press Inc., Emmaus, PA 18049.

"Resources for Organic Pest Control," 1986, Rodale Press Inc., Emmaus, PA 18049. (Pamphlet is available for $1.00.)

Ellis, Barbara W., and Bradley, Fern Marshall, Editors. *Organic Gardener's Handbook of Natural Insect and Disease Control* (Emmaus, Pa.: Rodale Press, 1992) This is Rodale's latest version of a series of books on insects and diseases. It is the best published to date, in part because of excellent illustrations and more accessible format.

McCord, Nancy. *Please Don't Eat My Garden* (New York, Sterling, 1992) A good introduction to larger garden pests, particularly mammals like deer and woodchucks.

Smith, Miranda, and Carr, Anna. *Rodale's Garden Insect, Disease, and Weed Identification Guide* (Emmaus, Pa.: Rodale Press, 1988) A "Field Guide" to identifying insects, diseases and weeds is an essential part of any gardener's library. This is one of the most useful and easy to use.

Yepsen, Robert B., editor. *Encyclopedia of Natural Insect and Disease Control* (Emmaus, Pa.: Rodale Press, 1984).

The key is to surround the garden with two or three strands of electrified wire and keep the fence charged whenever you are not in the yard or garden. The first strand should not be more than 6 inches above the ground, the second about 6 to 8 inches above that, and a third (for larger animals like dogs), about 2 feet off the ground. Conventional metal wire can be used (like that used for livestock fences), but it is preferable to use a braided polypropylene/stainless steel cord. This cord is becoming more common for use in movable livestock fencing systems and is resilient enough to bounce back to shape if you walk into it or step on it. It is also a bright color, making it easier to see.

For a charger we recommend using a "weed burner." This type of charger sends an intermittent, high-voltage, low-amperage charge into the wire, which can "burn off" weed stems and grass that come into contact with the wire. It works until the grass gets so thick that the charge is significantly diminished. Then you have to mow the weeds or grass down (see figure 5–15). Avoid using units that do not send a pulsing charge, as they are more likely to burn the wire out if grass comes in contact with the wire. Don't spend more than $100 for a charger, as the more expensive ones are designed for miles of fencing on livestock farms.

Electric fences use very little electricity over the course of a summer. Compared to the cost of putting a metal fence or wooden fence around your garden, they are a bargain. The Doschers' ½-acre garden would have cost more than $500 to fence with permanent sheep or chicken wire. The electric fence system, including insulators, wire, posts (made from scrap wood), and charger cost less than $150. And it works marvelously . . . as long as you remember to turn it on.

FIG. 5-15 This electric fence wire is made from polypropylene and stainless steel. The lines are stretched between insulators on posts and are set about 6 inches and 12 inches above the ground. The grass must be kept mowed to prevent a loss of "charge" in the lines.

FIG. 5-16 This solar cell array and battery can provide adequate power to charge a fence that is too far from a house to use AC current.

DISEASES AND
DISEASE PREVENTION

There are a great many diseases that can affect garden plants. Many are bacterial or fungal, live in the soil, and are transmitted to plants during the growing season. Others are spread by insects, one example being the aster yellows virus, which is spread by six-spotted leafhoppers, and another the cucumber bacterial wilt, which is spread by cucumber beetles.

Although there have been limited successes in breeding plants that are insect-resistant, there has been tremendous progress in breeding disease-resistant varieties. For example, many tomato varieties are now resistant to the serious diseases of verticillium and fusarium and bear the suffix "VF" next to the name to indicate this characteristic.

Whenever possible, if you encounter a plant disease, your first step in combating it should be to choose resistant varieties. As you look for seeds, note those that specifically mention resistance. If the description says nothing about it, the plant is probably susceptible.

The most important additional step you can take is crop rotation. With most diseases originating in the soil, it is essential that the organic gardener never grow the same crop in the same place two years in a row. This is particularly important with problems like cabbage club root, tomato septoria leaf spot, potato scab, and many others. We strongly recommend moving crops quite a distance away from the previous year's location and waiting at least two years before returning it to the same bed. Obviously, you will need to keep some fairly good records of what you plant and where you plant it.

Next, be sure to practice good sanitation. Whenever you notice cucumber or melon plants wilting, check for the presence of cucumber beetles. If they are there, you probably have bacterial wilt. Cut off the infected stem and destroy it so that the beetles cannot further spread the bacteria. This principle holds true for many other diseases. Destroy vines of peas as soon as the crop is harvested if any of the foliage is covered with powdery mildew. To "destroy" means to burn, compost (in a hot compost pile), or bury (outside the garden) all the plant material.

With some diseases, like tomato leaf spot, all these preventive measures may not be enough. Despite the Doschers' best efforts at rotation, prevention, and sanitation, their tomato crop is regularly devastated by this disease. Some publications indicate that it is possible to impart some resistance to leaf spot by giving the plants a regular spraying of liquid seaweed, and this is worth a try. Even if it doesn't control the disease, the extra nutrients in the seaweed can only help the plants. The best tactic to deal with this situation is to plant only the healthiest plants you can find, fertilize them well, and get as much production from the plants as possible before they succumb to the disease.

If you have crop failures year after year due to disease, the only really sensible thing to do is give up on that crop. But don't despair. If a disease is particularly troublesome to you, chances are it's also on the minds of plant breeders, too, and it's likely that someday a resistant variety will come along and allow you to try again.

PREPARATION FOR WINTER

As the summer growing season ends and harvesting is done, there still remains some work for the good gardener. A lot of next year's potential problems can be efficiently avoided by spending a little time in the fall to clean up and make ready for next spring.

Stakes, trellises, and cloches not being used over the winter should be put away. As previously mentioned, all plant residues should be tilled in or destroyed. If you use cover crops, they should be planted in time for them to become established before the beginning of extended colder weather.

Pull out any grass plants that may have become established in your beds or paths. Fall is grass-root-growing time, and anything you leave in now will come back to haunt you as well-established grass patches in the spring.

Plants you intend to leave in the garden will benefit from a mulch cover. Straw, leaves, and old hay are good choices. It's generally best not to mulch until you think the ground is about to freeze. This will help discourage mice from moving into your garden for the winter.

We have had good luck covering our beds for the winter with black plastic mulch. This prevents weeds from getting established in fall and early spring and also warms the soil earlier in the spring. The black plastic is removed just prior to planting time the following year. This can be a great time saver, as it reduces spring tilling or weeding and provides for better germination of early-planted seeds.

PREPARATION FOR SPRING

In northern climates the snow of late winter almost always hangs around until after you have the itch to start the garden. One way to get rid of the snow a littler earlier is to sprinkle wood ashes over your beds on top of the snow. This will cause the sun to melt the snow. It also provides the bed with some valuable potash, a necessary nutrient for good peas, for example.

Fall sowing is another way to get a jump on the season. Tim Fisher and Kathleen Kolb have often had peas, lettuce, and spinach come up on their own, self-seeded from the previous year. These seedlings, regulated by their own calendars, usually have a considerable head start over the seeds of the same species planted in the spring. By purposefully planting these seeds in the fall, you can benefit from early plants, planted where you want them to be, even if you are too occupied with other spring projects to get the rest of your seed in on time.

You can also plant semihardy plants (such as brassicas) toward the end of summer, and they will grow only a little through the fall. When it gets too cold for their continued growth, they should be covered with a thick mulch to protect them. Come spring, these plants, well established in the fall, will grow quickly, not having to wait for warm weather to germinate, nor suffering the shock of transplanting.

CONCLUSION

To reduce work and produce more food, the most important aspect of efficient garden management is planning. Use the winter months to read up on the various techniques and cultural requirements needed to grow your crops successfully. Armchair winter gardening is fun, easy, and inspiring. It will also pay big dividends during the summer.

CHAPTER 6

Cold Weather Gardening

We have all experienced it. The last of the winter snow is almost gone except in the most sheltered corners of the yard. The sun is getting higher in the sky every day, and the early wildflowers are beginning to appear. A few days each week the temperature rises into the 60s and 70s. The temptation to get out and plant the garden is almost irresistible, yet you know that it will still be another month or two before the danger of frost is past. In New Hampshire this itch inevitably hits before the end of March (last frost date averages around May 20), yet for most gardeners the only way to satisfy it is to plant flats of tomatoes, peppers, eggplant, and cabbage on a sunny windowsill. Going out into the garden to plant lettuce, radishes, and cabbage is considered a bit foolish (though it is all right to plant peas), and the idea of harvesting greens for a fresh salad is simply ridiculous.

With season-extension techniques these old ideas are forgotten. The only season when something cannot successfully be grown, harvested, or planted is the two-month period from mid-December to early February. Cold-hardy greens can be started early in either of two devices, hot frames or Solar Pods® (see figure 6–1). The hot frame is similar to the traditional cold frame, but is fully insulated to keep out winter cold and hold in solar heat. The Solar Pod® is a device that is installed over a permanent bed, framed with wood and rigid insulation, and is a double-glazed cover with a curved profile. In midspring still more plants can be transplanted into the garden under our twentieth-century versions of the cloches used by the traditional Parisian market gardeners. Then, in early summer, when cool nights still come quite frequently, heat-loving crops like melons and cucumbers are set out to thrive under cold

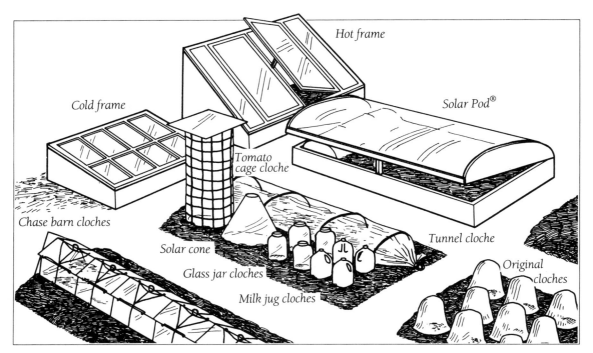

FIG. 6-1 There are a variety of season-extending devices both old and new that can be used to expand the gardening season.

frames or Solar Pods®. While neighbors are wondering why their melons are "just sitting there doing nothing," ours are growing each day, and the first flowers are beginning to bloom.

As the summer progresses, we continue to plant. Our late summer seedlings will become our fall and winter crops. When the first frost hits (usually in late September), our fall crops of lettuce, carrots, cabbage, broccoli, kale, chard, and other vegetables are under cover of cold frames, cloches, or in our greenhouse. Salads with fresh tomatoes, peppers, and cucumbers continue a month or so beyond the first frost, from plants that have been protected on the coldest nights.

When the 10°F nights of December arrive, the lettuce in our cold frames is dealt a fatal blow. But in the greenhouse Swiss chard, radishes, leaf lettuce, Chinese cabbage, beets, and parsley still keep growing, slowly but surely.

Our extended-season garden has made it possible for us to have fresh vegetables almost year-round. The methods we use are simple and relatively inexpensive, and in moderate climates can provide harvest during all twelve months of the year. With some planning, some thought, some skill in carpentry and horticulture, and a touch of enthusiasm, you can do the same.

THE EXTENDED-SEASON GARDEN IN SPRING

All good gardens begin with planning and preparation. Since you will want to get into your garden early in the spring, perhaps even in late winter, your preparations should be completed during the previous fall and winter. Preparation involves six steps:

1. Site selection

2. Construction of beds, including permanent, insulated beds and covers

3. Soil preparation in the fall

4. Crop selection

5. Soil finishing and possibly manure bed preparation in spring

6. Starting of seedlings indoors or in a greenhouse for transplanting into the garden

The first three steps must be accomplished the previous fall, before the ground freezes. The last three steps are good activities for the cold days of winter and early spring. Once you have them all completed, you will be on your way to producing amazingly early crops (see figures 6–2 and 6–3).

FIG. 6-2 Cold frames and a Solar Pod® are an integral part of Paul and Deb Doscher's garden in central New Hampshire.

Fig. 6-3 Simple glass bottle cloches help northern Vermont gardeners get extra early harvest of lettuce in their climate.

SITE SELECTION

As we mentioned in chapter 2, you should select a spot for your intensive beds that is well drained, receives full sun all day through the fall and later winter, and is close enough to your house to provide convenient access for your daily gardening chores. Having water close by is also helpful.

SEASON-EXTENDING
DEVICES

There are many systems and items to choose from. They range from the very simple, milk-jug cloche and fiberglass cone to uninsulated cold frames or lights, to insulated permanent beds with double-glazed covers. Beyond all these there is the fully insulated solar hot frame, which is a hybrid between the cold frame and a solar greenhouse. Most of the devices can be built by the user, and many can be purchased in local garden stores or through specialized mail-order catalogs. We describe them in detail at the end of this chapter.

You can begin your planting about three to four weeks earlier than normal if you use lightweight portable cloches. The original glass cloches were heavy and very fragile, but many of the materials you can use to construct modern cloches are durable, lightweight, and inexpensive. Cloches are used in your regular garden beds to provide a warm miniclimate for starting a wide variety of greens and root crops. They can also be used to protect early plantings of frost-sensitive plants like tomatoes, peppers, eggplant, melons, etc. Individual cloches, such as cut-off milk jugs and food jars, are inexpensive or free and should be easy to obtain. The fiberglass cone is simple to construct, is very durable, and can be made in almost any size you want. Continuous cloches made of glass, plastic, or polyethylene and wire are becoming more common. Continuous cloches made of glass once covered acres of land in Europe and were used to produce extra early harvests of lettuce, cauliflower, strawberries, and many other crops (see figure 6–4). For a detailed discussion of the history of intensive gardening under glass, see Appendix A.

One of the most popular new methods for creating a continuous cloche is the use of fabric and polyethylene row covers. Polyethylene plastic covers are cheap and easy to use. They involve creating a structure to support the plastic above the row and then covering it with a long, narrow sheet of clear poly. You can buy material specially designed for this use. It has numerous little slits in the plastic to allow ventilation (see figure 6–5).

Another polyethylene device is a series of tubes formed into a cone and filled with water (one brand is called "Wall o' Water"). This device allows soil heating, and the water retains nighttime heat to prevent frost damage. While difficult to fill and then empty, this combination cloche and heat storage device has gained considerable popularity.

"Reemay" is one of a number of commercial brands of spun-bonded polyester row covers now used by large- and small-scale vegetable growers. This material has pest-control benefits in addition to season-extension benefits (see Appendix B). Simply lay it out over the crops, which are growing in a bed. No supports are necessary because the material is very lightweight. Its porous texture allows some air to circulate through it and rainwater to penetrate (see figure 6–6). At night still air does not readily move through the fabric, and you get a few degrees of frost protection as a result. These two types of covers can give you a couple of weeks early start on the season as well as improve the growth of many crops during variable spring weather.

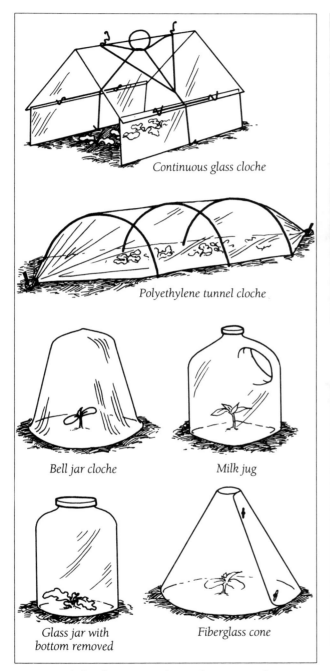

Continuous glass cloche

Polyethylene tunnel cloche

Bell jar cloche

Milk jug

Glass jar with
bottom removed

Fiberglass cone

FIG. 6-4 Cloches for getting a few weeks' jump on the growing season.

FIG. 6-5 Slitted row covers are used with wire hoops and black plastic mulch to create a warm microclimate for early heat-loving crops.

FIG. 6-6 Spun bonded polyester, also called floating row cover, is used to warm the soil and provide limited frost protection in the spring. It can also be purchased in large sheets for covering an entire small garden.

If you are content to start your gardening a month or month and a half before normal, you can use an uninsulated cold frame. Most gardeners have seen or used one, and its advantages are low cost and portability. It can be used to grow early crops in the garden or in the traditional fashion, to harden off seedlings that are to be set out after danger of frost is past (see figure 6–7).

Cold frames are best oriented east to west, and are lower in height on the south side. The angle of the glass allows the frame to catch the low winter sun.

Cold frames or lights can also be used to cover manure hotbeds. ("Lights" is a term used to describe the cold-frame sash used by European market gardeners.) Lights are similar to cold frames, differing in that they are completely portable and are used in large numbers to cover entire beds. When these devices are used to cover manure-heated beds, plants benefit not only from the heat of the air provided by the sun, but from the bottom heating of the soil.

FIG. 6-7 A low-cost, portable cold frame constructed with an old storm window.

An equally early start can be achieved using an insulated cold frame. Construction involves building a permanent wooden or masonry base in the ground. The base is insulated down into the ground to conserve soil heat. Each base is designed to accommodate one glazed cover. The size of the homemade insulated cold frame is usually determined by the size of the window to be used as a cover.

A variation is the Solar Pod® designed by Leandre Poisson. The cover has a curved surface; this allows the sun to shine into the bed all day long. Solar Pods® are often double glazed, which holds in more nighttime heat than a single glazed cover (see figure 6–8).

If you want the earliest spring start, you could choose the hot-frame idea. This device is both a permanent bed and cover all in one (see figures 6–9 and 6–10). It is insulated above and below the ground to hold soil heat and warm air. It may also have an insulated shutter, which significantly reduces nighttime heat loss through the glazed cover. In New England it is possible to get plants started in the device in late February or early March, when the snow is still a foot or two deep outdoors.

You should decide in the fall which devices you want to use. This will give you plenty of time to build permanent beds and covers before the snow falls. Simple cloches can be built at any time, but frames for permanent beds should be in the ground before it freezes for the winter. If you keep your permanent beds covered all winter, the soil in the beds will not freeze (or not very deep), and this will give you an earlier start in the spring. Be sure to provide some support or protection for your glass and fiberglass covers. Heavy winter snow may damage them or otherwise break them.

FIG. 6-8 An insulated Solar Pod®

FIG. 6-9 A hot frame called the "Solar Frame®" by designer Leandre Poisson. The cylindrical portion holds Styrofoam beads that flow down to insulate the glazing at night.

FIG. 6-10 This hot frame design was developed by the Rodale Press of Emmaus, Pennsylvania, and tested in northern Vermont. It successfully grew crops through the entire winter.

SOIL PREPARATION
IN THE FALL

If you have built a good garden soil for your summer intensive garden, you will be able to use the same soil for your season-extending beds. If your soil is still not as well prepared as it should be, you can make an acceptable mixture by combining two parts of your loam or clay with one part coarse sand and one part well-decomposed organic matter. For organic matter you can use peat moss, compost, leaf mold, or well-rotted manure.

The soil should be prepared during the fall and allowed to sit undisturbed for the winter, unless it is to be used for fall crops. If fall crops are grown, prepare the soil after they are harvested. Fertilizing can be done at this time.

You can add fresh organic matter now, but it is wise to avoid using fresh manures if you will be planting your crops very early in the spring. Decomposition will occur very slowly in cold soils, and you could end up with excess nutrients at planting time. Excess nitrogen is particularly troublesome because it can kill tender seedlings. Even if it does not kill the plants, excess nitrogen will be harmful to you because in cold soils many plants (especially greens) do not effectively convert nitrates to proteins, which means that the nitrates build up in plant tissues and can be harmful to human health.

SOIL FINISHING IN SPRING

In later winter you should work the soil as soon as possible, then check for nutrient and pH levels. At this time it should not be necessary to add organic matter, since that was done in the fall.

Next, you should prepare a seed or transplant bed as you would normally do. After this you must prewarm the soil. This is done by placing the cloches in the locations where you will have seedlings, or, with cold frames and Pods®, by keeping the covers closed and free of snow and ice. You will be able to plant earliest in insulated devices and latest under cloches. As a rule of thumb, you should wait until soil temperature has warmed up to 60° F or higher during the day and not less than 45° F at night. Measure the temperature at a depth of 1 to 3 inches.

It is difficult to give specific dates for doing any of this. In New Hampshire there is actually enough sun in late February to transplant some cold-hardy crops into insulated hot frames. It is not possible, however, to direct seed until the soil warms up in mid-March. In other locations these dates will vary considerably. The best way to judge your own climate is to take regular air and soil temperature readings inside the device you are using with a minimum-maximum thermometer and soil thermometer. The first spring you may not pick the best planting times, but after a couple of years of experience, you will know when to select planting and transplanting dates for your area.

MANURE HEATING

In the past French intensive gardeners used large quantities of fermenting manure to provide warm soil for early spring planting. This method works best in spring, because the heat given off by the manure is hottest just after the beds are prepared and gradually drops off as the season progresses. Correspondingly, the spring weather begins to warm up as the manure cools down, providing the possibility of creating an optimal growing environment from planting to harvest.

If you choose to try using manure hotbeds, use the following method as your guide (and refer to figure 6–12):

1. Excavate the area you will be using to about 2 to 2½ feet deep. If you are building your hotbed in an insulated, permanent bed, the size of your excavation is limited by the size of the bed frame. If you are going to use portable frames and lights like those used by the French, the excavation should extend at least 6 to 12 inches wider than the frame of the light. Your trench should be deeper on heavy, wet soil than on warm, sandy soil.

2. Obtain fresh horse manure that contains lots of bedding. Straw bedding is preferable to sawdust. Pile your manure near the garden and turn it at least once to get it to start heating up. You may want to measure the temperature in the pile to determine when it has dropped down to about 100° F to 120° F. Do not use it fresh, because in the early stages of decomposition some manures can reach 140° F to 160° F, and this is too hot for plants.

3. If you want to provide a more constant, lower heat, you should mix your manure with leaves, hay, or rotted manure. Some early books on the subject recommended using a 50/50 combination of fresh and rotted material.

4. After the temperature of the fermenting manure has begun to drop, shovel it into the pit in layers a few inches deep. Get in there and tread down each layer with your feet until it is well com-

FIG. 6-11 In cool New Hampshire springs, it is almost impossible to grow melons without some use of season-extending devices. Here melons were grown inside clear polyethylene shelters, which provide warm conditions for optimum plant growth.

Soil Temperatures for Best Seed Germination

Crop	Minimum °F	Optimum Range (°F)	Maximum °F
Asparagus	50	60–85	95
Beans, lima	60	65–85	85
Beans, snap	60	60–85	95
Beets	40	50–85	95
Cabbage	40	45–95	100
Carrots	40	45–85	95
Cauliflower	40	45–85	100
Celery	40	60–70	85*
Corn	50	60–95	105
Cucumbers	60	65–90	105
Eggplant	60	75–90	95
Lettuce	35	40–80	85
Muskmelon	60	75–95	100
Okra	60	70–95	105
Onions	35	50–95	95
Parsley	40	50–85	90
Parsnips	35	50–70	85
Peas	40	40–75	85
Peppers	60	65–95	95
Pumpkin	60	70–90	100
Radish	40	45–90	95
Spinach	35	45–75	85
Squash	60	70–95	100
Swiss Chard	40	50–85	95
Tomatoes	50	60–85	95
Turnips	40	60–105	105
Watermelon	60	70–95	105

*Nighttime temperature must drop to 60° F or lower for good germination

Compiled by J. F. Harrington, Department of Vegetable Crops, University of California at Davis.

pressed. Fill the bed until you are within about 6 inches of the top.

5. Water the manure all over so that it is moist (but not soaked) throughout.

6. Next you can add a layer of straw about 2 inches thick. This will help reduce the immediate impact of the heat upon plant roots by providing a small amount of insulation. This is not absolutely necessary, however.

7. Now add a 6-inch layer of loose rich topsoil over the entire bed.

8. Center your cold frame or light frame over the bed. Allow a day or two for the manure to start working again and for the soil to warm up before planting. Be sure the temperature in the top few inches of soil is no higher than about 75° F. If the temperature is higher than this, you may have to wait a few more days before planting seeds or transplants. It is best to use transplants, since the warm, moist environment in the frame can be conducive to seed rotting or damping-off fungus. Be

sure to select healthy transplants large enough to be unaffected by the fungus.

As an alternative to using manure for heating, you can use electric heating units like soil-warming cables. They can be used in many applications in both permanent and regular beds. We try to stay away from using such devices, however, as they greatly increase the nonsolar energy input into the garden and can be quite expensive to operate.

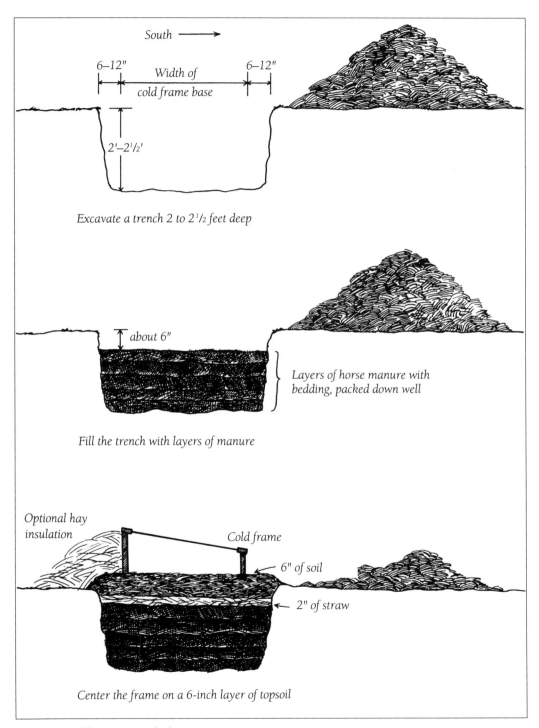

South →

6–12" Width of cold frame base 6–12"

2'–2½'

Excavate a trench 2 to 2½ feet deep

about 6"

Layers of horse manure with bedding, packed down well

Fill the trench with layers of manure

Optional hay insulation

Cold frame

6" of soil

2" of straw

Center the frame on a 6-inch layer of topsoil

FIG. 6-12 Building a manure bed.

CROP SELECTION

Your choice of crops for spring gardening is somewhat limited compared with your summer selection. The difference comes in the need to use crops that grow well under the cooler conditions prevalent in the early spring. If you will be planting directly into your beds using seeds, you will have also to choose seeds that germinate well under cool soil conditions. Of course, if you are using manure hotbeds, this is not the case.

The crops that grow best are leafy greens and root crops. Cold hardiness and short time to maturity are characteristics to look for when choosing varieties. If the seed package says "Wait until all danger of frost is past" before planting, the crop you have chosen is not a good one for the spring garden.

Plants that require pollination to develop fruit (cucumbers, melons, tomatoes, etc.) are not good choices. They may be transplanted under covers later in the spring and can often be used to follow the harvest of earlier greens and root vegetables.

The following crops can be planted or transplanted into insulated or manure-heated beds up to three months before the last spring frost:

lettuce:
   Oak leaf
   Grand Rapids Forcing
   Arctic King
   and other leafy types
carrots
beets
cauliflower
broccoli
radishes
Swiss chard
peas

spinach:
   Winter Bloomsdale
   Bloomsdale
   Monnopa
   and other varieties
India mustard
Chinese cabbage
endive
parsley
onion transplants
strawberries

We have tried many of these with varying success. Our greatest praise goes to the Chinese cabbages. They grow consistently through the coldest weather and do quite well under glass. Swiss chard is also a winner as an early spring crop. The most difficult crops tend to be spinach, broccoli, and other cabbage-family plants. One way to assure good lettuce is to start seedlings in the house or greenhouse and then move them into the garden after they are well established. We prefer leaf lettuce because it can be partially harvested continually and will continue to grow back.

All of these crops can be started as well later in the spring under cloches and row covers. About a month before the normal planting date, you can plant seeds directly in the garden, many of them under the prewarmed soil of a cloche or row cover. Be sure to plant generously, then thin out the space until you have one plant per cloche. If you are using continuous cloches that form tunnels, the thinning process should result in the spacing recommended on the seed package.

Heat-loving crops like tomatoes, peppers, eggplant, melons, cucumbers, and squash can be set out about four weeks before the last frost date under either cloches, lights, row

covers, or cold frames (devices) that can be removed once the plants are well established (see figure 6–13). It is best to use only healthy transplants that are not leggy or spindly, because, although night-time temperatures under the covers will not normally get down to freezing, weak plants can be seriously hampered by temperatures in the 30s and 40s.

FIG. 6-13 Cantaloupes in a cold frame in the garden of David Emery in Maine.

PLANT CARE

Once your plants are in the ground, you will need to tend them more carefully than you would in the summer garden. Thinning must be done regularly to prevent crowding. If you are interplanting, you will have to watch individual crops and pick them at the peak of maturity in order not to hamper neighboring crops by shading or competition for nutrients. You should also be prepared with a succession planting plan so that once an early crop is removed, it can be followed by another.

Temperature control is the real key to success. Cloches, row covers, lights, cold frames, Pods®, or any such device must be ventilated to prevent excessively high temperatures on warm spring days. This ventilation is also necessary to reduce dampness, which could otherwise lead to mildew or fungal disease problems. Excessively high temperatures cause stress and wilting in some plants because photosynthesis and respiration increase with temperature. As it gets hotter, the plant may not be able to get enough water from the cooler ground to supply the photosynthesis process, and the leaves will wilt. This can cause further stress within the plant tissues and result in delayed maturity or, in extreme cases, death (see figure 6–14).

Although you will have to open cloches and cold frames to achieve this ventilation, slitted and spun-bonded polyester row covers are adequately self-ventilated to prevent plant damage.

Your objective should be to obtain daily temperatures that approximately the optimum

FIG. 6-14 Unless this is manually opened on sunny days, temperatures inside can get too high for good plant health. Note that the cover is horizontal when closed. While optimum growth is usually obtained using sloped glazing, this design works quite well.

growing conditions of the individual species. For most early spring crops, this means no higher than 80° F and no lower than 40° F. Most gardeners worry more about cold temperatures than hot, but excess heat is actually more harmful to plants than cold.

Jim Crockett, the nationally known garden expert, suggested some guidelines for ventilating cold frames that are equally valid for other season-extension devices. He suggested that when the outside temperature reaches 40° F, the cover should be opened about 6 inches.

When the outdoor temperature gets up to 60° F, it is time to open the cover all the way. He noted that after midday (when there are a few hours of sun left), you should close the cover again to trap heat for the night.

Any appropriate size piece of wood can be used to prop up covers of lights, cold frames, or Solar Pods®, but small notched props should be used to tilt up cloches during the day. They can be made with two or three settings so that the warmer it gets, the higher you can raise the cloche.

The exception to these guidelines comes with your heat-loving crops. You can let them get a bit warmer than greens and root crops without doing any damage. Nonetheless, you should ventilate them somewhat to keep moisture from causing problems. The maximum temperature you should allow for these crops is about 90° F. Interestingly, we have grown squash under cone-shaped cloches and under row covers in which the temperature got as high as 105° F. The cones have a small opening at the top that allows some air in, but we did not tip up the cone to allow air in at the bottom. The squash grew faster than neighboring, uncovered plants and did not suffer any apparent damage. As the plants grew too big for the covers, they were removed. The crop from the covered plants was a full two weeks earlier than the neighboring, uncovered plants in the same bed.

If squash were grown under very large cones, the cones could be left on until the first female flowers appear. At that point it would be necessary to remove the cones to allow insect pollination (see figure 6–15).

On the other hand, beans and corn that we have allowed to stay under cones at such high temperatures not only suffered from the experience, they died. Eggplant started under cones grew faster during the early part of the season, but did not produce a crop any sooner than the neighboring, uncovered plants.

Our best success came with melons. We have grown them in a hot frame, under cones, and under row covers. All methods have produced startling results. In the hot frame we were able to produce extra early crops of melons that were almost free from pest problems. Apparently cucumber beetles, which are a great nuisance in our outdoor garden areas, do not like to fly under the covers of the hot frame and did not attack the plants. We kept the covers

FIG. 6-15 The first female flowers of a squash-family plant (such as this cantaloupe) are those with a round ovary at the base of the petals. Can you identify the male and female flowers in the photo?

closed on cool nights; this meant that the air in the frame was usually 10 to 20 degrees warmer than the normal night air. During cooler days the covers were opened only about 6 inches. This kept the plants warmer than they would have been outdoors. In comparing the plants in the frame with those outdoors, we found that the leaves of the frame plants were almost twice the size of the outdoor plants. Flowering was much earlier, and, with regular pruning, we were able to keep the plants flowering until early fall. The melons were larger, more numerous (on a per plant basis), and almost free of insect damage.

When cones were used, the melons were started indoors about four weeks before being set out into the garden. We used individual pots to eliminate any shock to the tender root system during transplanting. Setting out is done about two weeks before the last frost date. Each plant is then covered by a cone—all day on cool days (60° F or lower) and only during the morning on warmer days (60° F or higher). On warm days the cones were placed over the plants in late afternoon so that some warmth could be captured for overnight use. We left the cones on all day during cloudy periods.

After about two weeks under the cones, the plants had grown large enough almost to fill the cones. By the fourth week it became impossible to cover the plants with the cones any longer. The result of this effort has been flowering about two weeks before normal (for our climate) and a crop of melons two weeks before our usual mid-August harvest date.

A successful way to get similar early melon crops is by combining the use of plastic mulch, drip irrigation, and row covers. The drip line is laid out first, along a line next to where the melon plants will be transplanted. Then the bed is covered with plastic or IRT mulch. Next, the transplants are inserted into the soil through holes punched in the mulch. Finally, a slitted row cover or spun-bonded polyester fabric is placed over the entire bed. This method allows you to increase the temperatures to levels preferred by heat-loving melons.

Melons also need lots of water, which is provided by the drip line. The cover has the added benefit of protecting the young plants from devastation by cucumber beetles. In New Hampshire, where summers are cool and variable, many commercial growers would not be able to produce melons without using this system (see figure 6–16).

Another important factor in plant care is watering. Usually it is not necessary early in the season because of the high moisture content of the soil and the general abundance of capillary water during spring thaw. As the season progresses, you should check the soil regularly. If it becomes dry more than 1 inch below the surface, you should water. Completely soak the soil. Always water in the morning to make the moisture available to the plants for their daily photosynthesis. Evening watering results in excess moisture overnight and produces prime conditions for the development of mold and mildew.

If your plants show an obvious and urgent need for water during the day, be sure to use only warm water. "Warm water" is water that is at about the same temperature as the soil in your beds. Adding cold water will cool off the soil, making it harder for the plant to bring up the moisture from its roots into the leaves where it is needed.

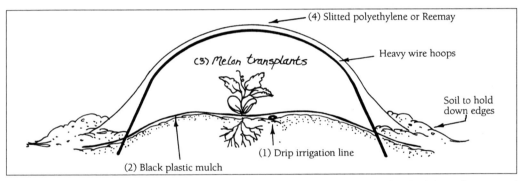

FIG. 6-16 *This melon system, used by the Doschers, involves (1) a drip irrigation line laid down the center of the bed, (2) black plastic mulch, (3) four-week-old individually grown transplants, and (4) a slitted row cover or spun-bonded polyester cover over wire hoops. It has proven the most successful method for producing quality melons in the cool New Hampshire summer.*

PESTS AND DISEASES

As we mentioned previously, the great disease threats to plants under cover are the fungi and mildews caused by excessive moisture. Once you have these problems, they are difficult to eliminate. The first measure to take is to increase your ventilation and hope for dry weather. Secondly, you can try leaving the cover open a slight bit at night so that the relative humidity in the device will not increase to where moisture condenses on the surfaces and plants inside. If both these fail, your crop probably will, too. The best thing to do then is pull it out and open up the device to allow it to be fully exposed to the sun for as long as it takes to dry it out completely. If your soil contains a soilborne fungus or disease like verticillium, fusarium, or clubroot, you may want to dig out the soil and replace it.

Damping-off fungus is another potential problem in season-extension devices, particularly in the early spring when your ventilation needs are low. Damping-off strikes young seedlings, causing them to become wet at the base of the stem and then fall over. The best control is prevention, and this is usually accomplished by spreading a thin layer of dry sand or sphagnum peat on the surface of the soil.

It is important to note that the tighter you build your devices the more moisture problem you are likely to have. "Not-so-tight" cold frames, row covers, and uninsulated devices seem to have less of a problem with fungus and mildew. This may be because of air leakage, which prevents moisture levels from getting as high as they do in fully insulated and tightly sealed Solar Pods® and hot frames.

Crop rotation is essential in avoiding many diseases. One way to accomplish this is by having a number of beds so that you do not have to plant the same crop in one area more often than once every three years. This is particularly important in combating many of the diseases of the cabbage family. If you wish to build and maintain only one Pod®, light, or cold-frame cover, you can build a number of permanent beds to put it on. Then you can move the cover from bed to bed on a rotation. If building a number of beds is still too much work for you, then build one permanent bed and one cover, and rotate the soil by removing it at the end of each crop rotation. For example, if you are growing cabbage, then carrots, then peas, then lettuce, and back to cabbage again, you should change the soil before planting the cabbage for a second time (see figure 6–17).

It is also a good idea to uncover a permanent bed once every few winters to let the soil freeze. This will help bring some diseases under control and will destroy the larval stages of many insect pests.

Most common garden insect pests are not likely to be a problem in your early spring beds. This is because most insect pests have a specific life cycle that brings them out only when the season is right, usually in summer. Secondly, since your plants are growing in a protected environment, unless you inadvertently introduce a pest into your beds, it will usually not find its way in.

Even so, there are some particular pests to look out for (see figure 6–18). Slugs will seek any warm moist place and seem to have an affinity for season-extension devices. We have had continual slug problems in our permanent beds. There are a number of home remedies for this problem, but we have tried only two. The first is to place a shallow pan of beer at ground level inside your device. The theory is that the slugs will smell or sense the beer and dive in for a drink. The little devils reportedly become intoxicated and forget how to swim, drowning in their stupor. As you may have guessed, this method has not worked for us, although some other gardeners swear by it. Maybe our slugs are teetotalers.

The method that works for us is a bit more demanding, but much more successful. Slugs like to hide under any object that traps the heat of the soil, and they also will climb to the top of a hot frame to seek out the warmth that rises there at night. Our efforts at slug control concentrate upon placing boards on the soil, which attracts the slugs. On a warm day (so that the plants will not be damaged by opening the cover of the device), we go out and collect the slimy pests from under the boards. On warm nights they seem to congregate near the top of the

Spring	Fall	Spring	Fall	Spring	Fall
lettuce	carrots	cabbage family	onions	chard	peas
cabbage family	radishes	chard	peas	beets	carrots
chard	onions	beets	carrots	lettuce	radishes
beets	peas	lettuce	radishes	cabbage family	onions
carrots	cabbage family	onions	chard	peas	lettuce
radishes	chard	peas	beets	carrots	cabbage family
onions	beets	carrots	lettuce	radishes	chard
peas	lettuce	radishes	cabbage family	onions	beets
Spring	**Fall**	**Spring**	**Fall**	**Spring**	**Fall**
YEAR 1		YEAR 2		YEAR 3	

FIG. 6-17 *A possible crop rotation in six season-extended beds (or in sections of large beds). The key is to avoid planting the same crop in one space more often than once every three years.*

device, on the walls and glass, and we pick them off there too. It is always good to check the plant leaves on warm evenings because some slugs are likely to be feeding there as well.

The other common pests of extended-season gardening are aphids and whiteflies. These two insects are close relatives and like the same conditions. In most northern climates the winter is harsh enough that not many of these pests survive the cold. But in an intensive bed covered for the winter, they can survive quite well. They thrive as the spring begins to warm the environment of the device, and your crops can become covered with them in what seems like no time at all. There are a few ways to control them, but you probably won't entirely eliminate them no matter what you do.

The first control to try is placing a piece of bright yellow-colored metal or paper under your plants. Coat the paper or metal with a sticky substance. For unknown reasons aphids and whiteflies are attracted to yellow and will become stuck to the trap you have made.

If the first method doesn't provide adequate control, you can resort to more active methods, using pyrethrum or soap sprays. Both of these will work to some degree (pyrethrum works the best), but neither will destroy all the pests. You will have to keep after them with occasional spraying or dusting until you can open up the bed in warmer weather. Once the bed is exposed to the natural environment, the many predators (including ladybugs) upon these little insects can go to work and keep them under control for you. The use of predatory insects, for example, certain species of tiny wasps (such as *Encarsia formosa*), works well in a greenhouse environment, but in the environment of cold frames and hot frames, these predators are unlikely to be able to maintain themselves. Wasps require warmer temperatures for reproduction than you are likely to have in your devices. In the long run the best way to combat aphids and whiteflies is to enrich your soil with organic matter. A high humus content discourages both of these pests.

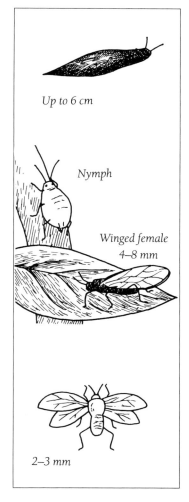

Up to 6 cm

Nymph

Winged female
4–8 mm

2–3 mm

SLUGS
Slimy snails that have many tiny teeth and are nocturnal feeders

APHIDS
Adults are dark colored; nymphs are light green.

WHITEFLIES
Minute white insects covered by a white powder. They are easily disturbed and take wing at the slightest movement.

Fig. 6-18 Slugs, aphids, and whiteflies are the most common pests of season-extending devices in northern climates.

EXTENDING THE SEASON IN FALL

Fall gardening under glass works much the same way as in the spring except that it requires more attention to planting dates. While the early crops of spring benefit from the improving weather and longer days of April, May, and June, your fall crops will find themselves working against rapidly shortening days, with colder day and night temperatures as the season progresses. This means you must plan your fall garden during the heat of summer and plant your crops early enough in the fall for them to be almost mature when winter arrives.

Certain crops are very sensitive to the photo-period, or length of day. Onions, for example, will not bulb unless days are twelve hours or longer. Other plants flower only during days that are longer than the nights, and some plants will not produce foliage at all during the eight- to ten-hour daylight period of deep winter. This may be because of biological clocks in some plants set to put the plant into a dormant period during shorter, colder weather, or because the amount of light received during short days is inadequate to allow the plant to produce enough extra nourishment (plant sugars) to do much more than just survive. Whatever the reason, in northern climates most plants grow slowly or not at all during late December and January. You should bear this in mind when planning the fall planting schedule.

We recommend that you begin your fall planting of greens and root crops four to six weeks before the first expected frost. Continued planting at one- to two-week intervals until about a month after your first frost will generally result in a constant harvest right up until the coldest days of the winter.

In our southern New Hampshire garden, we finish our fall planting around the beginning of October. This results in almost mature greens by the beginning of December, and these plants will be picked through January until they are almost gone. We are careful to leave some foliage on each plant, and in early February growth begins again, and harvesting can continue right on to spring planting time.

Soil preparation is relatively simple. Prepare your beds as though you were going to plant a regular summer crop, but instead of using the normal dose of fertilizer, cut it by about one half. This is done because plants grow slower in the fall and nutrients become available through the normal soil decomposition process at a slower pace. Also, you will not lose nutrients from excessive leaching by rain. Excess fertilization can result in "sappy" plants, which are more susceptible to frost and cold damage than normal plants. Be sure to add a good amount of well-decomposed organic matter at this time, since this will be your last opportunity until spring.

If your soil needs an additional boost during the winter because nutrient levels are too low, it is best to use very diluted liquid fertilizers. It is generally suggested that you use a low concentration of liquid fish or manure tea on a regular basis—that is, once a week or every two weeks—rather than a stronger solution in a one-shot application. If you are worried about nutrient levels, learn to recognize the early signs of plant nutrient deficiency or get out your test kit before rushing to the bottle of liquid fertilizer. It will pay to add only those nutrients that are needed to avoid an overdose of the others. See chapter 3 on soil for more specifics on sources of nutrients. (A useful guide to recognizing deficiencies is "A Key to Nutrient Disorders of Vegetable Plants" by Jean English and Donald N. Maynard in *Horti-science*, Vol. 13 (1), Feb. 1978.)

Also remember that excess nitrates in your soil can accumulate in plant tissues and present a significant health hazard, especially to small children.

You can use manure hotbeds in the fall as well. Although the timing of the heat release is not well coordinated with the demands of your crops (the manure will be getting colder just as the coldest temperatures of fall arrive), this heat source can still be an advantage in uninsulated beds.

SEASON-EXTENDING DEVICES FOR THE FALL

You can use the same solar devices in the fall that you used in the spring: Solar Pods®, cold frames, lights, and hot frames, with one possible exception, individual cloches. The problem with individual cloches is that they are generally too small to hold a maturing plant, and the point at which you need the protection of the cloche is as the plant matures in mid to late fall. Solar Pods®, cold frames, lights, and hot frames work better because they afford the space full-grown plants require and because they hold more heat through the night.

If you are in a relatively mild climate (such as is found in coastal areas or in states at about 37° north latitude or lower), you should be able to extend your growing season right through the fall without insulating your devices. In colder climates, as in New England, an insulated device is essential (see figure 6–19). Insulation below ground helps keep soil temperatures warm enough to encourage continued growth even when outdoor temperatures begin to hover in the 30s. See Appendix B for insulation details.

A device we are particularly happy with for fall and winter gardening is the hot frame. It is essentially a solar-heated "hothouse" and is capable of carrying many crops right through the winter in all but subarctic climates. It is used in the same way as Pods® or cold frames but is much more completely insulated. A unique feature of this type of device is an insulated shutter that covers the plants at night, preventing excessive heat

FIG. 6-19 The Solar Pod®, designed by New Hampshire gardener Leandre Poisson, can be used to extend the season well into the winter months. It has a double-glazed cover of fiberglass-reinforced plastic.

loss through the glazing. We have successfully grown many leafy crops, root crops, herbs, and cabbage-family plants through winters in New Hampshire, where temperatures of 20° F to 30° F below zero are frequent.

A device with a single glazing will allow you to produce harvests until nighttime temperatures drop below around 20° F. Double-glazed devices can protect most leafy crops down to about 10° F. Once the temperature drops below this, most crops will be frosted enough to die back unless you cover your device with some kind of insulation for the night. Although we have not tried it, we suspect that double-glazed Solar Pods® and cold frames could protect mature crops down to about 0° F outdoor temperature if the glazing were covered with heavy blankets, loose hay, or straw.

Be sure to check your devices for leaks and drafts. A small leak can lose enough heat to make the difference between survival or freezing for many crops. If you find any leaks, you can use small pieces of foam rubber, string, or cloth to seal them up.

If you use a device through the winter, you may find that the frost in the ground can twist it or push it out of shape. This can lead to loose fits on your covers and result in air leaks. To prevent this you can either treat the symptoms by plugging leaks as they appear or build the base of your device with deep insulation or a masonry foundation.

CROP SELECTION

We have found that many of the same crops that grow well in the spring intensive garden also do well in the fall.

Below are some crops that are particularly good performers in the fall garden:

- †* Chinese cabbage (see below)
  - leaf lettuce
- † Arctic King
  - Black Seeded Simpson
  - cos or romaine
- * Grand Rapids Forcing
- * Oak Leaf
- †* Swiss chard
- †* kale
- † endive
- †* parsley
- * radishes
- † turnips
- †* spinach

Other crops that can be used are

- * broccoli
- * beets
- * corn salad (mache)
  - collards
  - cress
- * escarole
  - celery
  - cabbage
  - mustard greens
- * carrots
  - rutabagas
  - cauliflower
  - bunching and scallion onions
  - leeks
- * and many perennial herbs

There are also some unusual oriental plants that grow well in fall intensive gardens. They are well suited to the short days and seem to be able to grow even when other crops are dormant. They are

　*† Siew Choy cabbage (heading)
　 * Bok Choy cabbage (leafy)
　　 Wong Bok cabbage (heading)
　　 Daikon radish
　　 Gai Lohn (Chinese broccoli or kale)
　　 Gow Choy (Chinese chives)
　 † Shungiku (Edible Chrysanthemum)
　 † Dai Gai Chow (Gai Choy) (Indian mustard)
　 † Pak Choy (white cabbage)
　 † Kyo Mizuna
　 † Seppaku Tiana (leaf cabbage)
　 † Komatsuna (leaf cabbage)
　 † Choy Sum (flowering white cabbage)
　　 Heung Kum (Chinese celery)
　　 Yuen Sai (Chinese parsley)

*Indicates plants we have successfully grown through the winter in a hot frame.

†Indicates plants that have been successfully grown through the winter at the Rodale Organic Gardening Research Center in Emmaus, Pennsylvania. These plants were grown in the Rodale Solar Growing Frame. (Ray Wolf, ed. *Rodale's Solar Growing Frame* [Emmaus, Pa.: Rodale Press, 1980]).

A list of companies that sell some or all of the oriental vegetables is included at the end of this chapter

PLANT CARE

It is difficult to give specific instructions on planting dates for fall crops. Shorter days make the plants grow slower and extend the estimated "date to maturity" figures listed on seed packages. Additionally, cooler soil and air temperatures make it harder for plants to use the light they get efficiently. We have estimated that in determining when to plant most leafy crops you should add at least 20 to 40 percent to the "date to maturity" figures listed on the package. For root crops planted early in the fall, you should add the same, but if your root crops go in late (after mid-August where we are), you may have to wait until later winter and early spring for a harvest.

We have found that lettuce and chard started in late September will take as much as three months to reach maturity in the New Hampshire climate. By December there is so little light that most leafy crops simply stop growing altogether. If you are using Pods®, lights, or cold frames, this is the time to harvest, since no further growth is likely. In the hot frame you can leave the plants in the ground, and they will provide occasional harvests until they begin to grow again in early February. By early March production should be going strong. In mild climates some growth will occur during the entire winter, and with some trial and error you will probably be able to develop a planting schedule that will yield fresh produce the full twelve months of the year.

You should keep all fall and winter crops well thinned. Crowding is particularly harmful, as it will cause plants to become leggy and weak-stemmed. Spacing should be slightly farther apart than in the summer garden to allow each plant to obtain full sun. A good rule of thumb would be to add 2 to 4 inches to the normal intensive planting spacings shown in chapter 4.

Weeds are rarely a problem in glazed beds. Occasionally some leftover weed seeds from the summer will germinate in the warm environment of the season-extending device. These few stragglers will rarely grow to maturity and almost never go to seed. You should pull them, however, because they will shade the soil and reduce the heating that is so important to maintaining warm soil temperatures.

Watering will be necessary early in the fall when plants are still strong. Since daytime temperatures are still high (above 60° F), you will not be covering the beds except at night. This will result in enough water loss to require regular sprinkling. As temperatures drop and you are keeping the covers on your beds during the day, however, the need for water will diminish. Do not water established crops unless you find that the soil is not damp within half an inch of the surface.

Further on into the winter, watering needs will drop to almost nothing. This requires a cutback in your sprinkling efforts to prevent the creation of conditions conducive to disease and fungus development. Regular watering at this point can be more harmful than helpful. In New Hampshire the late fall months usually bring plenty of rain, which soaks the soil, and our problem becomes too much, not too little, water. This is partly due to capillary water, which moves upward into the soil of frames and Pods® from the underground water table. In warm weather this capillary water evaporates at the soil surface, but in cold weather and in an enclosed solar intensive device the water cannot evaporate and escape as readily. This means that from late October to March we do not water at all. (We have a heavy clay subsoil; in sandy soils this may not be the case.)

Temperature control in fall is slightly different from what it is in spring. In spring soil and air temperatures just outside your solar intensive devices will be constantly increasing, so it is less crucial to conserve heat from the sun. In fall, with dropping air and soil temperatures, it is helpful to keep your devices closed more of the time to conserve valuable heat for nighttime use. This, on the other hand, can cause problems of overheating. Fortunately, overheating and the need to store heat for night can be addressed through the wise use of thermal mass.

Thermal mass is simply any massive material that can absorb and hold heat. Commonly used materials are water in drums or bottles and masonry such as concrete or bricks. Water holds almost four times as much heat per cubic foot as masonry does, so it is desirable from a space-saving point of view. In either case the function of thermal mass is to absorb some portion of the sun's energy that enters the solar intensive device, thus reducing the amount that immediately turns into hot air and increasing the amount held for release during the night as air temperatures drop.

Drums painted black and filled with water are commonly used in the Solar Pod® system. This allows the covers to be left closed most of the day during fall and spring. Our own hot frame contained three 30-gallon drums of water, which help store heat for overnight use. Other systems use concrete slabs embedded under the hot frame, and some schemes use rocks as the thermal storage medium (see figure 6–20).

Even in cold periods, when heat is precious, some ventilation is necessary. Fresh air is beneficial because it allows the oxygen given off by plants to escape and carbon dioxide, which plants absorb during photosynthesis, to get in. Air movement also helps to prevent mold and mildew, as many greenhouse operators have discovered. You should allow some ventilation except on the coldest days. Opening the cover of your frame or Pod® only a quarter of an inch can accomplish this, but be sure to do this only during the sunny period of the day. Be sure to close the cover again before the sun goes down so that enough heat will be held for the night. You should also try to ventilate in a way that doesn't let in cold blasts of air that hit the plants directly. A small ventilating hole, with a cover or plug, near the top of your device can help with this and may eliminate the need to crack open the cover itself.

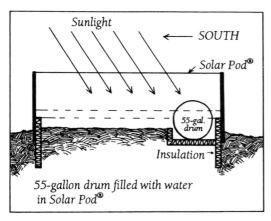

55-gallon drum filled with water in Solar Pod®

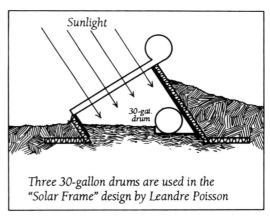

Three 30-gallon drums are used in the "Solar Frame" design by Leandre Poisson

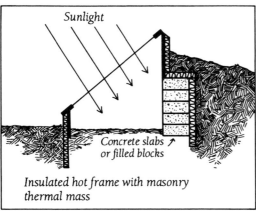

Insulated hot frame with masonry thermal mass

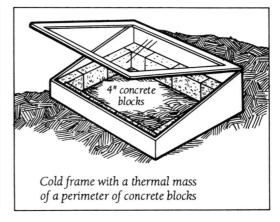

Cold frame with a thermal mass of a perimeter of concrete blocks

It is important not to allow temperature to change too rapidly in your devices. If, for example, you find that the temperature in a cold frame has risen above the desired level, do not immediately throw open the cover. Allow a gradual temperature drop by propping the cover open a little for about half an hour and then a little more for another half an hour until the temperature reaches the desired level. A sudden drop in temperature is damaging to plants, and a rapid change in relative humidity caused by allowing all the moisture in the device to escape quickly is equally bad. Such sudden changes usually cause wilting, can reduce plant vigor, and can set back growth.

If all this running around to open and close cold frames and other devices sounds like too much trouble, you have two alternatives. First, you can buy automatic temperature-controlled opening machines (see Appendix B). These relatively inexpensive openers—about $30 each—will take care of keeping the frames open at the appropriate times, but they may not work if you have unusually heavy covers on your cold frames. The other alternative is to stick to devices (like row covers) that are self-ventilated, or step up to the use of a greenhouse, which can have a fully automated ventilation system.

CROPS FOR WINTERING-OVER IN UNINSULATED DEVICES

If you do not build a fully insulated structure like the hot frame, or if you want to use your cold frames, Solar Pods®, or lights through the winter, you can employ them as wintering-over equipment. Certain crops that will not survive the winter in open gardens will do admirably with the protection provided by these devices. They will not grow much or at all during the winter, but in early spring will be awakened to begin a new year's growth.

The procedure is the same as for producing a fall crop, only you do not harvest the plants and you can usually start planting a little later. You should not harvest or take cuttings from your overwintering crops after they have been exposed to a frost because cutting encourages further growth. What you want to do is get the plant to the point where it is almost mature and then let it go into a dormant stage for the winter. Once the daily temperatures stay below freezing, you should cover the glazing with a material that will cut out solar energy. This will prevent any warm sunny periods in midwinter from reawakening the plants prematurely (see figure 6–21).

If you live in an area where there is a lot of snow, be sure to provide some support for the glazing to prevent the weight of the snow from breaking the glass or fiberglass. In early

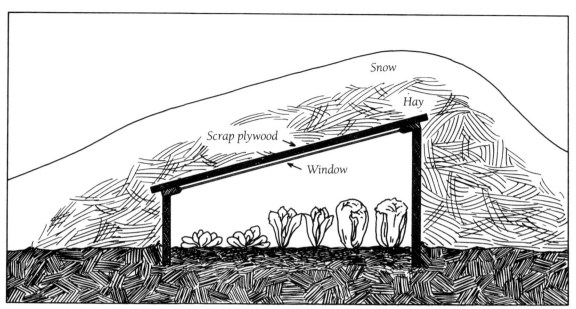

FIG. 6-21 A cold frame covered with hay and snow will keep hardy greens through the winter.

spring, once the days get into the 40s and the daylight is more than about ten hours long, you can uncover the device and allow the sun to shine in. In no time the crops will spring to life and within a few weeks you will be able to harvest. Some crops to try overwintering for spring harvest are:

cabbage	cauliflower
Chinese cabbage	bunching onions and scallions
Swiss chard	parsnips
beet greens	carrots
cress	kale
parsley	garlic
broccoli	and perennial herbs

You can also overwinter crops in your summer garden by covering them with cloches or a heavy mulch. Most root crops can be saved until spring this way, parsnips being one of the most notable. We have also mulched onions, carrots, herbs, parsley, and Swiss chard with success.

SOME WORDS OF CAUTION

We recommend starting small. Extending the season demands more of the gardener than summer gardening. Your timing and scheduling of planting, thinning, and harvesting requires more thought than in summer. Frequent trips into the garden are absolutely essential because one day of overheating can severely injure or even kill many crops. If you have devices with insulating covers, you will have to remember to open them every morning and close them every night. You must consciously refrain from watering and fertilizing as often as you do in summer. The more advanced devices are somewhat expensive and time-consuming to build, so don't overextend yourself until you have had success on a small scale. Finally, you must keep your equipment in good condition, and that requires regular maintenance throughout the year.

One of the biggest demands of the extended garden is the constant diligence required to maintain optimum temperatures in the devices. Many days we have had to make frequent trips into the garden to accommodate the fickle ways of the weather. If the day is one when the sun appears briefly and then disappears, only to return again a few hours later, you will have to make a number of journeys to your devices. All this running back and forth can get to be pretty tedious. It can be particularly bothersome when you want to go away for a weekend, or if you are a working person who is away all day. Either you will have to train your neighbors to babysit your garden or invest in only those devices that can be operated by automatic openers. Of course, if you have a solar greenhouse, most of this can be done more easily and in less time.

Starting out small will minimize the initial problems you will run into. It is much better to go through the trial-and-error stage in one or two Pods®, cold frames, or hot frames than in dozens of them. Once you have a season of experience, you can then expand in whatever ways have proven to be the most successful for you.

SOURCES FOR COLD-HARDY VEGETABLE VARIETIES

The following companies sell varieties of cold-hardy vegetables that can be used in season-extending devices. This list was compiled by Steve Tracy, formerly at the Ashland Community Organic Gardening Project in Ashland, Massachusetts.

Burpee Seeds
Warminster, PA 18001

Burgess Seeds
P.O. Box 218
Galesburg, MI 49053

Dessert Cal-Seed, Inc.
P.O. Box 3485
El Centro, CA 92244

Dominion Seeds
Georgetown, Ontario L7G 4A2

Epicure Seeds
Box 69
Avon, NY 10538

Grace's Gardens
Autumn Lane
Hackettstown, NJ 07840

Gurney's Seed and Nursery Co.
Yankton, SD 57078

Herbst Brothers Seedsmen, Inc.
100 N. Main St.
Brewster, NY 10509

J.A. Demonchaux Co.
225 Jackson
Topeka, KS 66603

Japonica Nursery
Seed Department
P.O. Box 69
Larchmont, NY 10538

J.L. Hudson, Seedsman
P.O. Box 1058
Redwood City, CA 94064

Johnny's Selected Seeds
Albion, ME 04910

Le Jardin Du Gourmet
West Danville, VT 05873

Lowden's Better Seeds and Plants
Box 10
Ancaster, Ontario L9G 3L3

McFayden Seed Co., Ltd.
P.O. Box 1600
30 Ninth St.
Brandon, Manitoba R7A 6A6

The Oriental Country Store
12 Mott St.
New York, NY 10013

Pellett Gardens
Atlantic, IA 50022

R.H. Shumway
Rockford, IL 61101

Roswell Seed Co.
115–117 S. Main
Roswell, NM 88201

Stokes Seed Co.
737 Main St.
Box 548
Buffalo, NY 04240

Tsang and Ma International
P.O. Box 294
Belmont, CA 94002

William Dam Seeds
West Flamboro, Ontario L0R 2KO

REFERENCES AND FURTHER READINGS

Aquatias, A. *Intensive Culture of Vegetables on the French System* (Harrisville, N.H.: Solar Survival, 1978, reprint of 1913 ed.). *An early description of the French market gardening system as practiced around Paris in the early 1900s. Includes detailed descriptions of devices and horticultural practices.*

Carter, A.R. *Dutch Lights for Growers and Gardeners* (London: Vinton, 1956).

Chase, J.L.H. *Commercial Cloche Gardening* (London: Faber and Faber, 1952). *A very useful book with information on many facets of both cold and warm season gardening, by the originator of the continuous cloche.*

Colebrook, Binda. *Winter Gardening in the Maritime Northwest* (Tilth Association, 1977.) *Includes a good list of winter crops and how to grow them.*

Coleman, Eliot. *The New Organic Grower's Four Season Harvest* (Chelsea, Vt.: Chelsea Green, 1992). *Eliot Coleman has tried numerous modern season-extending methods and devices. His work focuses on market gardening but has application to backyard gardening as well.*

Copley, George H. *Growing under Glass* (London: John Crowther, 1945). *Probably out of print.*

Dakers, J.S. *Early Vegetables under Glass* (London: Cassell, 1936). *Out of print.*

Flawn, Louis. *Gardening with Cloches* (London: John Gifford, 1957, 1967). *A very good book on a wide variety of cloches and how to use them.*

Getting the Most from Your Garden. The editors of *Organic Gardening* magazine (Emmaus, Pa.: Rodale, 1980). *A very useful and complete reference on all aspects of intensive gardening, including a chapter on "Extending Your Growing Season."*

McCullagh, James (ed.). *The Solar Greenhouse Book* (Emmaus, Pa.: Rodale, 1978). *contains a section on season-extending devices by Leandre Poisson and information on materials used in constructing solar intensive devices.*

Quarrell, C.P. *Intensive Salad Production* (London: Crosby Lockwood, 1938). *Another English book that describes and documents the development of gardening under glass in the early twentieth century.*

Spice, Henry. *Polyethylene Film in Horticulture* (London: Faber and Faber, 1959). *Probably out of print, but worth searching for, because it has many good (and some unusual) ideas for building inexpensive solar intensive devices.*

Weathers, John. *French Market Gardening* (London: John Murray, 1909). *Out of print. This is probably the first English book on gardening under glass; it is one of the best. It fully documents the methods of the French maraîchers.*

Willmott, P.K. *Dutch Lights and Frames* (London: Ernest Benn, 1958).

CHAPTER 7

Theme Gardens

Here is a chance to take time out from the nitty-gritty of making the best big little garden you have ever seen and see what other gardeners are doing without having a thing to do yourself but read on and dream. Many of the gardens and gardeners are described as we found them. Some descriptions, however, are fictional composites, to better present a specific theme. It is hoped that these gardeners will inspire you and that seeing garden plans that work, you will find yourself wanting to try some of the many ideas presented.

ROWHOUSE GARDEN

Kenneth and Marjorie Lauer developed a very special garden in the tiny backyard of their Allentown, Pennsylvania, rowhouse. Their whole yard was only 14 feet wide, and after subtracting the area taken by their car parking space, about the same length. Into this space they squeezed nine garden beds, all brimming with a wide range of vegetables.

Running the length of the right side of the yard was the sidewalk from the parking space to the house. At the rear of the yard, wedged between the parking space and the sidewalk, was a long strip of garden bed 1 foot wide—hardly worth planting by most people's standards, but not the Lauers'. Under their care it was overflowing with carrots. Between the sidewalk and their neighbor's parallel sidewalk was another long, 1-foot wide strip of earth. Although they rotate crops frequently, this was usually a favored spot for trellised peas, beans, or cucumbers. The trellis, in addition to supporting vegetables, provided a lovely fence between themselves and their neighbor's yard.

Directly in front of the parking space was a permanent bed of blueberries. This bed,

enriched with manure, was mulched heavily with sawdust to maintain the soil acidity needed by blueberries and to keep down weeds. As if the good picking from these high bush
blueberries weren't enough, they also provided an attractive visual screen between the parking space and the house.

In a bed to the left of the sidewalk, the Lauers placed their laundry drying carousel.
Unlike the other beds this one was devoted to flowers. The whole bed was bursting with a
solid ground cover of white and purple alyssum. Because the alyssum is a low-growing
flower, it doesn't suffer from the laundry flapping in the wind as would taller plants.

The left edge of the garden, against the fence bordering another neighbor's property,
contained a garden bed stretching from the blueberries to the house. This bed caught our eye
because of its self-watering device. The Lauers had rigged a 4-inch-diameter perforated plastic pipe to run the length of the bed. At the house end this pipe was connected to their roof
gutter downspout, so with every rain this bed got a double soaking.

At the front of the garden, just outside the kitchen door, was their compost bed. This
consisted of a regular boxed garden bed, about $3\frac{1}{2}$ feet long by 5 feet across. In the center
they placed an oval ring of 2-foot-tall woven fencing, roughly $2\frac{1}{2}$ feet in diameter. All their
kitchen garbage was thrown into the center of the ring of fencing, where it was left to decompose. Never ones for a single solution, the Lauers planted tomatoes all the way around the
outer circumference of the fence. The tomatoes, supported by the fence, thrived on the additional nutrients provided by the compost in their midst. At the end of the growing season,
the fence was taken down and the compost distributed to the other beds. Their final tomato-
growing tip was leaving slightly unripe tomatoes on top of their air-conditioner condenser
unit. There the tomatoes ripened quickly with the benefit of the heat from both the air conditioner and the sun.

Since our visit, the Lauers have moved to the country, to a bigger house and garden. But
we shall always remember the ingenuity, beauty, and productivity of their 14-foot backyard.

UNDER-THE-SNOW
GARDENING

"In New England summer comes every year. Last year it came on a Wednesday." Wilfred
Smith tells this old joke to almost every tourist who stops to ask him for directions while
passing through his quaint old New England village. Wilfred, a retired carpenter, has a big
vegetable garden along the roadside and is most often seen tending the plants on sunny days.

But he's only half-joking when he alludes to the short growing seasons he has to con-
tend with. It's always a struggle to coax a few tomatoes out of his garden before the fall frosts,
and growing cantaloupe is something he despaired of years ago. But he has found a way to
feed his gardening habit during the colder months when his neighbors have given up and
gone back to buying produce at the corner market.

Willie grows plants under the snow in winter. Because there's snow on the ground
from mid-November through mid-April, he figures that gives him 5 months of homegrown

vegetables while the rest of the town is huddled round the wood stove. Not only does he eat fresh vegetables all winter, but there are almost no garden pests to worry about and no weeding to do.

His strategy is threefold. First, he plants a full complement of crops in early July, enough to keep him fed right through to spring. Next, he has built, bought, or grown a battery of what he calls his "antifreeze" devices: hay mulch, cold frames, cloches, and polyester row covers. Third, he keeps a snow shovel handy at all times.

The crops Willie grows for his winter garden are as follows:

Carrots, beets, spinach, onions, and leeks: These are planted in July and mulched under a foot-deep layer of hay just before the ground freezes. Willie's Jerusalem artichokes get the same mulch treatment. Recently he has tried using polyester row covers (Reemay is one trade name) instead of hay, and he finds it works well as long as snow comes early in the winter.

Cabbage: Cabbage is planted in early June and grown to maturity in the late summer; then the heads are cut off in September. New tiny heads begin to form from the stump, and Willie mulches the plants with hay just before the temperature hits the mid-twenties. He does the same with brussels sprouts, too. In late March he can go out to remove the hay, let the heads grow a bit, and have some tasty spring cabbage.

Lettuce, Chinese cabbage, spinach, and miscellaneous greens: These are grown in a cold frame along the south side of the house. Planted in August, they grow to good size before the cold weather slows them down. Through the winter months Willie covers the cold frame with double glazing. During the daytime he shovels off the snow to let in some sun. At night he places a 2-inch-thick sheet of Styrofoam on top of the glass (the foam also protects the glass against damage from heavy snow). The cold frame is located against the house foundation, right in front of a basement window, so he can open the window a crack to keep the frame warm on those subzero nights during January.

Kale: Kale is easy to grow in the garden, and Willie simply covers it with hay before the snow comes. On any winter day he can go out, uncover it, and remove some leaves for a meal.

Parsnips: Willie is a traditionalist with this crop. He grows parsnips all summer and forgets about them until spring. Then he feasts on the sweet roots for about a three-week period in April, after the ground has thawed enough to dig the 8-inch-plus roots.

One of his neighbors, a younger man with training in horticulture, keeps trying to get Willie to build a greenhouse so that he can grow tomatoes and other warmer-climate crops over a longer season. But the winter is a time to relax, says Willie. He prefers his under-the-snow method. "I'd hate to have to spend my time watering, weeding, and controlling bugs both winter and summer." He likes his winter garden just fine, even if it means having to supplement his own produce by purchasing some kinds of vegetables at the market. "And besides, who would take care of a greenhouse while I visit my grandchildren in Florida for two weeks?"

THE PARKING-SPACE GARDEN

Miles and Fifi Outerbridge thought they had it all when they moved into their spacious condominium in East Hampton, on Long Island, New York. "We have swimming, boating, tennis, an ocean view, and someone else takes care of all the grounds maintenance. We own our own home, but are spared most of the headaches of home ownership. We don't have to mow the lawn. We can do what we want on the weekend." The one thing the Outerbridges missed from their prior suburban houses was having a vegetable garden. "That's what we give up with this condo living; once we leave the unit, it's all common property. We just can't plow up a patch and put in a garden. But the one outdoor thing we do have exclusive right to is our parking spaces. So that is where we put the garden."

Two parking spaces are allotted to each condo unit. Miles, an investments consultant, works at home via computer. Fifi, who owns and operates her own fitness center, usually

Fig. 7-1 A parking space garden.

bicycles to work. So they need only one car and parking space. The other space became their garden. Unfortunately, the parking space was paved, but at least it was sunny and near a hose faucet. Since they didn't have the option of tearing up the pavement, they had to build a raised bed and import soil. Miles had a bottomless box made to contain the bed. The box is 4 feet wide by 15 feet long by 2 feet tall. It is constructed of 2-inch-thick cedar planks that resist rot (treated lumber is not a good idea because the chemical used in the treatment is bad for the plants). To keep the sides of the bed from bowing out due to the force of the earth, the carpenter used two-by-fours to tie the midsection of the bed together. He did this by nailing a vertical two-by-four on the outside center of each long side of the bed. Between the ends of these he nailed horizontal two-by-fours, effectively keeping the bed pulled together at top and bottom.

They placed the garden box in the middle of the parking space so that they could walk around all sides of it even when cars were parked in the adjoining spaces. They put some scraps of bathroom tile spaced 2 feet apart under the edges of the garden box to raise the box a quarter inch off the pavement, which allowed drainage of excess moisture. For additional drainage they laid a length of perforated drain tile on the pavement down the center of the box. They filled the bottom of the box with coarse gravel to a depth of 4 inches, which covered the drain tile (see figure 7-2).

Finding and moving enough soil to fill this garden bed was a big task. "I wasn't about to try to move it all in the Porsche," said Miles. Instead he hired a dump truck to bring 4 cubic yards of topsoil and dump it directly into the garden box, nearly filling it. "It wasn't the best topsoil I'd ever seen, but it wasn't terrible, either. We removed a fair number of rocks, but with a little sprucing up it has turned out fine." The sprucing up consisted of peat moss to add humus to the soil; bagged manure to add humus, nitrogen, phosphorus, and magne-

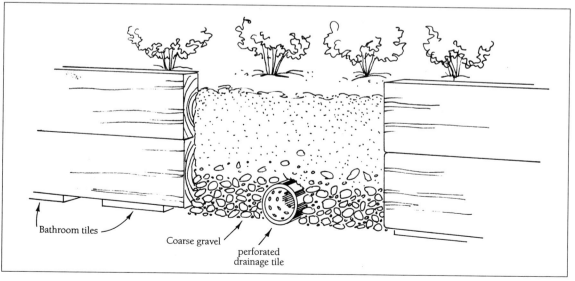

Bathroom tiles

Coarse gravel

perforated
drainage tile

Fig. 7-2 Detail showing components of a parking space garden.

sium; wood ashes, contributing potassium and calcium; and rock phosphate, providing phosphorus and magnesium. When the soil tested a little acid, some rock limestone was added, correcting the problem and contributing additional calcium and magnesium.

The Outerbridges planting plan was straightforward. Because they were trying to raise as great a variety of vegetables as possible, they were careful to select compact and bush varieties of vegetables. Many tall and trellised plants would have shaded their shorter neighbors too much. They supported their tomatoes and green peppers on wire rings that look like the framework for a large ice cream cone (available at many garden-supply stores). "We use the shade from those plants to our advantage midsummer when it gets pretty hot. Our salad greens like it a little cooler then and do well in the shade."

The garden bed was laid out with the short ends facing approximately east and west. "The gardening books usually recommend north/south, but whoever designed the parking lot failed to anticipate our needs." Starting from the east end, down the center of the bed they planted two tomatoes 18 inches apart, then two peppers 14 inches apart. The rest of the way down the center of the bed they planted a triple row of bush green beans planted 6 inches apart, followed by four rows of bush sugar-snap peas planted 4 inches apart.

On the south side of the tomatoes and peppers, they planted one plant each of summer squash, cucumber, and zucchini. They mulched under these and the peppers and tomatoes with black plastic. Once the plants got going, the Outerbridges trained the zucchini, cucumber, and summer squash to grow over the edge of the garden bed and then directed them toward the strip of grass and sidewalk that separates the east end of the bed from the condo building. "Occasionally when they get too far out of hand, the maintenance man mows down a squash or two with the grass," said Fifi. "But since we have started giving him a little of the garden surplus, he goes to great lengths to ignore condo law to our advantage. One August I even found him gently picking up all the vines, mowing under them, then arranging them again across the lawn."

The center section of the south side of the garden was devoted to salad greens—long-standing Bloomsdale spinach and many varieties of lettuce. "We specially like Red Salad Bowl and Buttercrunch."

The west third of the south side of the garden was devoted to strawberries, a double row of plants spaced a foot apart. The Outerbridges practice the cultural method of maintaining the mother plant for many years (four so far), cutting off all the stringers so that the plant's energy goes exclusively into creating berries. "This method works out very fruitfully for us. On a large scale it would be hard to keep up with trimming the runners," advised Miles.

Along the north side of the bed, they planted a double row of brassicas spaced 15 inches apart, two each of cauliflower, broccoli, and brussels sprouts. "This doesn't sound like much, but if you keep harvesting the side shoots, you get quite a few meals out of the broccoli. The brussels sprouts are wonderful to have in the fall."

Next to the brassicas they planted a small carrot patch. Next to that were the herbs: one plant each of basil, rosemary, sage, oregano, dill, and parsley. As mentioned already, the east end of this side is reserved for midsummer salad plants, which thrive in the cooler shade of the peppers and tomatoes.

The Outerbridges are firm believers in giving their soil extra feedings during the growing season. Every week they gave the plants a soaking of liquid seaweed or manure tea. The most difficult part of the process is finding a good source of manure. Fortunately Miles's cousin lives on a farm with sheep, so an occasional trip to the country means returning with a bagful of manure. To make manure tea they diluted about one part manure to five of water and left it to soak overnight in a plastic trash can. The abundance of their crops seems testimony to the effectiveness of their extra feedings.

The Outerbridges reseeded the salad crops as they harvested through the summer, and they planted a fall crop of peas after the first crop went by. Some years they squeeze in a late broccoli crop if the beans peter out before late summer. As Miles said, "We try to keep a flourishing garden all season. I'm sure ours isn't the best garden around, but it certainly is the best in our parking lot."

THE SALAD GARDEN

One of the most difficult things to find in a supermarket is good ingredients for a fresh salad. Sure, the produce department always has lots of iceberg lettuce, pink (and tough) tomatoes, waxed cucumbers, and somewhat soft green peppers. No doubt salads made of those supermarket vegetables are better than the ready-made variety found in so many fast-food places, but nothing can beat a fresh-picked, homegrown garden salad. Not only does it taste better, but the variety of garden produce you can grow makes it more attractive to look at as well.

Dorothy Greenlove certainly agrees. She's not a particularly enthusiastic gardener, but she can't live without fresh greens and salads on her table. In her small backyard (only 50 by 50) she'd rather grow flowers and grass, but she dedicated a 10-by-15-foot area to her salad obsession. It contained five 2-by-10-foot raised garden beds in which she grew greens, tomatoes, peppers, carrots, spinach, and a small variety of salad-dressing herbs.

One big advantage of growing your own lettuce, according to Dorothy, is the great variety of shapes, textures, and colors you can produce. She grows Grand Rapids leaf lettuce for its furled light-green leaves; Red Sails and Prizehead for their ruby-red color, Parris Island Cos for its dark-green foliage; and Green Ice for both its curly leaves and bright green hue. The best tasting lettuce, she believes, is Buttercrunch, a Boston type that grows best in early spring and fall.

Sometimes she can find these types of lettuce in the market, but the problem is that the more colorful and tasty leaf lettuces are highly perishable. Often the market lettuces look good but don't keep well in the refrigerator. Growing her own, Dorothy simply puts in about six varieties and then picks leaves off as she needs them. If she decides to cut an entire head, she can wash and cool it quickly, put it in a plastic bag and into the refrigerator. It will stay fresh and tasty for up to a week.

Of course, the real eye-catchers in a homemade salad are the tomatoes. Ask Dorothy which type she prefers and she'll tell you that there's nothing better than a cherry tomato. She's tried all kinds—including Tiny Tim and other patio types, which conserve space—but has returned to the old standbys: Sweet 100s and Gardeners Delight. "You just can't find a more productive and sweet-tasting tomato!" She puts in only one plant, in a cage, and it grows to be almost 6 feet tall and produces hundreds of delicious 1-inch-round fruits. (She covers it with a clear plastic "tent" in the fall and thus keeps it producing a month after the first killing frost.

What else goes into her garden?

- *Carrots,* for use as "baby carrots," for shredding as a garnish, and for slicing.

- *Sweet green peppers* (about four plants), which can be picked green or allowed to turn a bright red before harvesting. She also freezes them raw, for using in winter cooking.

- *Spinach,* a row of which is planted in early spring and another one in the fall, for harvest in the following spring.

- *Cucumbers,* so she won't have to eat the waxed ones from the store. She chooses either "bush varieties," which take up less space than climbing varieties, or trellises them on a wire fence.

- *Chinese cabbage* is a favorite in the fall and early spring. It grows quickly and has a light, semisweet taste. Dorothy cautioned against trying to grow it in the summer, as it either gets bitter or goes to seed before harvesting.

- *Broccoli* and *cauliflower* get a small space in the garden. Only a couple of broccoli plants produce prodigious amounts of small side shoots, which go straight into salads. Cauliflower, although it produces only one head, keeps well in the fridge.

- Miscellaneous crops like *radicchio* (red-hearted chicory), *endive, mustard greens, sorrel, borage,* and *mache* (corn salad) are regular inhabitants in Dorothy's garden, but get only a small space.

A true lover of homemade salad dressing, Dorothy grows most of her nonliquid ingredients. Garlic, onions, shallots, and chives were located wherever a tiny space was available. She also grew basil (sweet, globe, and purple) from seed and had a small perennial garden of tarragon, thyme, savory, and oregano. Dill, grown from seed, is one of her favorites.

Whereas most summer gardeners must be content to have salads from June to October, Dorothy was determined to extend the season from Easter to Thanksgiving. She did it by using a cold frame to force greens in the fall and by overwintering some crops under mulch. The cold frame was planted with greens in late summer, and the cover was put on in late October, as nighttime temperatures dropped below freezing. Shorter days kept the crops from growing much, but they kept just fine until the early part of December. The biggest problem was not cold, but remembering to open the frames on warmer days so that the lettuce and greens wouldn't "fry."

Some crops like lettuce, carrots, and spinach, started in September and grown almost to maturity, were mulched with leaves once the cold nights came. They did just fine until early spring, when Dorothy uncovered them. After a week or two of sun and warmer days, she began eating again.

When asked what her one most important "tip" for gardeners was, she had no trouble offering the thought that the best way to keep eating fresh salads is to keep planting them. Dorothy always has a flat or two of transplants growing on her windowsill. She takes a few minutes a week to start a new crop of lettuce or other greens. After the seedlings are a couple of inches tall (and thinned to one plant in a 1-inch cell) she puts the vigorous seedlings outdoors. "It helps me keep the pests, especially cutworms, from ruining my crops. The bigger plants can even survive a marauding cat or two."

THE SPAGHETTI-SAUCE GARDEN

Television commercials notwithstanding, there are lots of people who will tell you that there's no way store-bought spaghetti sauce can compete with homemade. To go one step further, there are those who simply drool at the thought of homemade Italian spaghetti sauce concocted from fresh garden produce.

Anthony and Peg Pepper are two such people. They absolutely love Italian tomato dishes like spaghetti, lasagna, eggplant parmigiana, and pizza. They also make all their own sauces from a section of their garden they call the "spaghetti corner."

Every herb and vegetable you could want to put into a rich tomato sauce was growing there. The space wasn't too large, but most of it was taken up by their twenty-five tomato plants. "Tomatoes are my specialty," said Tony, "and I grow a lot of them." He grew his own plants from seed so that he could select the best varieties. Even though he grew the standard beefsteak types for summer salads and dishes, his preferences for sauce making were the plum, or paste, types. "I like Bellstar, Heinz 2653, and Roma and also grow some heirloom varieties I get through the Seed Savers Exchange."

The advantage of plum tomatoes is that most are determinate varieties that take up less space and don't need staking. Also, with varieties like Heinz 2653, most of the tomatoes ripen around the same time, so you can make a big batch of sauce all at once.

Tony fertilized his garden well to get big yields. He used whatever animal manures (usually composted horse manure) he could get and swore that tomatoes grown in compost taste better than those grown with only chemical fertilizers. He also planted the seedlings in boxes, about 18 inches square. Tony put each plant into the box (which has no top or bottom) and as it grew, he filled in around the stem with more compost until the box was full. "This gives the plant some additional fertilizing, and it sends out new roots from the stem into the compost." When he grows regular eating-type tomatoes, each plant is staked so that it can grow as tall as it wants. "Some neighbors wonder whether I am growing some new variety of 'tree tomato' because my plants often get over 6 feet tall."

To cut down on the incidence of tomato diseases like early blight and septoria leaf spot (common maladies where tomatoes are grown year after year in the same spot), Tony always rotates his crops. The spaghetti-sauce garden is found in a different corner of the yard every year. If diseases get started, he'll spray regularly with "liquid copper" for a moderate degree of control. Liquid copper is a mild fungicide.

But tomato sauce is more than mashed tomatoes. Tony and Peg also grew celery, onions, garlic, green peppers, carrots, chives, basil, tarragon, and oregano as ingredients. About ten plants provided all the diced green peppers they needed, and a carrot bed only 4-by-4-feet gave them sufficient yields for sauce and eating. Celery, Peg noted, is easy to grow if you start it indoors in February, and about ten plants filled their needs.

Onions, garlic, and basil were grown as companions in one part of the garden and were harvested whenever they were mature. Basil was easily dried or frozen for later inclusion in sauce, and onions were simply allowed to cure in the sun a couple of days before braiding and hanging.

The only ingredients not produced in the spaghetti-sauce garden were the perennials; oregano, tarragon, and chives. They were grown in a small bed near the back door. The chives stayed in the garden year round, but the tarragon (French type) and oregano (Greek type) were potted up and brought into the house for the winter. Greek oregano is preferred because it is considerably more flavorful than the common variety.

Peg cautioned that Greek oregano (*Origanum onites*) was not the type commonly sold in seed catalogs (*Origanum heracleoticum*). Greek oregano is difficult to grow from seed, so she recommended looking for cuttings or seedlings. Its poor winter hardiness means that it will not survive the cold temperatures of more northerly climates.

Does having a spaghetti-sauce garden take the place of the regular garden? It could, if all you eat is pasta, but for the Peppers this small theme garden was done primarily for convenience. They could easily have grown all the tomato-sauce crops mixed into the larger garden, but it was more convenient to have all the fixings in one place.

Finally, should you want to reduce the starch in the regular pasta meal, the Peppers suggest that you try growing spaghetti squash. This winter squash produces a hard-shelled fruit with spaghettilike fibers inside. It doesn't taste like real pasta, but has a mild summer-squash taste. A good sauce can make it an interesting change from the ordinary, but as Tony said, "It will never surpass the real thing!"

THE FLOATING-DINGHY GARDEN

On Golden Pond (names changed) Lucinda Lovejoy has a floating garden. Lucinda isn't just one of those cocktail-party people looking for something unusual to talk about. She is also a gardener who, like the pre-Columbian gardeners who tended floating *chinampas* (see Appendix A, Looking Back), took her garden to the water to meet real gardening needs and limitations.

Golden Pond is typical of many northern lakes in that it is ringed with summer houses, each with its own sunny dock projecting into the cool, clear lake. The lakeshore would look like a clutter of houses were it not for the dense growth of cedar and birch trees between and enclosing each cottage. But with the trees and the combination of a lovely lake and vacationing residents, life around the lake in summer has a refreshing, relaxed air. The only problem is that with small, shady lots, there is no logical place to put a garden—or no logical place to most people. To Lucinda it was quite logical: "I put the garden out in the lake. There was plenty of sun and plenty of water; all I lacked was soil."

Lucinda's solution to that minor limitation was to take her husband's old fiberglass sailing dinghy and put soil in it. "Harvey never used that old dinghy. He said it had been patched up so many times it was like sailing a tugboat. Until I took it, he acted as though he would be glad to get rid of it." Lucinda put several inches of Styrofoam packing peanuts in the bottom of the dinghy to give the soil drainage. "Obviously I have to be careful not to overwater the plants. I can't put a drainage hole in the bottom or I would sink the boat." Her soil was a mixture of one-third peat moss, one-third vermiculite, and one-third garden soil mixed in with manure and compost. She mixed in a couple of bucketfuls of wood ashes and rock phosphate each year, with a supplement of new manure and compost. "I don't worry about soil tests and all that; as long as I keep the manure coming, everything grows fine." Lucinda filled the boat about half full with soil. "I'm no mariner, but I do try not to sink the boat. I'm happy to let the Japanese grow the seaweed." Lucinda did have to take extra precautions so as not to capsize the boat in foul weather. "If there is a storm coming, I take my dinghy garden and beach it."

The most festive thing about Lucinda's garden was the scarlet runner beans. She planted a large hill (about fifteen plants) of them in the bow and another hill of them in the stern. She had trellis ropes ("I found the beans didn't wrap themselves around string as well as rope") stretching from stern to the tip of the mast, to the bow, and all in between tied to the boom. By midsummer a scarlet/green sail was visible from a distance. Only on closer examination did the many beans sprouting out of the sail appear. Harvesting was not really a problem. Lucinda explained, "I just pull the boat into the dock, and from there I can reach nearly to the top of the mast. I have to stand on a chair to get the beans at the very top. That gets a bit hairy if it is a windy day and the boat is rocking, but we gardeners are used to taking risks."

Along the center of the garden, under the boom, Lucinda planted Big Boy tomatoes, sweet peppers, and cucumbers spaced 18 inches apart. The tomatoes and peppers were staked and then tied to the boom. Lucinda placed a 2-foot-wide strip of black plastic under these plants, finding they thrived on the extra heat. She trained the cucumbers to spread on the plastic under the tomatoes and peppers.

The planting scheme for the rest of the dinghy garden was more haphazard. "I'm not one of those efficient gardeners you write about; I throw around a lot of seed and see what comes up." What came up was a lively mixture of bush sugar-snap peas, a few carrots, broccoli, marigolds, chives, scallions, parsley, dill, basil, oregano, sage, spinach, and several kinds of lettuce. "I'd try growing zucchini and summer squash, but when they come on, all the land gardeners in the area are so eager to give them away that I figure why bother. Some day I'd like to have a whole boat of just strawberries and another of asparagus, but I'm not there yet." Lucinda may claim not to be an efficient gardener, but she continues to reseed as she harvests through the summer. "We get most of our summer vegetables from the dinghy. But Harvey eats only steak and potato chips, so he doesn't really count."

"Ultimately, even more than the food, what I love about this garden is the theater of it.

I love the scene of me, in my teeny jungle-scenes bikini, lying sunbathing on the dock with my torso half in the boat, weeding the garden. That gives the neighbors and passing boaties a sight. But I'm in my true glory when we have a dinner party. I'll have all the guests on the dock, having cocktails and enjoying the sunset over Golden Pond. I am wearing my evening clothes carrying a straw basket. I casually walk to the end of the dock. I pull in the dinghy from its mooring and pick a salad for dinner before their eyes. Me and my garden, we are a sight to remember."

THE ORNAMENTAL FRONT-YARD VEGETABLE GARDEN

The dilemma is quite common. You have a half-acre lot in the suburbs, two kids, and a couple of pets. The backyard is a nice place to have a garden but for the tall shade trees, most of which are on your neighbor's property. Besides that, the kids like to play kickball in the yard, and any garden you ever plant gets trampled almost immediately.

You would love to have a vegetable garden, if only to grow some tomatoes, lettuce, cucumbers, herbs, and a few other crops. but you know that if you replace your front-yard flower garden with vegetables, the neighbors will scowl at the scruffy appearance of those gangly tomatoes and overbearing cucumbers. You could always try to hide the vegetables behind a hedge or fence, but then you'd be suspected of growing something illegal.

Don't despair, because the Smartweeds (John, Joan and family) have an idea that could transform your ornamental garden into a culinary delight. It's called the ornamental vegetable garden and it will fool your neighbors into thinking you are just growing some new exotic landscaping plants.

The key to this method is in selecting plants that produce a bountiful harvest as well as having eye-appealing color, form, and flowers. You will also want plants that continue to grow over a long season so that you won't be faced with half-dead or half-harvested plants in mid-August.

The first step is to rule out the uninspiring plants you won't want in your front yard. Forget potatoes (they die back in midsummer), pumpkins (too invasive), regular tomatoes (too unkempt looking), and green beans (too short-lived).

Next, think about your plantings the same way you would think about perennials. Plan to place plants in groups. Groups should be about 6 to 10 square feet in size, but round or free-form in shape. Never use rows or square groups because that will immediately make observers suspect that you are planting a vegetable garden.

Choosing plants or varieties is easy if you keep three things in mind: form, color, and flowers. Here are some ideas the Smartweeds have for crops that you can grow and where to grow them:

Carrots: Plant them in a group as a border or foliage plant in beds with groups of flowers. If you surround them with bedding flowers, no one will suspect you plan to eat them. When they get about 2 inches high, thin them out to about 3 inches apart; then let them grow to full size. You can occasionally steal a few from the middle of the group and not diminish the lush, green, bushy appearance of the group.

Tomatoes: Use only the determinate bush types like Basket King, Pixie, Small Fry, etc. One of the best ways to do this is in baskets or barrels, as accent plantings along walks or by the house. You can also put single plants into the flower beds if you leave space or stones around them to facilitate picking the fruit.

Green peppers: These make a great "hedge" along a walk or path. Plant a double row of them (about 16 inches apart) and prune them to keep a nice shape. The flowers are white and not particularly pretty, but the green fruit will turn brilliant red or yellow upon ripening.

Cucumbers: The only way to grow cucumbers is on a trellis along the wall of the house. A south-facing wall is best. You can tell neighbors that it's a new variety of English ivy, and they won't steal your cukes.

Beans: Bush beans are a problem unless you plan to pull out the plants immediately after the bean crop is harvested. On the other hand you can grow some pole beans next to the house or on a lamppost. Try scarlet runner beans; no one will believe such a beautiful flower could produce something edible.

Corn: This is a dead giveaway as an edible crop. You can still get away with it, however, if you try using it the way some people use ornamental grasses. Grow it in a circular bed, about 6 feet in diameter. Thin the plants to about 10 inches apart and plant some other ornamentals around the perimeter. Lead the neighbors to believe that it's ornamental Indian corn, and they will forgive your sins.

Lettuce: You can get away with this only if you grow it as individual plants. The vegetable gardener's method of planting a row and then eating off the outside leaves is aesthetic heresy. Choose colorful varieties like Red Sails, or Ruby Red, and those with intensive textures like Oak Leaf and furled-leaf Grand Rapids. Let the plants grow to maturity (they look like little bushes) and then cut off the entire plant while no one is looking. Replace it with a flower plant, and no one will be the wiser.

Beets: It's tough to grow ordinary green-leaf beets without being caught. Red-leaf varieties (including Swiss chard, a close relative), however, can be very attractive accents in the flower garden. Beets are one type of plant you can harvest by the leaf—cut individual leaves off at the base—because new ones grow back quickly.

By now you certainly have the idea. Many common vegetables can easily be disguised as high-class ornamentals with a little creativity and the right varieties. And the Smartweeds also remind you to include some culinary herbs in your garden, as they are perfectly acceptable edible ornamentals, even in the "best neighborhoods."

THE BATHTUB GARDEN

There is a lot of junk in this world, and people have tried planting vegetables in much of it at one time or another. We have seen washing machines, refrigerators, stoves, cement mixers, tires, sandboxes, mailboxes, sinks, and toilets all used as vegetable planters. One person even had a two-tier toilet garden, with salad growing in the bowl and strawberries cascading over the rim of the water tank. Imagine a whole row of such succulent toilets lined up along the south-facing wall of an urban sidewalk. That would be the best garden on the block.

Some people can't resist the idea of a mobile garden, or even a once-mobile garden. A wagon or wheelbarrow filled with soil makes a fine small garden. In spring and fall you can wheel the garden outside into the sun during the day and put it into the garage at night to avoid frost. Many people use this idea when starting transplants for a bigger garden. Some, of course, aren't satisfied with a mere wagon. The whole back of a pickup truck can be filled with earth, planted with vegetables, and moved in and out of the garage like the wagon. After the springs break from the constant weight of the soil, however, the truck tends to remain either out in the drive or in the garage, growing mushrooms.

Once you abandon mobility, your old junker can still live on as a garden. Fill an old convertible to the windows with soil and plant the vegetables of your choice. The convertible top is a big plus, as you can quickly cover the garden in cold weather. If the original roofing material is no good, use the framework and cover the roof area with clear polyethylene for a cold frame. Once you get into midsummer, use the same roof framework as a trellis for tomatoes, peas, or beans. Let the melons out over the windshield to sprawl and bask in the heat of the front hood.

All the above only shows that you can be as innovative and/or junky with your container garden as you wish. One container garden that we particularly like is the Brooklyn, New York, rooftop garden of Simon Koch. When a neighboring apartment was renovated, he acquired the old cast-iron claw-footed bathtub that was torn out. He got a free planter, and the neighbor was relieved not to have to figure out how to get rid of the bathtub. Simon is a meticulous gardener, so he placed the bathtub on the roof several feet from the south side of the stairwell wall, where it would get wind protection without sacrificing sunlight.

As with any container garden, Simon was concerned with soil drainage. Plants left in a pool of water of an undrained pot will die. Fortunately, the bathtub already had a drain hole. Simon put a coarse screen over the drain hole and then placed 3 inches of gravel in the bottom of the tub. For soil Simon used a mixture of vermiculite (it was the easiest to carry up to the roof), soil scrounged from suburban friends' yards, and manure from a riding stable. He added a shovelful of rock phosphate and one of wood ashes. Simon borrowed a home soil test kit and found the soil to be slightly acid, so he added a few cups of ground limestone.

Simon's planting scheme was fairly simple. He grew tall plants at the faucet end of the tub and small plants at the back. He said, "In a bathtub this size I don't try to grow corn and potatoes, but I sure love the fresh vegetables all summer."

Summer started early for Simon. He starts seedlings on his windowsill and transplanted them to the bathtub as soon as things warmed up in March. He placed an old window

FIG 7-3 A bathtub garden.

across the rim of the tub as a cold frame. The soil filled the tub to within only 6 inches of the rim, so there was room for the seedlings.

Simon's early planting consisted of a double row of sugar-snap peas at the front of the tub. Once they were up and in need of support (after the windows were off the tub), he put a 4-foot stake in each side of the tub between the rows of peas. Between the stakes he strung 3-foot chicken wire to support the peas. "I don't get enough sugar snaps to make a regular meal, but I love coming up here and nibbling on those sweet little fellows."

From the sugar snaps to the middle of the tub, he planted lettuce and spinach plants spaced 6 inches apart. His spacing was too close together for the mature plants, but Simon didn't harvest the whole plant at once; he tore off individual leaves as needed.

In the middle of the tub, he planted one plant each of parsley, dill, and basil. These plants supplied him all summer. He kept them trimmed low enough to avoid shading the plants behind. He planted more spinach and lettuce in the back portion of the tub.

When all danger of frost was past, the tub took on its summer phase. The window was no longer used. Some of the salad plants in the front portion of the tub were replaced by warm-weather plants. In the middle of this front half of the tub, a green pepper plant was planted with a tomato a foot behind it. On either side of this portion, one cucumber and one zucchini plant were put in. The pepper and tomato plants were staked, whereas the cuke and zucchini plants were trained to droop over the rim of the tub and sprawl across the roof.

"Don't plant two zucchini," cautioned Koch, "the way they grow they would take over the whole roof and collapse the building."

By early summer the peas were done and pulled up with their chicken wire. Simon replaced the peas with a row of Blue Lake pole beans. He put two 10-foot poles in either side of the front of the tub and crossed them at the height of the showerhead (fortunately still attached to the tub). The crossed poles were tied to the showerhead to prevent their blowing over. The Blue Lake beans grew prolifically all summer up the two poles and shower pipe, though by later summer he was picking them from a stepladder.

Meanwhile, back in the tub, things progressed. As the tomato, pepper, cucumber, and zucchini plants got larger, the surrounding salad plants were pulled up. Simon then mulched the area with the *New York Times*. "I'd rather use hay, but one thing we have plenty of in New York is the *Times*. I could mulch my garden for several years with one Sunday paper." The salad plants at the front of the bath continued to flourish. Every two weeks Simon pulled out a whole row and replaced it with new transplants from his still-productive windowsill, so there was always a fresh crop of young, tender spinach and lettuce coming along. At the same time he gave a supplementary feeding of dilute fish emulsion to keep the nitrogen supply adequate.

With fall's frosts Simon lost the tender vegetables. He replaced them with more lettuce and cold-hardy spinach. By covering the tub with a blanket on cold nights, he kept the salads coming till late fall. "I suppose I could build a greenhouse around the tub and garden all year, but by Thanksgiving I am thankful to quit gardening until spring. I feel sorry for those farmers who feel chained to their land, but it would be a whole lot sillier to feel chained to my bathtub."

THE WINTER-STORAGE GARDEN

Why give up on having your homegrown vegetables just because winter has killed off the garden? Most gardeners are summer gardeners, who plant the entire garden in one or two days, then enjoy its produce only until the first frost of the fall. But even the weekend gardener can plant a second garden that will produce fresh food right through the winter.

That's what Samuel and Louise Dawkus did in their family garden. They set aside about half of their 50-by-100-foot garden for winter-storage crops. Samuel owns his own business, and Louise does the bookkeeping while tending three kids, so both of them prefer crops that are easy to keep. Although freezing and canning are the preferable way to put up beans, peas, apple sauce, and broccoli, the Dawkuses rarely have enough spare time to get enough processed to last the entire winter.

On the other hand they can easily put away an ample supply of root crops, squash, potatoes, cabbage, onions, beets, carrots, and leeks. They have a root cellar in the basement and can keep boxes of crops there as long as the temperature stays in the low 40s or upper 30s. Winter squashes are kept in a spare bedroom where the winter temperature stays in the 50s and where the air is dry.

The Dawkuses considered their storage garden a "second" garden because much of what grew in it was planted not in April or May, but in July. As their summer garden was just beginning to produce, they tilled under the buckwheat and clover in their "winter garden." Then, a week or so later (usually not later than July 15), they planted the garden.

The crop varieties they put in were all selected for their ability to keep well, either in the ground or in the root cellar. They included the following:

- *Carrots:* Scarlet Keeper, Nantes Fancy, and Chantenay types

- *Beets:* Long Season or Winter Keeper

- *Rutabaga:* Laurentian

- *Cabbage:* Amager Green, Lariat, Ball Head, etc. (started in flats around May 30)

These "second" garden crops were seeded in, watered well, and then covered with a layer of straw or hay. The straw protected the soil from the drying heat of midsummer, so the seeds could germinate in constant moisture. (Any drying would have resulted in significant reductions in germination rates.) After the appropriate time the Dawkuses checked every day to see if the sprouts had appeared, and as soon as they did, the straw was removed.

Part of the winter-keeper garden was planted at the same time as the summer garden. Potatoes (white long-season types), onions, winter squash, pumpkins, parsnips, field corn, and leeks were all included.

Their tips for each:

- *Potatoes:* Plant varieties known for good keeping quality. You can wait until June in most climates and still get a good crop. Later planting also helps avoid the first generation of Colorado potato beetles.

- *Onions:* Use seeds and start your own plants in early March. Onions grown from seed keep better than those grown from sets, and they will not go to seed during the growing season. Choose varieties known for good storage characteristics, not, for example, Spanish types.

- *Cabbage:* Start your seedlings in mid-May and transplant them into the garden in June or July. There are many good storage cabbages, and all benefit from getting regular watering. Harvest them just before the first heavy frost.

- *Parsnips:* Plant them at the same time as your summer garden, but be sure to keep the seedbed damp. No need to mulch them in the garden for the winter; they will keep just fine. Dig them up as soon as the ground thaws in the spring, for a sweet and nutritious meal.

- *Garlic:* Plant in the early fall for harvest the next summer.

- *Squash and pumpkins:* The best keepers are butternut, buttercup, and other hard-skinned varieties. Let them stay in the garden until the first frost, then "cure" them in the sun for a week or so, protecting them from freezing. You get better quality by allowing only three fruits per vine and then clipping off any new growth.

Samuel and Louise also grew kale, parsley, dry beans, and a collection of herbs for winter use. The kale was left in the garden all winter, mulched under hay. It could be picked at any time and provided an excellent source of vitamins. Parsley can be grown the same way, but Louise also dried about a quart of it for winter cooking. Dry beans are a major nuisance to harvest and shell, and if they didn't look so nice in jars on the pantry shelf, the Dawkuses would have given up growing them long ago.

Most of these crops are not particularly demanding of soil nutrients and do well without a lot of nitrogen fertilizer. The Dawkuses add rock phosphate, sul-po-mag, and lime every few years, and try to use clover cover crops to supply the nitrogen (see chapter 3).

What's the greatest advantage of having a winter-storage garden? Louise Dawkus said that it's having your own homegrown, organically grown food year round. The Dawkuses know they have a plentiful supply of healthful food, free of potentially harmful pesticides and chemicals.

THE FIVE-GALLON PLASTIC-CONTAINER GARDEN

Tom and Caitlin Fowler garden in plastic buckets. They also have a large intensive garden, but they use the bucket garden to supplement and extend the larger garden. "Here in northern Vermont we can only count on a three-month frost-free growing period. From the containers we get some fresh food all year long." The Fowlers grew plants outside in the containers during the summer and brought them inside for the rest of the year. Not only did this extend the harvest from the containers through the winter, but, equally important, as soon as frost danger is past, they have mature, bearing plants ready to transplant into the outdoor garden beds.

For containers the Fowlers used five-gallon pails. These are available free from sources as divergent as Dunkin' Donuts outlets (the jelly for their donuts comes in these pails) and builders (pails used to hold joint compound for Sheetrock). These containers are big enough in which to grow healthy plants; they are all the same size; and they have handles, so they are easy to move around. Tom drilled holes in the bottom of each bucket for drainage and placed a few inches of gravel in the bottom for the same reason. The buckets were then filled with rich soil from the garden beds.

Tom and Caitlin built a shelf in their house specifically for their bucket garden. The shelf, directly in front of a south-facing window, was 12 inches wide (diameter of bucket) and 13½ inches below the windowsill (height of the bucket). The 5-foot-long shelf held five containers. It had a copper tray under it to collect overflow from watering. A wood facing across the front of the shelf, with storage cabinets below, made it an attractive built-in feature of the room. A fluorescent plant-growth light was hung over the plants to supplement the dim light in winter.

The planting cycle for the bucket garden began when they planted the rest of their garden outdoors in late May or June. The buckets, filled with fresh soil, were moved outside,

FIG. 7-4 Gardening in five-gallon plastic containers.

where they remained all summer. Their usual container plants are a tomato, a green pepper, parsley, and nicotiana (flowering tobacco). These four are directly seeded in the bucket. The fifth pail usually holds lettuce, which doesn't need seeding until much later in the summer. "We are in no rush with these container plants to get them started early. We don't plan on eating from them until fall, when they have been moved inside and the outside garden is dead. The most important lesson we have learned is letting the plants get established in the containers. We have had poor results trying to transplant mature plants in the fall."

Summer care for the container plants is minimal. They are treated the same as garden plants except that they need additional watering because they tend to dry out faster. They get a side dressing of pony manure every month. "I don't specifically recommend pony manure," said Tom, "it's just that we have a pony." The tomato and pepper plants get staked when they need it, and the bees pollinate the flowers.

At the first threat of frost, the plants are moved inside. With the fresh bounty of the outside garden past, the Fowlers begin eating from the windowsill. "The parsley is the most prolific. it really does supply our needs all winter. The cherry tomato is great, but it doesn't supply that many salads all winter. Of course if I didn't pop a tomato in my mouth every time I walk by, we would get more meals out of the plant," admitted Tom. While nibbling, Tom also pollinates the tomato flowers by shaking the plant slightly. Tomatoes are self-fertile, so this is all the pollination they need. "The peppers are a treat through the fall, but by midwinter they start to look poorly. I cut the plant down to a new side shoot near the base. A nice, healthy, new plant grows out of this. It flowers, and I pollinate by passing a fine-haired paintbrush from flower to flower, and we are getting peppers again by the time I plant it outside again. The nicotianas are welcome for their bell-shaped white flowers and their strong pleasant odor, but the main reason we grow them is for pest control. We have long grown them in our unheated greenhouse because their sticky stalk, leaves, and flowers attract and then trap flying pests like aphids. We finally thought to grow them inside, too. They have done a marvelous job of controlling what had been a serious pest problem.

"The lettuce is mostly a token to spice up the salads made with carrots and the forced Belgian endive from the root cellar. Even with succession plantings a 12-inch-diameter pot isn't big enough to grow very much lettuce. Some years when we are particularly keen, we have grown flats of lettuce under a separate plant-growth light and have gotten a respectable crop. Fortunately under cold frames lettuce and spinach start early and last late in the outside garden." Tom usually harvests his last crop of bucket lettuce by March 1 and plants a second tomato from seed to have another big plant for planting out in the summer garden. During their time inside the plants get a feeding of pony-manure tea every month.

When the last frost is past, the container plants are removed from their containers. They have developed a tight root ball, so they come out as a whole. "Theoretically the tomatoes and peppers, being tropical plants, could keep going for years if brought in each fall. But we prefer to plant them out and start new plants again each summer. After being cooped up all winter in five-gallon buckets, those plants really take off when the roots are released to grow in the richness of a garden bed. It is wonderful, especially with the tomatoes and peppers, to have bearing plants growing outside at the same time that other local gardeners are just planting out 6-inch-tall transplants."

THE MINIMARKET GARDEN

Can you grow enough food in a half-acre to both feed a family of four *and* make a summer income? If you ask any commercial vegetable grower, he or she would say, "No way." If you ask Paul and Deb Doscher, however, the answer would be "Sure, if you do it right!"

Paul and Deb Doscher have a 35-acre part-time farm in New England and devote about one acre to food and flower production. Half of that is an orchard of peaches, apples, pears, and blueberries, and the rest is almost one hundred raised intensive beds used primarily for market crops. They grow practically everything one can imagine—more than 140 varieties of vegetables and herbs and ninety varieties of flowering plants.

Paul is a college professor, and the garden is a summer job for him. He spends most of his time in the vegetables, whereas Deb, a mother of two, concentrates on a crop of everlasting flowers. Deb uses these to make a wide variety of flower arrangements and wreaths, which sell well during the off-season.

They began their business about four years ago on what was once a hayfield. Determined to start tiny, get a bit larger, stay small, they initially began with only about one-fifth of an acre. After one year the garden grew to about a third of an acre and finally reached its present size of one acre after three years. "That's where it's going to stay," said Deb. "If Paul tries to make it any larger, I'll throw him out of the house!"

The half-acre is enough to keep them busy, but not too busy. "If we were to use conventional growing methods, we would be constantly busy fighting weeds. We would also have to use almost three times as much land to grow what we do." They have been able to grow more than $4,000 worth of crops a year from their space and hope to increase it to $5,000 as soil conditions improve.

The most profitable crops they grow are tomatoes, melons, lettuce, and flowers. Other crops like beans and peas are marginally profitable unless they sell them to people who pick their own. Some vegetables, such as potatoes and onions, really aren't money makers, but the Doschers grow them because so many customers want them. "You have to supply as many of your customers' needs as possible to keep them coming back," noted Paul.

Virtually all their crops are sold retail, at either a local farmers' market or through a scheme called "produce by subscription." The subscription system involves customers placing orders in the spring, before the seeds are ordered from catalogs. Then the Doschers know almost exactly what to buy and plant for the growing season.

Subscription customers then come to the farm to pick up their crops or get them delivered to a central location in a nearby city. "We like this system because it means we have less waste and guaranteed customers," noted Deb. "It does away with some of the worry about whether you can sell everything you produce."

The garden itself is well maintained and beautiful. "Lots of people have commented on how picturesque our garden is, so we try to keep it tended for our visitors. We seem to spend almost as much time giving garden tours as selling vegetables . . . maybe we should give the veggies away and charge for the tours."

Among the reasons the Doschers cite for their success are these:

• *Good soil management:* They use lots of compost (every scrap of plant waste is composted), green manures, cover crops, and they rigidly adhere to crop-rotation principles. "We also use some commercial organic fertilizers, but have been reducing our dependence on them through the use of green manures," said Paul.

• *Selection of well-adapted varieties:* "We try to use only crops adapted to our northern climate, and we constantly consult with other gardeners and growers to find out what's best."

• *Use of season-extending devices:* Black plastic mulch, clear plastic row covers, polyester row covers, cloches, and cold frames play an important part in the operation. Paul explained: "What you want to do is have tomatoes to sell a month before the home gardeners have them. That's when you get the best price. Once the home gardens begin to produce, you have to cut your price significantly. Most market gardeners make their profits in the early crops and then again with late crops. Midsummer sales are high in volume but low in profits."

• *Intensive planting:* The garden is entirely done in raised beds where crops grow close enough to completely shade the soil. This reduces water requirements and makes it tough for weeds to compete. The permanent paths between beds are mulched with hay to conserve moisture and control weeds. "After about mid-July, we have the entire garden mulched, and our weeding chores are minimal," Paul said. Another advantage is high production. Paul figures that the intensive garden yields about three times as much per square foot as conventional row planting.

• *Irrigation:* The Doschers' principal irrigation method is a drip-tube system. "We have a shallow well, and before we installed the drip system, we used to pump the well dry. Now we use much less water and put it exactly where the plants need it." Using a drip system also reduces the incidence of various moisture-dependent plant diseases because the foliage stays dry during watering.

• *Critter control:* Marauding woodchucks, cats, dogs, and raccoons can make a real mess of a garden, to say nothing of eating up the profits. The Doschers had no hope of being able to put a permanent wood or metal fence around the garden, as it would have cost more than they could afford. So they bought an electric fence charger like the ones used to keep cows in a pasture. The charger is hooked up to two strands of wire (one 6 inches above the ground, the other about 16 to 18 inches high) that run around the entire garden. In four years not one raccoon has stolen even one ear of corn! Only an occasional woodchuck has ever entered the garden. Neighborhood dogs who stake out their territories by urinating on the fence almost never return to try again.

Is this garden something that can be copied by other part-time farmers? "As long as you don't expect to make your entire living from the garden, it's a great source of income," said Paul. In fact the closer one is to a major city or place where customers are in ample supply, the easier it is to start a retail market garden."Focus on quality and customer satisfaction," said Deb, "and you will develop a loyal following of friendly customers."

THE MONEY-SAVER GARDEN

Billy Taylor, financier and yachtsman, is not the kind of man you expect to find getting his hands dirty in the garden. But garden he does. "I only go in for the expensive stuff," confided Billy. "Beans, corn, potatoes, they're all cheap. Why waste my time? But basil, asparagus, berries, and peppers, they're expensive. I figured I'd save a little and grow my own."

Billy's garden consisted of four 4-by-12-foot raised beds and a 26-foot-long row of raspberries running the length of one side of the garden. He grew one bed each of asparagus and strawberries. The other beds contained loofah sponge plants, tomatoes, green peppers, basil, Belgian endive, sugar-snap peas, yellow squash, zucchini, cucumbers, and lettuce.

The raspberries were supported by three 6-inch-diameter cedar posts spaced 13 feet apart. At the 3-foot height he had stretched a wire around both sides of the posts, making parallel wires 6 inches apart. The raspberries were trained to grow between these wires for support and ease of picking. When he established the row, Billy dug a trench a foot deep and a foot wide the length of the row. He mixed in a lot of manure and some wood ash and rock phosphate; then he refilled the trench to its new, slightly raised form. After planting the raspberry plants, he mulched the whole row heavily with leaves. Each spring he rakes back the leaves enough to add new manure, then replaces the leaves. In the fall he cuts out all the canes that bore fruit the previous summer, which leaves only new canes that will bear next year. He thins the new canes, leaving only the sturdiest ones, spaced about one every 6 inches. Billy cuts off the taller canes at the four-foot height to prevent winter breakage. He adds new leaf mulch each fall. "The only other thing I have to do for the raspberries is pick them, and I don't mind that at all. I especially love going out first thing in the morning and picking a cup of raspberries for breakfast."

Billy devoted a whole permanent bed to asparagus. "You can't have too much asparagus!" He started his asparagus bed from seed. "Some people say you get asparagus faster if you start the bed from roots. But if I'd had to trench the whole bed and follow all the other advice, I might never have gotten to planting asparagus at all. All I did was hoe two 9-inch-deep ditches the length of the bed. I sprinkled a pack of seed in the ditches and left the seedlings to grow in the open ditches that first summer. That fall I filled in the ditches so that the roots would be protected by the earth above. I didn't harvest any asparagus the second summer. That was all the self-control I could muster. The third summer I started harvesting. I know some people say you are supposed to wait longer before harvesting to let the plants get more established. But I'm of the eat-it-now-school. If I'm going to weed it, I'm going to eat it. My rule of thumb on asparagus is I pick till the strawberries are ripe; then I leave the asparagus to grow in peace until next spring."

Billy reserved a second bed for strawberries. He used a permanent hill method with a black plastic much. After tilling and feeding the soil as he would for the vegetables, Billy spread black plastic the length of the bed and made a triple row of holes in the plastic spaced 16 inches apart. "I use a soup can with the rim cut off for cutting the holes in the plastic." He planted a strawberry plant in each hole, making a slight depression in the soil around each plant. (The depression causes the rain shed by the plastic to run toward the plant, where it is needed.) He cut all the runners off the plants as they developed so that all the plant's energy went toward developing the fruit. Billy has been harvesting berries from these plants for six years and they are still going strong. To avoid the difficulty of applying fertilizer under the plastic, he relied mostly on bone and fish meal at the time of initial planting.

The other two beds were for annuals. Both had trellises running down the length of their centers. The first trellis supported loofah sponge vines for half its length. "I don't eat the sponge," assured Billy, "but I like them, and they make good presents. They cost up to $10 apiece at the store; sometimes I get fifteen on one vine. So especially if I cut them up, I get a lot of sponge for my trouble." Billy keeps the loofah tied up on the trellis because sponges that grow hanging tend to be longer and bigger than ones left on the ground. "After I pick them I let them dry in the attic for a couple of months. Then I whack them to knock the seeds out. There are usually a few troublemakers that I have to get out with tweezers. I cut off the stems, and the sponges are ready to go."

The trellis at the other end of this bed supported tomato plants on one side and green peppers on the other. The space on one side of the loofah grew basil. "I don't actually eat all that much basil, but pesto has been such a fad that when the hoity-toits hear I have a garden, they always ask if I have basil. I reverently give them some and come off looking like Mr. Goodguy."

On the other side of the loofah was a double row of Belgian endive. "They are as easy to grow as lettuce. I would make a fortune on endive if I didn't eat it all myself. I have to keep the plants spaced at least 6 inches apart or they don't develop good roots," Billy explained. He harvested them in the fall. The green tops that grew in the summer were discarded, and only the parsniplike roots were saved. The roots were planted in soil, about six to a bucket, topside up, as they grew in the garden. They should be covered with $1/2$ to 1 inch of soil. "I leave them in a dark, cool corner of my basement, where they do well. I start off by watering just one bucket so that it comes on ahead of the others. This way I can stagger my crop. They don't require much water. The whitish-green endive sprouts from the roots. I usually get a nice, tight little head from each root. After I've cut that off, more leaves usually sprout from the same root; I pick them, too. That's all there is to it. Belgian endive is a real treat in my salads all winter."

Billy's second bed of annual vegetables had a row of trellised sugar-snap peas down its center. At one end, on either side of the trellis, he grew one hill each of yellow summer squash and zucchini. He let these sprawl across the adjacent lawn once they took off in midsummer. "Zucchini and squash aren't really big money crops. But they give so much for so little effort they make sense to me, and they taste great with pesto." Billy planted cucumbers on plastic mulch for the remaining length of one side of the trellis. In the space remaining on the other side of the trellis, Billy planted a variety of lettuces. When we expressed surprise that he grew lettuce, which is usually inexpensive to buy, he relented. "Maybe I'm not as hard-nosed as I like to sound. The iceberg lettuce they sell at the store tastes like watered-down cardboard compared to the lovely lettuces I grow. I guess, despite myself, I've gone in for quality as well as economy."

Looking Back

The types of gardens people make are determined by the value and availability of land and water, the tools and people available to do the work, and the climate. Other factors that shape gardens can be aesthetic, including current fashion and personal taste. In the past intensive-type gardens, because they are so efficient, have been made in situations where land or water was dear and where human labor using hand tools was the main means of cultivation. These examples from former times can give us many practical ideas to use in our present-day gardens (see figure A–1). Where climates or seasons dictated special care for plants to flourish or survive, intensive methods were easily broadened to include protective elements. In fact the care and attention given to plants in an effort to modify their climate were, and still are, generally practical only on an intensive level to make the greatest use of the effort required. For this reason much of this book is about the practice of forcing, or season extending, which is an integral part of the most intensive gardening schemes, and enjoys much popularity today.

Oriental cultures have a very old tradition of intensive gardening, developed in response to the need for their land to support a very high density of population. The general pattern in China was to grow culinary vegetables intensively and cultivate cereal crops extensively in the field. A sixth-century agricultural encyclopedia, the *Ch'i Min Yao Shu,* gives directions for protecting plants, including shading them in summer, wintering them under mulch in pits, and warding off frost in garden and orchard with smoldering fires.

In other situations, when land is extremely precious, gardens have been made on water. *Chinampas* are an example of floating gardens that evolved in pre-Columbian Mexico.

Chinampas originated because of land famine. When the Aztecs first came from the north into the Valley of Mexico, they were made slaves by their more powerful and civilized neighbors. Even later, when free, they were at first poor and weak and were confined to the

FIG A-1 These raised beds near Nuwara Eliya in Sri Lanka are part of a longstanding tradition of intensive agriculture. In this overpopulated land where food crops compete for space with the cash tea crop, small family market gardens such as this one combine raised beds with irrigation and terracing to capitalize on land and water.

marshy lakeshore that nobody else wanted. So they built their homes on piles out into the lake, because what dry land they did have was too valuable for the raising of crops to be used for building; hence their cities in the water, and their great causeways. But they also *made* land: They built rafts of reeds and rushes lashed together with tough roots, and onto them they piled soil dredged up from the shallow bottom of their lake, which, consisting largely of decayed vegetation, was very fertile. Raft was joined to raft, and artificial, floating islands were formed as much as 200 feet long, and for the most part about 4 feet deep. The larger and older *chinampas* had small trees planted on them, as well as plots of flowers and vegetables for market, and even a hut for the gardener to live in. By using a long pole, the gardener could punt his floating garden from shade to sun or sun to shade, or nearer to his market. At times it seems that scores of these floating gardens could be seen gliding about the surface of the lake.[1]

Floating gardens also exist on Dal Lake in Indian Kashmir. These are intensively cultivated patches of former swamp existing amid the houseboat culture on the beautiful mountain lakes.

[1] Edward Hyams. *A History of Gardens and Gardening* (New York: Praeger Publishers, 1971), p. 124.

EARLY EUROPEAN
KITCHEN GARDENS

Classical western tradition was similar to that of the Chinese in including distinct cultures for field crops and garden vegetables. The essential elements of intensive gardening, even as they endure today, are spelled out in this description of a Roman kitchen garden:

> The productivity of these garden plots when under irrigation is astonishing: catch cropping and succession cropping are essential features, and with a sufficient supply of manure, every square yard of the garden is under cultivation; the seasons become virtually undistinguishable, and the return per man-hour of effort is extremely high.[2]

The novelty of out-of-season fruits and vegetables was produced in Roman times with the heat of fermenting manure and the use of sheets of transparent minerals such as talc and mica (sheet glass was not known until the third century A.D.). Plants were sometimes grown in a basket of dung with a mineral slab for a cover. Pits were also used, warmed with manure or a masonry furnace, and likewise covered by a thick plate of talc or mica. This evolved into a primitive forcing house called a *specularium,* in which heat was supplied by small fires around the walls, by heat ducts built into the walls, or by hot water.

Grapes, peaches, roses, and lilies were all forced in these structures. Once, when Emperor Tiberius was ill, his doctor prescribed that he eat cucumbers every day. These were grown throughout the winter in his *specularium.* Columella's *De Re Rustica,* a classic Roman agricultural text, gave directions for less sophisticated forcing techniques, including ancient equivalents of pits, cold frames, and hot beds.

Although the style of the Roman kitchen garden provided the basis for vegetable gardening in medieval Europe, its refinements faded except in the monasteries, which became the guardians of horticultural traditions.

In Germany, Albertus Magnus, a Dominican philosopher and theologian, practiced the arts of forcing that the Romans had developed. Albertus was known as one of the greatest scholars of his time, as well as a fine horticulturist. One story describes how he received William II of Holland at his monastery in 1249. It was the sixth of January, and in spite of the season, Albertus was able to show King William flowering plants and fruit trees bearing ripe fruit he had forced in the cloister garden. This was so astounding that people suspiciously called it witchcraft.

Medieval gardens were often laid out in beds with paths between them (see figure A–2). Culinary and "physic" (medicinal) herbs, fruits, and vegetables grew together in these gardens. Vegetables received less attention in this period than they had in Roman times, as meat had slowly become a more important element in the diet. Many plants, however, were cultivated for medicines and dyes.

---

[2] K. D. White. *Roman Farming* (London: Thames & Hudson, 1971), p. 49. Copyright K. D. White 1970.

FIG. A-2 A garden of raised beds, 1470.

Garden beds were raised for both practical and decorative reasons (see figure A–3). Some writers advised their use to improve soil drainage for plants particularly sensitive to wet ground. Garden benches were made by seeding a raised bed of the proper height with grass, often interspersed with small wildflowers (see figure A–4). The sides of these beds were made of brick, boards, or wooden lattice. Medieval illustrations show square and rectangular raised beds in pleasure gardens.

Kitchen gardens were usually surrounded by a wall, an important part of the garden. Actually, our word *garden* stems from the Middle English and German words for enclosure— a wall was at one time implicit in the meaning of the word. Often fruit trees and vines were trained along a kitchen garden wall, and vegetable beds were bordered or mixed with flowers and herbs. This is still a European tradition, charmingly described in Frances Hodgson Burnett's novel for children *The Secret Garden*.

One castle garden in Germany had 12-foot-high stone walls surrounding and partitioning it. The walls,

FIG. A-3 Raised beds in a garden, 1542.

FIG. A-4 A garden bench and flowers grown in a raised bed, 1460.

like nearly all garden walls in Germany during the 1800s, were covered with wooden trellises, on which peach, apricot, and apple trees were trained. This particular garden wall, however, had rafters projecting outward 2 feet just under the coping. The rafters supported rolls of straw matting, which could be unfurled over the trees to protect the blossoms from spring frosts.

Garden walls provided not only shelter from wind and storm and support for trees and vines, but also gave a south-facing border, which has always been an important part of the garden. Antique gardening manuals advise that early vegetables and salads be planted out in this

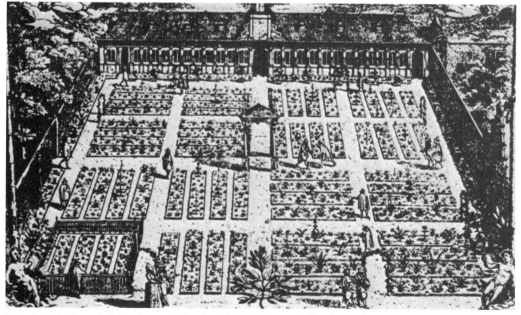

FIG. A-5 The Botanical Garden at Leiden, by J.C. Woudamus (Holland, 1610)

sheltered, sunny spot. Not only was the wall itself among the most elementary forms of plant protection, but it also offered support for more sophisticated means, such as the mats described above and glazed sash. In some instances walls were heated by means of flues conducted through the masonry, which, when coupled with the use of glass against the wall, made an effective forcing house. Whether or not the gardeners were aware of it, an added advantage of these masonry walls was their thermal mass, or their ability to absorb and store heat from the sun, radiating this heat back out as the surrounding air cooled, thus helping to moderate temperatures.

KINGS' FEASTS AND ROYAL GARDENERS

Gardens were made not only for private use, but also to produce vegetables for sale. Much labor, glass, and manure were spent in intensively cultivated gardens to provide the courts of Europe with fresh vegetables and fruits out of season. These were often shipped surprising distances.

Before 1500 many common vegetables were exported to England from Holland, supposedly because the English did not properly understand how to grow them (see figure A–5). In his *History of England,* David Hume wrote, "It was not till the end of the reign of Henry VIII [mid-1500s] that any salads, carrots, turnips, or other edible roots were produced in England. The little of these vegetables that was used was formerly imported from Holland or Flanders. Queen Catherine, when she wanted a salad, was obliged to dispatch a messenger thither on purpose.[3] In speaking of the 1600s, Alicia Amherst explains that "there had for long been a fair supply of vegetables in England; but when anything early, or out of season, was wanted on great festive occasions, it was procured from abroad, chiefly from Holland."[4] The Dutch must have had considerable skill as growers to acquire this reputation, and they had a distinct forcing system, using pits (presumably with sash lights) and low houses by the early 1700s.

At this point in history, forced vegetables, always produced in intensive gardens, were an extravagant luxury. Holland supplied early fruits and vegetables to all the courts of Europe.

In time court gardeners in all the countries of northern Europe produced vegetables out of season, though the extent to which they did so was limited by the wealth of the country, as the effort required to grow these specialties required that they fetch a high price. Loudon, in chronicling the horticulture of Denmark in the early 1800s, gives the Danes much credit for their forced produce, especially considering the climate. In Sweden, on the other hand, although the gardeners were considered successful, he describes the season as short: "and there is not yet sufficient wealth to admit of much forcing, or of forming artificial climates to any extent."[5]

[3] David Hume. "The History of England," as quoted in Loudon's *Encyclopedia,* pp. 283–84.
[4] Alicia Amherst. *A History of Gardening in England* (London: 1896), p. 259
[5] J.C. Loudon. *An Encyclopedia of Gardening* (London: Longmans Green and Company, 1865), pp. 177 and 189.

SIMPLE FORCING METHODS

Many simple ways to protect plants were used and recommended in the books of this time. Straw mattresses were supported over growing beds in the same way that autumn finds sheets, blankets, and plastic draped over gardens in our own time. To supply early blooms as well as edibles, plants were brought indoors in anything from a pot to a large box on wheels, which could be rolled in and out. Manure was used in hotbeds and around plant protectors to give added insulation as well as radiant warmth. Cloth and paper were used to ward off frost in the same capacity that more expensive glass was used.

In the seventeenth century a number of tender plants were coming to England from the New World. One of these was tobacco, which was started in a hotbed, then transferred to a south-facing border sheltered from the weather. A variation on the stove-heated masonry wall was a wall made of boards, the heat supplied by a hotbed of dung piled up against the back. Fruits were trained on this wooden screen, the front of which was covered with glass. This technique was apparently in common use long before more sophisticated glass forcing and hothouses appeared in England.

About the same period, glass bell jars began to be used for covering one or more plants, giving them a warmer environment. Bell jars have been recorded in horticultural use in France since 1623. The term used for them there was *cloche,* which literally means "bell" (see figure A–6). These same glass bells have a long history of use in the laboratory, where they were used to contain a gas or vacuum, or to display a specimen. "Whether it was chance or some experiment that first brought the cloche from the alchemist's bench into the garden is a matter for conjecture. The fact remains that the bell glass became very popular in France at an early date

FIG. A-6 A bell jar cloche.

and ultimately formed the basis for a great industry[6]. Alchemy required the use of many plants and plant extracts, and it is entirely possible that a gardening alchemist first inverted the hollow glass over growing plants, creating a minigreenhouse.

The use of these jars is mentioned in English books by John Parkinson, a London apothecary, in 1629. His book, *Paradisi in Sole Paradisus Terrestris,* describes using them over growing melon plants. He also suggests growing the melons on a slightly sloping hotbed, protecting them with straw when necessary.

[6] Louis N. Flawn. *Gardening with Cloches* (London: John Gifford Ltd., 1957), p. 14.

KITCHEN GARDENS
IN PURITAN NEW ENGLAND

New England's gardens in the seventeenth century were basically an English import, like its people. For reference they had, at least initially, the same books relied upon in Europe. Their gardens were separate from orchard and fields, and each household was largely self-sufficient. By necessity the garden was expected to support a large number of plants for food, medicine, and dyes, creating a very diverse garden. Everything the Puritans planted was useful, in keeping with their belief that God had made the earth and everything on it for man's use. These gardens were usually made of raised beds to ensure proper drainage and because the limited area of the beds made it feasible to control and improve the soil quality.

Early New England gardens were enclosed with a wall or fence, an essential protection from wandering domestic and wild animals. It was also part of the European tradition of the gardener. Along the inside of the wall, a wide, raised border surrounded the garden. The other beds varied from simple oblong shapes to intricate geometrical patterns, depending on the affluence and artistry of the gardener. They were narrow enough so that the gardener would never need to step in them while tending the plants. Paths were quite wide to prevent plants along the edges from being damaged and so that people could walk and talk together in the garden (see figure A–7).

Fig. A-7 A garden of sixteenth-century England with raised beds and wide paths.

The beds were filled with a mixture of manure (or fish, which Native Americans had taught them to use) and good earth. They were edged with boards, stones, or even sheep shank bones, and the good soil from the surface of the paths was scraped off and put in the beds. The paths were covered with gravel or something else that would drain well. Placing the garden on a slight slope was advised for severe drainage problems.

Perennial plants were grouped together, as were the annuals, which needed to be resown each year. Intercropping was used to save space and trouble. In *Paradisi* Parkinson suggests edging beds of squash or melons with cabbages and mixing onion, radish, and lettuce seeds to broadcast in a bed where they would all come up together, even though they would mature at different times.

THE DEVELOPMENT OF FORCING AND MARKET GARDENING IN EUROPE

In France at this time, an expert grower named Jean de La Quintinye was the director of the king's fruit and kitchen garden for Louis XIV at Versailles. His book, *Traité des Jardins Fruitiers et Potagers,* published in Amsterdam in 1690, was said to be the best work on growing fruit and vegetables in his generation. It was translated into English in 1693 by John Evelyn, a famous English horticultural writer, under the title *The Compleat Gard'ner.* Through La Quintinye's skill the king enjoyed asparagus in December, lettuce, radishes, and mushrooms in January, cauliflower in March, strawberries in April, peas in May, and melons and figs in June. For these miracles he received a yearly bonus equal to twice his annual salary!

In the 1700s the English diet was gradually changing to include more vegetables, and market gardeners around London were not only growing a greater variety of them but also were beginning to stretch their season, learning to force produce for sale. Philip Miller, a distinguished English horticulturist, noted these developments in the preface to the 1765 edition of his *Gardener's Kalendar:*

> The improvements which have been made in the art of Gardening, within fifty years past, are very great; so that we may without presumption affirm, that every part of this art is in great perfection at this time in England, as in any part of Europe. Our markets being better supplied with all sorts of esculent plants, through the whole year, than those of any other country; and these in their several seasons are afforded at so cheap rates, that they are become a great part of the food of the poor: to which we may in part attribute the abatement of those violent scorbutick disorders, which formerly raged so much in this country.[7]

---

[7] Philip Miller. *The Gardener's Kalendar* (London: 1765), p. vi.

In 1748 when the Swedish horticulturist, Peter Kalm, traveled through England on his way to North America, he noticed that intensive market gardening had become quite impressive. The growing beds were raised and sloped slightly to the south.

> . . . most of them were at this time [February] covered with glass frames, which could be taken off at will. Russian matting over these, and straw over that four inches thick. These contained cauliflowers some four inches high. In the rest of the field were "bell-glasses," under which also cauliflower plants were set 3 or 4 under each bell-glass. Besides the afore-named beds, there were here long asparagus beds. Their height above the ground was two feet; on the top they were similarly covered with glass, matting, and straw, which had just been all taken off at midday. The asparagus under these was one inch high and considerably thick.[8]

The elements of intensive forcing culture—hotbeds, glass lights, bell jars, and hand glasses, and the straw mats and mulches used for insulation—were similar in other intensive gardens in Europe, though Dutch light gardening and French gardening were distinct in their particulars. In Holland growing in forcing pits and frames with glass lights had for long been quite successful, and into the 1800s the skill of the gardeners was such that melons, grapes, and pineapples were sent to the London and Paris markets and sold for prices lower than the English growers could compete with.

THE SPECIALIZATION OF INTENSIVE MARKET GARDENING IN FRANCE

In France an intensive market gardening system had also been developing, with gardens springing up in the environs of Paris, close to both the markets and the source of manure on which the system so depended.

The French were said to excel in the production of winter lettuce on hotbeds covered with glass. This lettuce was in great demand in the Paris market. Loudon points out that vegetables played a more important role in the French cuisine than in the English and that enormous quantities were purchased by institutions such as hospitals as well as by the general public. He reported that the vegetables were extremely fine and large due to the quantity of manure used and the benefit of daily waterings. By the middle of the nineteenth century, it was estimated that there were over 1,000 *maraîchers* in the Paris area, their gardens averaging one and one-third acres each. These Paris gardeners had the benefit of fine seedsmen, and

---

[8] "Kalm's Visit to England," translated by Joseph Lucas (London: 1892), as quoted in Amherst's A *History of Gardening in England* (London 1896), p. 260.

varieties of vegetables were developed specifically for their requirements, their main requirement being that the varieties tolerate being forced.

Maximum efficiency was achieved by well-planned intensive cropping procedures (see
figure A–8), improvements in materials, and the use of modular appliances for which stan-
dardized designs had evolved through time. The lights, panels consisting usually of sixteen
glass panes and similar to window sashes (see figure A-9), were relatively small, which made
them fairly easy to handle. Also,
the narrow width of the area
under glass made it possible for
the plants to get the moisture they
needed by capillary attraction
from the pathways when the
weather was too severe to remove
the lights for watering. Wooden
frames were used to hold the
lights high enough off the ground
for vegetables to grow under the
glass. The frames were shorter
along one side so that the lights
would slope gently toward the
south. This gave a good exposure
to the sun as well as a little shelter
from the north and made the surface of the glass drain properly.

FIG. A-8 *Carrots and cauliflowers growing under lights in a
French garden in the early twentieth century.*

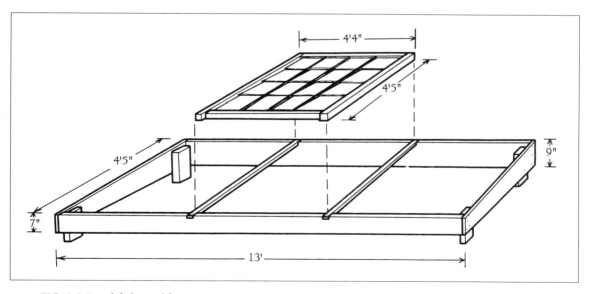

FIG. A-9 *French lights and frames.*

The frames carried three lights each and were placed end to end in rows running as close to east/west as possible. This is still an excellent pattern for a gardener who wants to use cold frames.

Cloches were still an important gardening appliance. Each held close to six gallons of water, weighed five and a half pounds, and was made of clear glass tinted slightly blue to offer protection from strong sun (see figure A–10). Straw mats were used in the evening and in poor weather to cover both cloches and lights (see figures A–11 and A–12). The mats were longer

FIG. A-10 Bell jar cloches over lettuce in a French garden in the early twentieth century.

FIG. A-11 Rye straw mats were used to cover the frames and lights at night or in bad weather.

FIG. A-12 Frames, lights, and mat coverings.

lasting than loose straw mulches and easier to deal with, as they could be rolled up.

To prop open the frames and cloches for ventilation, special "tilts" were made with several notches. The different notches of these props allowed varying amounts of air to get to the plants. Care was taken always to ventilate the appliances so that they would not be open facing the wind (see figure A-13). This was done both to protect the plants and to keep the wind from catching under the glass and perhaps lifting and breaking it. The notches in the cloche tilts were made at such an angle that the lip of the cloche resting on the notch would slide off and close itself when the tilt was pressed slightly backward.

FIG. A-13 *Lights ventilated to avoid drafts.*

The French gardeners used tools, especially garden forks, with relatively long, smooth handles varying in length from 3½ to 6 feet, which made it easier to throw manure or soil any distance or height. Watering cans were also developed for ease and speed of use, and special pack baskets evolved for carrying manure and soil along the narrow paths where wheelbarrows could not go (see figure A–14).

An amazing feature of the French system was the large areas that were made into hotbeds with fermenting horse manure. The way in which the hotbeds themselves were made depended on the condition of the soil, the desired temperature of the beds, and the season of the year. No matter what the situation, though, it entailed moving and handling enormous quantities of manure as well as soil. Each successful grower had a method for efficiently preparing the beds to minimize the earth-moving involved (see figure A–15).

Essentially, the entire area was excavated to about 8 inches and filled with a specific mix-

FIG. A-14 *Basket for carrying manure on the narrow paths in a French garden—there being no room for wheelbarrows between beds.*

FIG. A-15 Mixing soil and manure for under-glass crops.

ture of composted manure and fresh manure with straw litter, to give off the proper warmth. The manure was piled to a depth of 9 to 18 inches, depending on the amount and duration of heat required. It was trampled evenly and covered with a few inches of soil. The frames were then placed on the beds and filled with a couple more inches of soil, which served to protect the plants from the hot manure and eliminate any drafts.

Thicker beds were made in colder weather or for crops that required greater warmth. More manure would be used on wet ground, as it is generally colder. It was very important to compact this manure firmly and uniformly. Any inconsistency would encourage an uneven fermentation, hence uneven heat and lopsided settling.

Once the heat was exhausted from the manure, it was spread on open borders, on cloche beds, and over the manure in the hotbeds, where it made a very fertile growing medium. John Weathers describes the accumulation of this spent hotbed fuel in his book *French Market-Gardening*:

> In some old Parisian gardens I visited, the manure of former years covered the
> original soil to a depth of two or three feet, and it almost felt as if one was walk-
> ing on a velvet pile carpet. This old manure, decayed into fine particles, assumes
> a deeper and deeper tint with age, and yields up its fertilising foods under the
> influence of air, water, and heat for the benefit of crops grown upon it.[9]

Within the frames space was used as efficiently as possible. Several different vegetables that would not interfere with one another were grown together. Root crops were sown where

[9] John Weathers. *French Market-Gardening* (London: John Murray, 1909), p. 17.

they were to grow, whereas heading crops were transplanted at least once. One example of how this might work would be radishes and carrots sown together with lettuce seedlings. The radishes would be harvested while the carrots were still small, and the lettuce would have grown to marketable size by the time the carrots needed more space. Sometimes the border of the bed would be planted with cauliflower seedlings, which would mature after the carrots were pulled. This sort of economy was practiced throughout the garden, and schemes included many different vegetables.

The whole system had been refined and specialized to the point that, despite the small scale of these market gardens, it was an entirely economical business. This is not to say that it wasn't hard work! The gardens were necessarily small because the labor and materials invested were very great and not at all practical on a large scale. For these same reasons they remain a fine example for efficient gardeners today.

THE FRENCH SYSTEM
IN ENGLAND

In the meantime England was still importing fresh produce from France and Holland. One source claims that 24,000 to 30,000 crates of lettuce (each crate containing three dozen) came from France to the London market every week from just before Christmas until March! Eventually a party of gardeners from Evesham went to France and toured some of the intensive market gardens there to explore its feasibility for them.

The English growers were much impressed with what they saw, and in 1906 one of them, Mr. Indiens, hired a French expert to start a garden in Evesham on the French pattern. In the next year a French garden was started in Essex with the help of another French expert. "The press of the day, however, gave such optimistic and exaggerated reports relative to its possibilities for rapidly acquiring huge fortunes, that the system came into disrepute consequent upon the failure of inexperienced growers. Several growers continued to work the system successfully, but the Great War cut short a good many promising ventures."[10]

World War I was not the only thing that cut the prospects of French intensive gardening short. As Dalziel O'Brien wrote:

> Market gardening began with plenty of dung. Every city is ringed with the now built-over lands of men who sent their vegetables and fruit in and brought back the manure on the return load behind the horses . . . the beginning of intensive horticulture under heavy pit lights with tiny panes of glass used this free manure, costing only loading time, as fuel in hotbeds as well. Some growers use artificials, with peat to supply the humus; some use chemically composted straw, and all of them pay heavily in direct cash and in labor for what their fathers and grandfathers had for free.[11]

---

[10] C. P. Quarrel. *Intensive Salad Production* (London: Crosby, Lockwood and Sons Ltd., 1938), p. 69.
[11] R. Dalziel O'Brien. *Intensive Gardening* (London: Faber and Faber Ltd., 1956), p. 17.

The rise of the automobile and decline of the horse for transportation drastically altered the centuries-old balance of livery stable manure in exchange for intensively grown vegetables. Though cars began to come into use in the early 1900s, it was some years before the traffic in cities was mostly motor. In any case this great change in transportation spelled certain death to a system dependent on manure hotbeds to produce winter vegetables commercially.

While French gardening underwent both modifications and decline, intensive growing in general remained an economical way to supply local food for an urban population. This is especially true because the population density in these areas made the land too valuable to cultivate extensively. The future of large-scale manure hotbeds may have been doomed, but the use of glass was not. Glass remained in use for as long as it was necessary or profitable to produce food in an area or season where the climate prohibited growth in the open air.

In England the lights remained the most popular means of protection; the bell jars never caught on in use as they had in France. Other protective devices were developed, such as the continuous cloche. Invented by Major L. H. Chase and patented in 1912, the continuous cloche was much

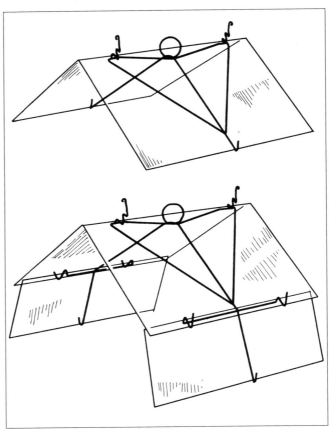

Fig. A-16 Chase barn and tent cloches.

more versatile than the bell jar cloches (see figure A–16). The simpler version was a "tent" of two glass panes. This was improved by adding two more panes as vertical walls, with the tent acting as a roof. The cloches could be used individually or could be arranged end to end to form long, miniature greenhouses covering entire rows of plants, much like the modern "tunnel cloches." This type of cloche was much lighter than bell glasses and easier to repair, as broken panes could easily be replaced.

DUTCH LIGHT GARDENING IN ENGLAND

In the early 1930s imports of foreign produce to Great Britain were restricted, greatly encouraging intensive market gardening there. At about the same time, immigrants from Holland came to settle in Yorkshire, and apparently a number of them were growers. They brought their own equipment and methods for intensive cultivation, which spread fairly rapidly.

The Dutch growers in England adopted double-span frames for their lights rather than single frames. These facilitated a less intensive cropping system than the French gardeners used, called "alternative frame cropping." The Dutch system is still in use in Great Britain today. In this system the lights are used alternately on one range of frames and then on the adjacent ones, switching back and forth. This is coordinated with the crops growing in the frames. It means that the ground is exposed to the weather after every crop, and that the grower is not in a frantic rush to prepare the beds between crops. This system makes maximum use of the glass involved, for when a crop under glass is harvested, the lights can be immediately transferred to a bed already prepared and planted.

Unlike the French system where the soil was soon covered with a depth of manure, nearly eliminating any soil fertility problems, Dutch growers with a limited manure supply had to choose soil more carefully. This was especially true in a situation where the ground was covered with glass, limiting the weather effects of freezing and thawing, wetting and drying. Under these circumstances it was particularly important to have a soil that was naturally loose and well drained, without being dry.

Manures, of course, were needed to supply fertility and humus. Although one writer advises that initially a French garden may require 500 tons of manure per acre, the recommendation for Dutch light gardens averages fifty tons per acre. These are very broad figures, and the qualities of both soils and manures vary widely. For comparison current American books inform that ten to fifteen tons of manure per acre is an average application for nonintensive use. This shows the relation of intensive cropping to intensive manuring, as well as giving some concept of the quantity of manure needed for heat, as opposed to fertility, in French gardening.

FORCING AND MARKET GARDENING IN NORTH AMERICA

In the United States there were also intensive market gardens to supply large cities and towns with vegetables in the early nineteenth century.

In the New York area, Fulton Market was supplied with excellent fruits and vegetables from small market gardens. Boston residents also had a wide variety of choice produce at the Faneuil Hall Market. As has always been the case, commercial production of vegetables and fruits was restricted to the environs of towns large enough to support such enterprises. Naturally gardeners could not afford to subject their produce to more travel than was necessary. This was truer then than it is today because of poor refrigeration and because so many vegetable varieties have been developed for their firmness or hard rinds, which are an advantage in shipping. This meant that market gardens thrived mostly in the already urban Northeast, in spite of the less-than-ideal climate. American growers, like their European counterparts, used hotbeds and cold frames to produce the out-of-season vegetables that commanded higher prices.

By 1850 industrial development in northern urban areas was changing the agriculture of that area by increasing the demand for everything, including vegetables and fruits. Production in this populous area turned to more intensive means, whereas products that were cultivated extensively and could tolerate shipping (for example, grain), were grown in the Midwest (see figures A-17, A-18, and A-19). In the Northeast as land became more valuable, "Farmers were tilling their wet areas. Land not suitable for intensive use was being abandoned, and farmers not able to adapt themselves to the more intensive and capitalistic type of farming were moving into industry or migrating west to farm in their old way there."[12]

As the Northeast became more industrial, the population changed "from a producing to a consuming one."[13] A middle class emerged, able to afford the more expensive forced vegetables. Market gardening grew accordingly.

FIG. A-17 Cold frames in American market gardens used for growing cucumbers.

. . .the value of orchard and garden products for 1859 reveals that four states in which industry and urban growth were most concentrated—Massachusetts, New York, New Jersey, and Pennsylvania—plus Ohio, constituted an orchard and truck garden belt. These five states of the thirty-three in the Union produced 47 percent of the value of fruits and vegetables the country yielded.[14]

[12] Paul W. Gates. *The Farmer's Age: Agriculture 1815–1860* (New York: Harper & Row, 1960), p. 269.
[13] Lee Cleveland Corbett. *Garden Farming* (Boston: Ginn and Co., 1913), p. 2.
[14] Gates, p. 269.

FIG. A-18 American market gardeners made easily movable frames to carry glass lights by constructing only the paths. Older, experienced gardeners much preferred this construction.

FIG. A-19 Rye straw mats are used in American gardens to protect frame crops from cold weather.

Truck gardening, however, was different from traditional market gardening. The fact that vegetables were transported, initially by steamer and later by railroad, meant that they were grown farther from their markets. Because of this, growers could take advantage of cheaper land in more rural areas and milder climates farther south. These conditions did not require an intensive use of the land or a serious forcing culture. The progress of the season from Florida northward, combined with refrigeration and fast freight, served to supply large cities with fresh produce throughout the entire year.

"Yet," wrote Corbett in 1913, "it [truck gardening] has not discouraged the development of the forcing industry, which has for a number of years been an important branch of market gardening in the vicinity of the larger northern cities."[15] Because of the expense of covering beds with glass and heating them, cropping was necessarily intensive. This industry was, in the early 1900s, most highly developed in the Boston area. Manure, or hot water or steam flowing through pipes, supplied heat for hotbeds. Glass forcing houses were heated, too, so that tomatoes, cucumbers, and lettuce could be grown through the winter (see figure A–20). In milder areas cold frames were used in market gardens, though hotbeds were used for starting seedlings (see figure A–21). In warmer areas frames were used, covered with "muslins." These frames consisted of a lightweight, standard-size (3 feet by 6 feet) framework with unbleached muslin stretched over each side of it to form a sort of "double-glazed" effect.

Near Montreal melons were raised for market in a way more reminiscent of the French gardens near Paris. Hotbeds were made with an 18-inch depth of fermenting manure in which the heat was allowed to temper for a week or so. Then melon plants were transplanted into the frames, two seedlings under each sash, and the sash was covered on cold nights. The melon plants grew until nearly mature before the frames were removed. Under

FIG. A-20 A forcing house and frames covered with glass lights. Note the coverings of burlap coated with linseed oil made from old fertilizer bags on frames in the left foreground.

---

[15] Corbett, p. 3.

FIG. A-21 *Sweet potatoes in cold frames.*

each fruit was placed a shingle or flat stone to keep it off the ground, and the melons were turned regularly for uniform ripening.

Our urban centers are no longer surrounded by small-scale, intensively cultivated market gardens, for fast, economical transportation has totally changed the commercial production of vegetables in our country. Nevertheless, because of the rising costs of growing and shipping vegetables in the current system and because of the rising standards of the eating public, small growers are again finding it economical to use intensive methods to supply local markets with delicious fresh produce.

There have always been good reasons to use intensive methods, from raised beds for solving drainage problems to cropping procedures that made the most efficient possible use of space. Reasons have not changed, and gardeners such as you can gain the same benefits from gardening intensively as did gardeners in former times. Materials have changed, but the methods employed in gardens of the past are just as useful now.

USDA PLANT HARDINESS ZONE MAP

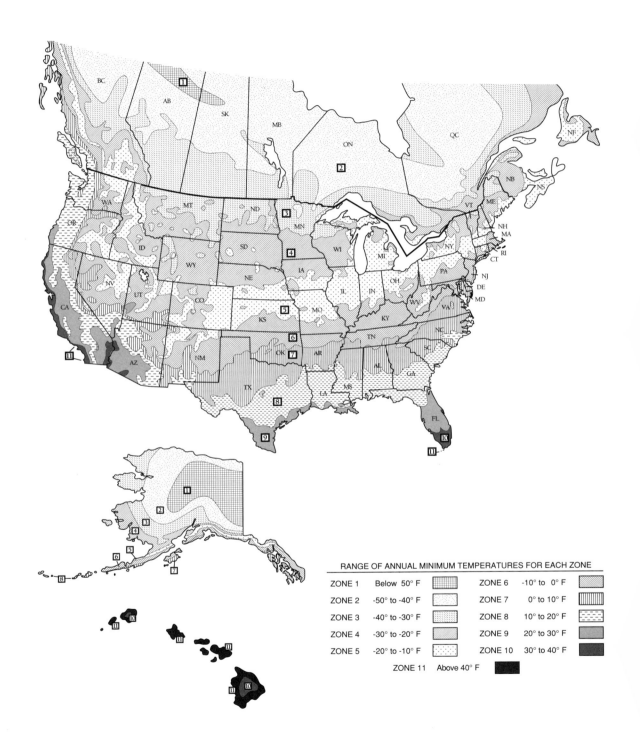

RANGE OF ANNUAL MINIMUM TEMPERATURES FOR EACH ZONE			
ZONE 1	Below 50° F	ZONE 6	-10° to 0° F
ZONE 2	-50° to -40° F	ZONE 7	0° to 10° F
ZONE 3	-40° to -30° F	ZONE 8	10° to 20° F
ZONE 4	-30° to -20° F	ZONE 9	20° to 30° F
ZONE 5	-20° to -10° F	ZONE 10	30° to 40° F
	ZONE 11	Above 40° F	

Season-Extending Devices

A CATALOG OF SEASON-EXTENDING TOOLS AND DEVICES

There are many ways to produce the microclimate needed for extending the gardening season. Generally the less complicated and inexpensive devices can provide a few weeks of growing after killing frosts, and the more complicated devices can provide up to year-round gardening in less severe climates. This catalog will give you the information you need to start growing vegetables over a longer season.

CLOCHES

Description

The cloche (bell jar), as originated in Europe, was a small, plant-sized glass device designed to create a more temperate microclimate during the period just before or after the normal, frost-free growing season. Cloches can protect seedlings from the wind; prewarm the soil before planting; protect young plants from light frosts; protect plants during excessively wet weather; protect from animal damage; and provide optimum growing temperatures during cooler weather.

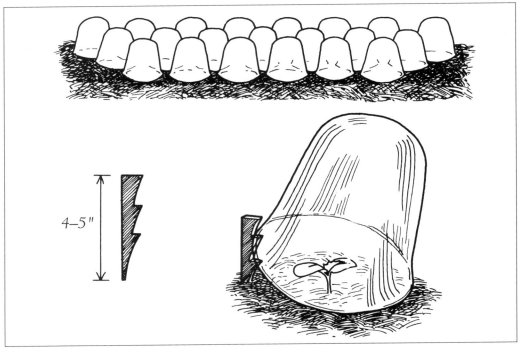

4–5"

The original French cloche. A small wedge-shaped "tilt" was used for ventilation on sunny days.

Today, cloches are most often made from plastic milk jugs, large glass bottles, fiberglass, and waxed paper.

Types of Cloches

Milk jugs: After cutting off the bottom of the jug, it can be placed over smaller plants in the garden. The cap is removed to allow some ventilation on sunny days.

Advantages: No cost; easy to find.

Disadvantages: Light weight makes them easily blown away by the wind, but you can solve this problem by putting a short, thin stake through the hole and down into the ground, then firmly pressing the jug into the soil. Another disadvantage is that sunlight will eventually destroy the plastic.

Milk jug cloches.

Glass jars: Use a bottle-cutting jig to remove the bottom. Alternatively, tie a kerosene-soaked cotton string tightly around the jar about 2 inches above the base. Light the string with a match and when the fire is burned out, pour cold water on the bottle. It should (but may not) break along a line where the string was.

Advantages: Low or no cost; will not blow away.

Disadvantages: Heavier weight; breakable.

Lid can be put on for cold nights.

Bottom of jar inverted over seedling bed.

Glass jar cloche.

Hot caps: Hot caps are inexpensive, waxed-paper cloches available in many garden stores. They can be ventilated by opening folds in the paper without removing the cap from the soil. Prices vary but start around 15 cents each.

Advantages: Inexpensive; easy to ventilate; easily removed and stored.

Disadvantages: Generally not reusable; fragile; may blow away under strong winds.

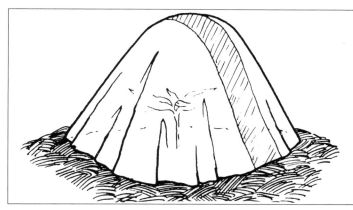

Hotcaps are available in most garden stores and catalogs; they are useful but short-lived.

Cones: Cones are made from semirigid fiberglass-reinforced plastic (commonly used in the manufacture of solar heating panels). The material is cut in the shape of a semicircle and the straight edges drawn together and fastened to form the cone. Brass paper fasteners are the least expensive way to fasten them.

Advantages: Ventilation is provided by the hole on top; they will last a number of years; they usually stay put on windy days; they can be made almost any size.

Disadvantages: High cost of material; they need to be removed on warmer days to prevent overheating.

Cones of various sizes can be made from sheets of fiberglass-reinforced plastic.

THE ROW COVER
AND CONTINUOUS CLOCHE

Description

According to the early intensive gardeners of England, the bell cloche was unworkable because of its fragility and size. In response to this criticism L. H. Chase invented the continuous cloche, which was constructed of panes of glass and which allowed a long row of plants to be enclosed under a single device.

The Chase cloche is still available today, but there are many other variations on the idea as well. An advantage of the continuous cloche is that provided by shifting it from one crop, as

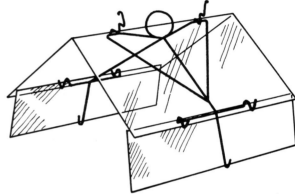

it matures, to another younger crop just beside it. This works well for gardens managed in the conventional fashion. For the bed gardener, the modern fabric or plastic row cover is more appropriate, as it can be made to cover the entire bed and is considerably less expensive.

Three types of glass cloche designs, commonly called "barn" cloches.

"Low barn" cloche

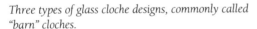

"Grower's barn" cloche

"Large barn" cloche

Types of Row Covers and Continuous Cloches

Glass cloches: Held together with metal brackets, glass cloches once came in a variety of styles. Today they can be bought from some of the more "stylish" garden-supply houses. They are set end to end to form a tunnel of cloches. The ends of the tunnel are covered with glass panes or boards at night.

Advantages: They last a long time if you are careful in handling them; they can also be used as wind breaks; they are easily ventilated by opening the tops; some people consider them more aesthetically acceptable than plastic alternatives.

Disadvantages: Glass is expensive and fragile, heavy, and difficult to store safely, and the metal brackets can be difficult to find.

Glass cloches in use for warming tomatoes at the Coolidge Center for the Advancement of Agriculture in Massachusetts.

Continuous glass cloches up-ended to provide wind protection for young plants.

Tunnel cloches: Constructed of semirigid fiberglass sheets, tunnel cloches are helpful for protecting short rows of plants. They can be made of smooth sheets or pieces of translucent fiberglass corrugated roofing. The sheet is bent into a "U" and then tied together with wire or cord. Ends are made of scrap sheets or wood.

Advantages: Reusable; generally not likely to blow off under strong winds; easy to remove ends or tip up to provide ventilation on warm days; can provide good frost protection.

Disadvantages: Require a number of pieces to cover a long row of a crop; can be expensive; difficult to store if not disassembled.

A tunnel cloche made of fiberglass sheeting.

Polyethylene Row Covers: Many gardeners have developed their own versions of this popular enclosure. A polyethylene row cover is nothing more than a long sheet of polyethylene supported by wire, plastic, or wooden arches. "Poly" is inexpensive and easy to find; it is easy to move, store, and replace.

A framework of arches should be firmly embedded in the ground about every 3 feet along the length of the row cover. A 5-foot-wide layer of plastic is then laid over the framework. The edges of the plastic should be held down either by burying them under soil or by covering them with boards or rocks. Ends of the tunnels can be closed by staking the excess plastic into the ground or with boards or other rigid materials.

Ventilation must be provided. Either the material must be opened on one side, or you should use "slitted row cover" designed for this purpose. The slitted material contains a series of ventilation "slits" near the top. Although this material is inexpensive and very effective, it will provide less frost protection than solid material will. Slitted row covers

Arches made with brush wood can become a framework for polyethylene tunnel cloches.

installed over a layer of black plastic to control weeds are the preferred choice of many market gardeners.

Advantages: Inexpensive; framework can be made from scrap materials; easy to move and store; slitted covers are self-ventilated.

Disadvantages: Can be blown off by strong winds if not adequately secured; polyethylene is subject to degradation from sunlight and may only be usable for one season; can be difficult to install by one person.

Heavy gauge wires can be used to form supports for polyethylene cloches.

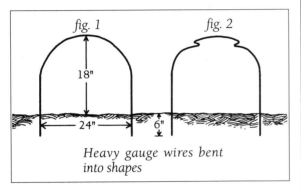

Heavy gauge wires bent into shapes

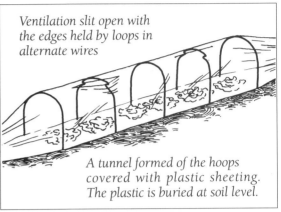

Ventilation slit open with the edges held by loops in alternate wires

A tunnel formed of the hoops covered with plastic sheeting. The plastic is buried at soil level.

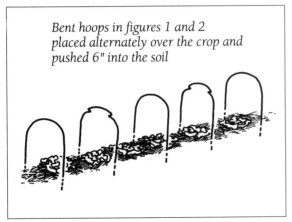

Bent hoops in figures 1 and 2 placed alternately over the crop and pushed 6" into the soil

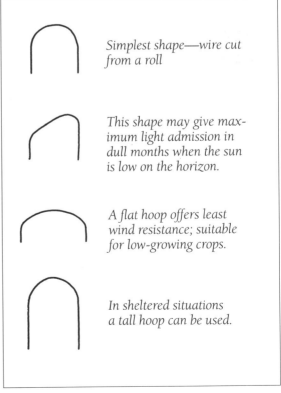

Simplest shape—wire cut from a roll

This shape may give maximum light admission in dull months when the sun is low on the horizon.

A flat hoop offers least wind resistance; suitable for low-growing crops.

In sheltered situations a tall hoop can be used.

Spun-bonded polyethylene row covers and sheets: Spun-bonded polyethylene is becoming more popular all the time. It is a fabric that is laid over the crop in a bed or section of the garden. The material is porous and lets water through, yet keeps out insects and provides a few degrees of frost protection. Its advantages in prewarming the soil and providing added heat during spring weather are well documented by the research of Dr. Otho Wells at the University of New Hampshire.

There are a number of manufacturers of this material ("Reemay" is the name of the Kenbar Co. product, but it is also made by Kimberly Farms and others), and it can be purchased at most garden stores. It comes in rolls of various lengths and is usually 5 feet wide. The material is laid out and the edges held down with rocks, soil, or mulch. Wind will usually not pull it off. Ventilation is not necessary, and it should be taken off only when plants need to be pollinated or temperature no longer require its use.

The product can also be purchased in large sheets, can be laid over an entire garden or section of a garden. According to those who have used sheets, one or two people can cover an entire garden plot in a few minutes.

To help control weeds and conserve moisture, it is always a wise idea to use black plastic mulch under row covers.

Advantages: Moderately low cost; can be reused at least a few times; needs no ventilation; controls insects; easily handled; allows rainfall penetration.

Disadvantages: Difficult to see through to check on crop progress; usually installed without supports and will prevent plants from developing proper upright form if left on too long.

While most gardeners use row covers for spring-season extending, this crop of carrots was protected through the New Hampshire winter with Reemay®. (Unlike this crop, carrots that are overwintered should be harvested before they grow leaves in the spring.)

TOMATO-CAGE CLOCHE

Many gardeners save space and labor by growing tomatoes in wire cages. A cage can be turned into a cloche by wrapping the cage with a layer of clear polyethylene. This will allow you to set out tomatoes in their final growing places as much as three to four weeks before the normal planting time. The cloche will protect the plants from cool winds and excessive rains and will provide the warm, humid environment tomatoes love.

Cover the top of the cloche at night with boards, plastic, or other material to conserve heat.

Once the weather warms up, remove the plastic from the cage.

Advantages: Inexpensive and easy to construct; can produce considerably earlier than usual crops.

Disadvantages: Must be removed as temperatures get above 90° as tomato flowers become sterile at high temperatures; can be blown over by high winds.

Recycled materials can provide the structure for inexpensive cloche-type enclosures. This device built from the frame of a pick-up camper can also be covered with wooden slats to provide summer shading. Garden of Norman and Sherrie Lee in New York.

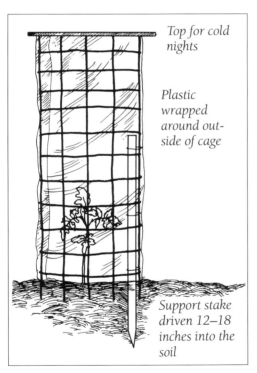

Top for cold nights

Plastic wrapped around outside of cage

Support stake driven 12–18 inches into the soil

A tomato cage cloche.

Tomato cage cloches in Janney Munsell's garden in Maine.

COLD FRAMES AND LIGHTS

Description:

Dutch, French, and English cold frames and lights are all variations of a basic design including a wooden frame covered by a glass window. A number of them can be placed over an intensive bed to allow a large area to be enclosed. As an alternative, the bed can be framed by a permanent wooden structure, which both holds the soil and provides the base for the windows.

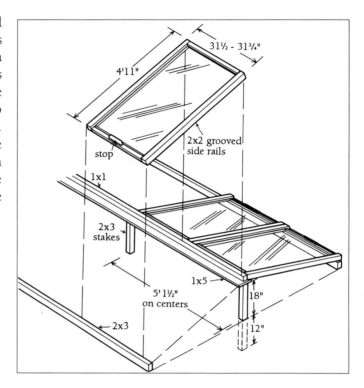

Traditional Dutch light system.

COLD FRAMES

Today's cold frame is probably one of the most useful devices in the garden. It is really just a contemporary version of the traditional lights but usually stands alone and is not moved around the garden. Its uses include raising early crops of greens, hardening off seedlings, providing additional heat for summer crops like melons and cucumbers, and protecting fall crops of various kinds of half-hardy perennials through the winter.

A cold frame, minus its sash, can be used to support shading material over midsummer crops, like lettuce, that prefer cooler temperatures.

The base frame can be either permanent or movable. Movable bases can be moved from bed to bed throughout the season as necessary.

Locate the cold frame so that it faces south, and preferably where it will be protected from strong winds. Adjacent to the foundation of your house or other building is ideal. Some gardeners place their frames in front of a basement window to give the plants a bit of warm air on cold nights. If your garden beds run north and south (as recommended), then you may want to build a couple that run east/west for your cold frames.

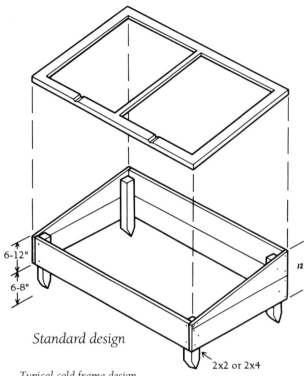

6-12"

6-8"

Standard design

2x2 or 2x4

Typical cold frame design.

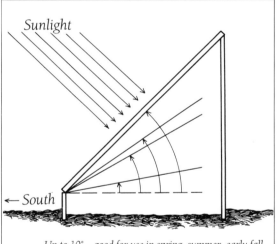

The modified design is used when you plan to set trays of flats in the cold frame and want to avoid wasting space.

Modified design for use with starter flats

Sunlight

← South

Up to 10°—good for use in spring, summer, early fall
About 30°—best for early spring and fall use
Not less than 35°—good for year round use*
Not less than 45°—best for late fall through early spring*
* In most cases you will have to insulate frames that are to be used in late fall and winter.

Cold frame angles for northern climates (regions north of 40° latitude).

The base of the frame is generally designed to allow the glass to slope toward the south, and it can be made to slope as much as 60° from horizontal. In the far north a steeper angle will provide more direct sun in the fall and spring. A general rule of thumb is that the optimum angle is equal to the geographic latitude at which you live. For example, in New Hampshire that means 40°. Of course, a steeper angle will mean reduced growing space unless you use larger windows.

Some cold frames are not built with sloped covers. Often these are frames that are movable around the garden. They can have vaulted covers if fiberglass sheets are used for the glazing. A flat cover is possible if the sides of the cover are high enough to allow adequate head room for plants.

Size is a matter of individual preference. The most convenient widths range from 3 to 4 feet. Wider than this will result in your having difficulty reaching plants at the back of the frame.

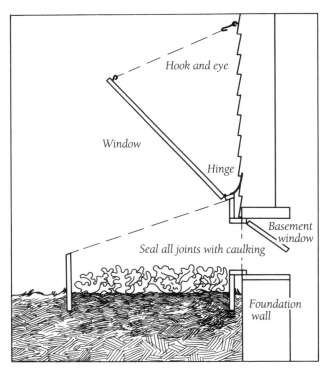

A cold frame can be installed against the south wall of your house, and a basement window can be used to heat the cold frame on cold nights.

A typical cold frame used to harden-off spring seedlings.

The length should be determined by how heavy a window you can lift. A length of 4 to 6 feet is most common. If you are using old storm windows, you should preplan your frames to match.

Wood or masonry materials can be used to build the base. Either should be placed at least 8 to 10 inches into the ground, and masonry materials should be set on a good bed of coarse gravel. Do not use preservative-impregnated wood for cold frames, as the substances that prevent the wood from rotting are often toxic to plants. Also avoid wood treated with creosote and pentachlorophenol preservatives.

Insulation is optional for cold frames. Alternatives range from piling hay bales around the frame for the winter to piling up soil or warm manure around the base. A simple way to protect your crops from deep freezes late in fall is to cover the cold frame with a piece of ½-inch-thick rigid insulation. For overwintering crops cover the glass with plywood and they lay mulch over the top.

Although most old storm windows are fine for cold frames, eventually the glass will break. We recommend replacing it with fiberglass or another lightweight material. This will make the frames easier to handle and resistant to further breakage.

Although many cold frame owners do not put hinges on the covers, it may be a good idea to do so. Hinges will make your daily opening and closing chores easier and will prevent gusts of wind from picking up your sash and smashing it. Use hinges with removable pins so that you can easily detach the sash for maintenance or storing for the winter.

This small greenhouse is used as a walk-in cold frame.

Portable A-frame cold frames being used in the garden of Adam and Bonnie Tomash in Maine to protect peppers and eggplant in the summer.

This polyethylene greenhouse was built right in the garden for $50 worth of materials. It is a practical, temporary, walk-in cold frame for gardeners who need lots of space for growing seedlings. Lewis Creek Farm, Starksboro, Vermont.

Lights

Lights were originally developed for use in market gardening. We describe their sizes and construction in Appendix A. The basic parts are (1) a bottomless frame built about 9 inches high on one side and 6 inches high on the other, (2) windows or lights to cover the entire wooden frame, and (3) straw or other types of mats used to cover the glass lights at night when there is danger of frost.

Because the frames are portable, the lights can be moved from bed to bed as the growing season progresses. Light frames were frequently used by European growers to cover manure hotbeds. This system has faded from the scene in commercial horticulture because modern plastics and row covers are more economical in both cost and labor.

Advantages: Relatively permanent materials; mobility; good way to use old wooden storm windows.

Disadvantages: Frames and sash can be heavy and difficult to move; glass can be easily broken; inadequate head room for many crops.

HOT FRAMES

Description

Hot frames are insulated devices that are designed to allow enough heat to be retained inside to provide plant growth through the coldest months. Variations of this idea range from simple and inexpensive to complex and costly.

Originally hot frames were simply cold frames that derived heat from manure beds built underneath. This was the basis of the French and Dutch light systems. Today heat can be obtained by capturing and then storing solar energy with the use of modern insulation and heat-storage devices.

The basic elements of modern hot-frame design include insulation of the below-ground and aboveground structure, heat-storage capacity or an auxiliary heat source, double-glazed covers, and optional insulation for the glazed panels.

These devices can produce certain crops (see listing in chapter 6) throughout the winter in most cold climates. In the extreme north (north of about 40° latitude), it is more reasonable to expect crops in hot frames to grow well for all but the coldest period of mid-December through early February.

The Solar Grow Frame at the Rodale Organic Gardening and Farming Research Center in Pennsylvania.

A Solar Pod® in early spring.

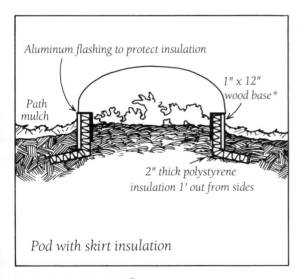

Aluminum flashing to protect insulation

Path mulch

1" x 12" wood base*

2" thick polystyrene insulation 1' out from sides

Pod with skirt insulation

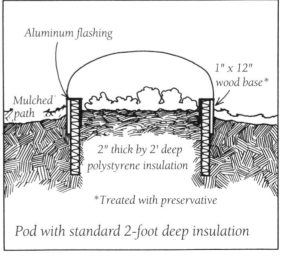

Aluminum flashing

Mulched path

1" x 12" wood base*

2" thick by 2' deep polystyrene insulation

*Treated with preservative

Pod with standard 2-foot deep insulation

Insulation for Solar Pods®

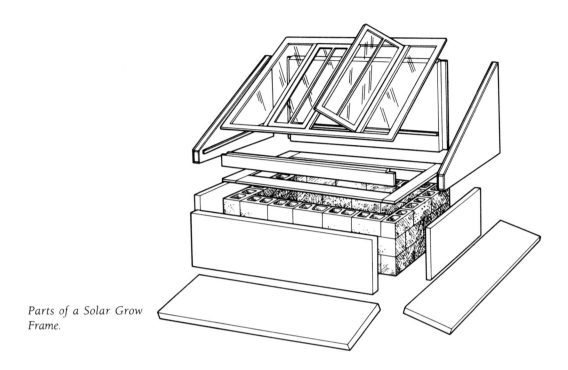

*Parts of a Solar Grow
Frame.*

Insulated Cold Frames and Hot Frames

These frames are the intermediate step between cold frames and a greenhouse. In effect they are minisolar, but nonwalk-in greenhouses. Their advantage over other season-extending devices is their heavy insulation and their orientation, which takes full advantage of the heat and light of the winter sun.

The elements of the design are a fully insulated base, double glazing, and optional thermal storage in the form of masonry or water drums.

A simple version of this type of device is the Solar Pod® designed by gardener and architect Leandre Poisson of Harrisville, New Hampshire. It is double glazed with a fiber-glass-reinforced plastic called "Sunlite," manufactured by Solar Components Corp. of Manchester, New Hampshire. The curved profile of the cover mandates that this device be oriented in a north–south direction. This ensures that the sun penetrates to the plants equally well at all hours of the day.

Although it is possible to build a Solar Pod® without insulating the base structure, Poisson has designed it to be surrounded by a 2-inch-thick layer of rigid foam. This layer goes 18 to 24 inches down into the ground. The purpose is to keep the soil as warm as possible.

The base of the pod is usually made of wooden boards and is 4 feet wide by 8 feet long. It would be wise to treat the base with a nonhazardous wood preservative to prevent rotting. Cuprinol® (a copper-based preservative) or CWF® (a wood finish with tri-butyl tin as its preservative) are good choices.

Another feature of the Solar Pod® is the inclusion of a fifty-five-gallon drum filled with water. The drum is painted black and set at the northern end of the pod. It helps to keep the pod warm at night (as much as 10 degrees warmer than in pod without drums). The drum works by absorbing the rays of the sun during the day and storing the heat in water. Concrete blocks or other masonry could be used for heat storage, but these are only about one fourth as effective as the water drum.

If the snow is brushed off after every winter storm, the Solar Pod[R] is capable of producing a continual crop of fresh produce until mid-December and begins producing again as early as late February. In milder climates than that of New Hampshire, it would be reasonable to expect the pod to provide a year-round salad and root crop season.

The solar hot frame is a similar device. It is essentially an insulated cold frame, as the glass is usually flat and oriented toward the south. The hot frame can be as simple as a double-glazed cold frame, with hay bales up against it for insulation, or as complicated as the fully insulated Solar Grow Frame designed by Rodale Press.

Important to the successful operation of hot frames with insulating covers is opening and closing them. On a sunny day the insulation must be removed or retracted to allow light and sun to get to the plants. If you leave it on too long, not only will the plants not get the needed heat, but they will suffer from inadequate light as well. Remembering to close the insulation at night is also crucial. Failure to do so in the spring and fall will produce no problems, but forgetting to do it in January could result in freezing of tender crops you have nursed along for weeks.

Advantages: The well-insulated device requires no auxiliary heat for year-round production; it is less expensive to build than a small greenhouse; it is ideal for growing spring transplants.

Disadvantages: Considerably more expensive than cold frames; may require substantial carpentry skill to construct; requires daily attention if you are to maximize winter-crop production.

GREENHOUSES

Description

A greenhouse needs no description. Virtually every gardener has one, or wishes he or she had one. It's a great place to start spring transplants, grow greens and other crops through the winter, and escape from the winter doldrums.

Whereas cold frames, hot frames, and the like are great gardening devices, the greenhouse is a horticultural world unto its own. Management of a greenhouse requires knowledge and skills beyond those acquired by growing plants outdoors. Soil management, pest and disease control, and temperature regulation are all different in the greenhouse.

This is not to say that gardeners should resist the temptation to build or buy a greenhouse. Its advantages far outweigh its disadvantages, but you must be fully aware of the extra skill and knowledge required to run it efficiently and effectively.

Today solariums and solar greenhouses are becoming very popular additions to homes. Most are intended primarily as living spaces and secondarily as places to grow plants.

This is because the optimum environment for providing solar heat for a house or for a day-use living room is different from that needed by many plants.

People can enjoy the sunroom during the day and go inside at night, but plants cannot, which means that if you wish to use a sunspace as a true greenhouse, you will want it to be warmer at night than it would be kept if unoccupied. To this end, many horticultural greenhouses have heating systems that consume large amounts of fuel. Modern "solar" greenhouses are usually designed to be more energy efficient but are often not as efficient as they could be.

The typical residential sunspace or greenhouse kit is a metal or wooden frame, with glass on three sides; the back side is attached to the existing house. The glass is usually double paned, and the structure is designed to minimize air leaks. But with these designs, plants can only grow well in winter if supplementary heat is supplied. Why? Because the amount of glass is so great that much of the heat gained during the day is rapidly lost at night. Glass is a poor insulator, even if doubled up and coated with modern heat-conserving coatings. Without supplementary heat these greenhouses will get very cold or might even freeze at night.

To maximize use of the sun and emphasize plant growing, a greenhouse would look a bit different. It would have a lot of glass on the south wall and part of the roof, but not much on the east and west walls. It would also have a heavily insulated foundation and roof. Most interior surfaces would be light colors to maximize reflection of light onto the plants. This is important because winter light levels are low and because the sun is only up for a short period of time.

To reduce the need for supplementary heat, the greenhouse should have "thermal mass" in the form of water, masonry, or other materials. These perform two functions: (1) to absorb heat during the day, reducing the tendency of the greenhouse to overheat, and (2) to hold heat for release at night. Thermal mass is often found in the form of concrete floors, walls, and planting beds, or tubes, bottles, and drums of water.

This greenhouse was designed and built at the Rodale Research Center in Pennsylvania. It stands alone, but can grow crops through the winter using only solar energy.

A good solar greenhouse can coast through the coldest winter nights with no direct-heat input. For example, the Doschers built an 8-foot-by-22-foot greenhouse on their home in central New Hampshire in 1981, and it has produced a wide variety of crops ever since, without ever freezing. The only source of heat is the sun; its energy is stored in masonry floors, walls, and drums of water.

Inside the Rodale greenhouse a productive crop of greens continues into late November.

This modest fiberglass greenhouse can be used to grow spring transplants. Simple structures such as this can be used very effectively in all except the coldest weather.

This more elaborate greenhouse was constructed as a connector between a house and garage. It is designed to grow plants all winter without using back-up heat. Heavy insulation and heat storage are integrated into the design. Home of Ralph and Geneva Markus, Hancock, New Hampshire; greenhouse designed by Paul Doscher.

The Doschers' greenhouse is in constant use. In fall it contains salad greens and ornamentals; in winter it produces more greens, tomatoes, and ornamentals; and in spring the greens and ornamentals give way to hundreds of seedlings destined for the garden. The greenhouse has taken the place of hot frames formerly used for these purposes, and it provides a pleasant place to sit or work on those sunny but ⁻10-degree days in January.

Ralph Markus demonstrates the insulating shutters that reduce winter heat loss through the overhead glazing in his greenhouse.

The Markus's greenhouse has built-in planting beds, a potting bench, water-filled tubes for heat storage, and a masonry floor.

This older conventional greenhouse was made more energy efficient by adding an outer layer of rigid plastic glazing. Home of Betsy and Harold Janeway, Webster, New Hampshire.

The Doschers' greenhouse.

ACCESSORIES AND OTHER USEFUL TOOLS

Thermostatic Vent Openers

Any cold frame is actually a solar oven in disguise. Leave it closed on a warm day and you'll discover why baked lettuce is not on anyone's list of gourmet delights. The need to provide regular ventilation can be met by manual means, or, if your cold frame covers are not too heavy, by automatic venting devices. These are used commonly in commercial greenhouses.

They can lift a window weighing up to twenty-six pounds. An automatic vent opener requires no source of power because it contains an expanding cylinder powered by the heat of the sun. As the cylinder expands, the arm of the device opens.

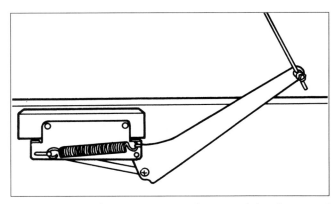

This ingenious device can be obtained in many garden stores and through some seed catalogs. It comes in some models that lift up to twelve pounds and in other spring-assisted versions that lift as much as twenty-six pounds. Costs start at around $35.

This solar-operated automatic venting device can help take some of the risk out of solar intensive gardening.

Miniautomatic Cold Frames

Miniautomatic cold frames are small enclosures made of plastic and wood that have an automatic opener. The cover raises to provide ventilation at 70 to 80° F. These devices are small (about 3 by 4 feet), but they can be a good piece of equipment for the individual with a small garden and no carpentry skills. Costs usually start at around $100.

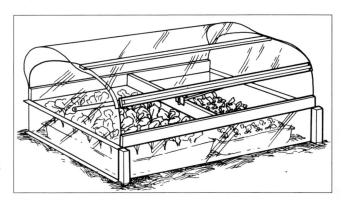

Small, automatic, minature cold frames can be very helpful for hardening-off transplants.

Soil-Heating Cables and Tapes

Starting seeds in the house or greenhouse can be a risky business if you don't control the temperature of the soil. Many seeds germinate best at temperatures between 70 and 80° F, and success rates will drop off if temperatures drop much below this range. One way to ensure good germination temperatures is to install a small heating coil, cable, or tape in a "germinating tent." The coil is laid in a flat tray or box, then covered with sand. The sand is watered to keep it damp, and then a "tent" can be placed over the tray to hold in the moisture and heat. Plant your seeds in flats or containers and place them in the tent on top of the heated sand.

Not only will germination rates be improved, but so will the time it takes for the seeds to sprout. Many seeds will pop out of the ground in less time than indicated on the seed package. We have seen cabbage and lettuce seeds come up in fewer than four days, for example.

There are many versions of heating cables and coils. Buy one with an automatic thermostat that keeps the coil temperature above 70°. We don't recommend buying the fancy, more expensive models. Heat is heat, and any of these products will work well.

A propagating tent heated by a cable.

Minimum-Maximum Thermometers

A minimum-maximum thermometer is an important piece of equipment for any greenhouse or season-extending device. It will tell you if you are operating your devices properly by recording the daily high and low temperatures for you to check at a later time. There are a variety of models on the market, ranging in price from a few dollars to more than $20. If you want to have a number of them placed in various locations around the garden, the less expensive models will suffice.

The problem with some of these is accuracy. We have noticed that there can be a significant variation between individual thermometers of the same brand and model. To minimize this problem it is wise to bring all your thermometers indoors and set them for a few hours next to a thermometer you know to be accurate. Then calibrate the minimum-maximum thermometers so that they all read the same.

For the most accurate records, a minimum-maximum thermometer must be reset every day. We do this when installing new cold frames and when first beginning to use new greenhouses. A few months of watch-

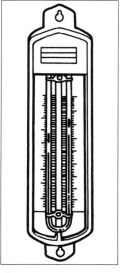

A minimum-maximum thermometer.

ing the thermometer and recording the data can give you a good sense of how your plant environment is functioning. After a while, as you gain experience, the regular use of the thermometer will be less important.

Soil Thermometers

A soil thermometer is essential for determining when to plant. There are a few inexpensive models to choose from, and based on our experience, all are satisfactory. Choose one with a temperature-sensing probe that is at least 6 inches long so that you can get accurate readings for early spring planting. It is not necessary to leave your soil thermometer in the ground all the time. It will respond quickly to changes in temperature and can be inserted to any depth for several minutes for a quick temperature reading.

A soil thermometer is an essential tool for the intensive gardener.

"No-Tech" Heat Storage for Heat-Loving Plants

In the solar engineering trade, there are many new high-tech materials for storing heat. In the backyard garden there are a number of "no-tech" materials you can use to capture and store summer heat to benefit tropical-type plants like melons, watermelons, tomatoes, peppers, and eggplant.

Old milk jugs, painted black and filled with water, can be partially buried in the soil next to your plants. They will provide a little extra heat to the soil and nearby plants at night.

You can also ring a plant with concrete blocks, bricks, rocks, or an old tire to get the same effect. Combine these with an easy system for covering the plants on cool nights (for example, row covers or continuous cloches) and you can coax a crop out in the most uncooperative weather.

If you grow cucumbers or melons on a fence or trellis, you can design it to be covered at night. Make the fence high enough so that a sheet of polyethylene can be draped over it to protect the plants. You could use spun-bonded polyester sheets to do this and not have to remove the cover on most days, thus providing some insect protection as well.

CONCLUSION

The devices mentioned here are not the only ones you can find or create. People are constantly coming up with new ideas and revised versions of old ideas. What we have tried to do is give you an overview of the types of devices you can use. We hope you will experiment and develop your own ideas as well.

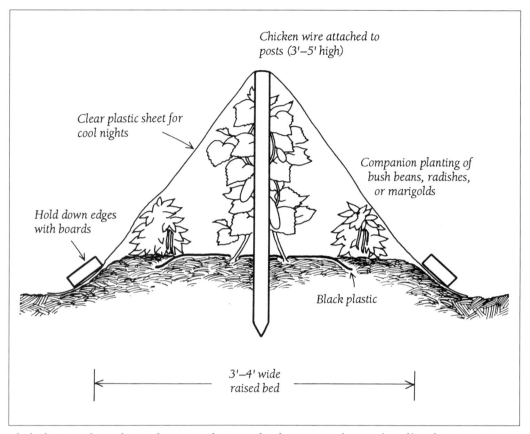

Chicken wire attached to posts (3'–5' high)

Clear plastic sheet for cool nights

Companion planting of bush beans, radishes, or marigolds

Hold down edges with boards

Black plastic

3'–4' wide raised bed

Black plastic can be used in combination with a cucumber fence to provide a number of benefits.

Don't feel constrained by our recommendations. What works best in New England may not work best in Oregon or Wisconsin. The point is not that you should try hard to duplicate the work of the gardeners we have illustrated or ours. Your real objective should be to grow good foods inexpensively, efficiently, and during as much of the year as you choose.

INDEX